WICKED WOMEN

WICKED WOMEN

KELLY EVANS

ISBN: 979-8-218-66302-5

INTRODUCTION

When we think of evil, we often conjure images of shadowy figures lurking in dark alleys, predatory strangers hiding just out of sight. And more often than not, society imagines these figures as men. But what happens when the villain isn't who you'd expect? What happens when the monster is a woman? A mother, a wife, a neighbor? Someone familiar, someone ordinary?

As confusing as it is to admit, I've been interested in true crime since I was a child. While other kids were watching Rugrats on Nickelodeon, I was watching Forensic Files and Unsolved Mysteries. My favorite show, however, was Autopsy on HBO, hosted by the world-renowned forensic pathologist, Dr. Michael Baden. I had a morbid curiosity about crime and the human condition; what drives people to commit these heinous crimes. Is it nature? Is it nurture?

While I was studying at the University of Kansas, I watched Nancy Grace nightly. When she began covering the case of Casey Anthony, aka "Tot Mom", I was glued to my television every night, fascinated by the way Casey could so casually lie in regards to her missing daughter. I couldn't wrap my head around it and watched so intently, trying to figure out how a woman, a mother, could be so flippant about her missing child. I became obsessed with the coverage of her case and the ultimate trial. Many people remember where they were when JFK was shot or when the twin towers were hit. I remember exactly where I was when the verdicts were read in the Casey Anthony case. Those words, "not guilty", took the wind out of me. I refused to believe it then and I refuse to believe it now. But that case really opened Pandora's box for me, wanting to understand more how people are capable of such unthinkable acts. After the Casey Anthony case, I became desperate to find a link, a common thread between these cases. After all these years, I've come to understand one thing to always be true... behind every headline is a human story—and it's never as simple as it seems. There's no such thing as a typical killer. Just ordinary people with terrifying secrets.

In Wicked Women, I wanted to dive deep into the chilling stories of eleven women whose shocking choices shattered lives and challenged our perceptions of what evil looks like, especially because these atrocities were committed by women in a society conditioned to expect such horrors primarily from men. From Susan Smith, whose unimaginable actions forever scarred a community, to Katherine Knight, whose brutality is almost beyond comprehension, these women have left lasting impacts that ripple far beyond their initial crimes.

The disturbing commonality in these stories isn't their violence alone, but rather the unsettling truth that crime doesn't discriminate. Some, like Aileen Wuornos, seemed almost destined to a life steeped in tragedy and turmoil from the start. Others, such as Sherri Papini or Shayna Hubers, grew up in environments that many would deem safe, stable, even enviable and yet they still found themselves capable of committing unthinkable acts.

Perhaps most troubling of all are the mothers among these women, those who defied every instinct and expectation by turning on their own children. The stark reality of a mother harming her child cuts so deeply, shaking our foundational understanding of family, love, and protection.

Each chapter unravels not only the crimes themselves but also the lives and circumstances that led these women down their devastating paths. By exploring their backgrounds, motivations, and the shocking aftermaths of their actions, we are forced to confront the complex nature of evil itself.

These stories compel us to ask difficult questions: Could this happen in my own neighborhood? Could someone I know and trust be capable of such horror? In examining these wicked women, we seek not only to understand the darkness but also to better recognize the fragile lines separating ordinary lives from extraordinary evil.

DRIVEN TO KILL

Susan Smith

Susan Leigh Vaughan was born on September 26, 1971, in Union, South Carolina, the youngest of three children. Her early childhood was marked by tragedy and turmoil. When Susan was only six years old, her father, Harry Vaughan, died by suicide. This traumatic loss deeply affected Susan and family later recalled she kept an audiotape of her dad's voice and his coin collection in her room as mementos. A couple of years later, Susan's mother Linda remarried a local businessman, Beverly "Bev" Russell. Bev was a prominent figure in the community. He was active in the local Republican Party and the Christian Coalition and outwardly, the newly blended family appeared normal. In fact, Susan thrived in school on the surface: she was a member of the National Honor Society and voted "Friendliest Girl" in her high school yearbook. But behind closed doors, Susan's home life was deeply troubling.

As a teenager, Susan endured sexual abuse by her stepfather, Bev Russell. In 1987, when Susan was 15, she confided in her mother and a school counselor that Bev had molested her by fondling her breasts and even forcing her hand on his genitals one night when she'd fallen asleep on his lap. Bev didn't deny it when confronted, and he temporarily moved out for counseling, but the abuse did not stop. A few months later, in early 1988, Susan reported to her counselor that Bev had molested her again. Tragically, Susan and her mother decided not to press charges, and Bev stayed in the family. Years later, it emerged that Bev's sexual involvement with Susan actually continued even into her adulthood, reportedly until as late as six months before the murders of her children. In other words, Susan's own stepfather maintained an illicit sexual "affair" with her off and on through her teens, a fact he himself later admitted and said he was "ashamed of". This long-term betrayal by a parental figure was an enormous psychological burden for Susan.

Mental health struggles accompanied Susan's adolescence. She attempted suicide for the first time at age 13. Then at 17, after a messy end to a relationship with an older married co-worker from her part-time job at Winn-Dixie, Susan attempted suicide again by overdosing on pills. She survived, and doctors labeled her reaction an "adjustment disorder," essentially noting that she had extreme difficulty coping with stress. Despite these red flags, a father's suicide, ongoing sexual abuse, and her own suicide attempts, Susan tried to maintain a veneer of normalcy. She graduated high school and sought stability in the next chapter of life, but the emotional scars of her youth would not disappear.

In the late 1980s, after her second suicide attempt, Susan found comfort in a coworker at Winn-Dixie: David Smith. David was a familiar face from town, and the two began dating when Susan was around 18. Like Susan, David had his own family issues. He was raised by a devoutly religious mother (a Jehovah's Witness) and a strict father, and he chafed under an isolated upbringing. David had even faced tragedy shortly before marrying Susan when his older brother died of an illness 11 days before their wedding, and not long after, David's grief-stricken father attempted suicide. In many ways, Susan and David were two young people coming from turbulent backgrounds, rushing into adulthood and clinging to each other for stability. They dated for about a year, and in 1991, when Susan was 19 and David 20, they got married. Susan was already two months pregnant at the time. In October 1991 she gave birth to their first son, Michael. A second son, Alexander (Alex), would follow in August 1993. From the outside, they looked like a picture-perfect young family starting out. But the reality was far from idyllic.

Susan and David's marriage was volatile and fraught with infidelity. Both were still immature and "neither of them was exactly what you'd call virtuous," a friend observed bluntly. They frequently separated, got back together, and argued about cheating. According to locals, Susan was the first to be unfaithful not long after baby Michael was born. She allegedly had an affair in 1991 with an older man (rumors varied about who), while David responded in kind by having an affair with a coworker named Tiffany Moss. Public fights became routine: friends recall Susan storming into the grocery store where David worked, accusing him of "messing around" with other women, then a week later the couple would reconcile and act lovey-dovey. It was a rollercoaster. They even separated formally in 1993 for a time. While neither spouse was innocent, David insisted he'd always been a good father but the infidelities deeply hurt Susan. She had a desperate need for love and validation (perhaps stemming from the early losses in her life), and when she didn't get it at home, she looked elsewhere.

In 1993, Susan got a new job as a bookkeeper at Conso Products, a local textile company in Union, and this would introduce the key relationship that led to tragedy. At Conso, Susan met Tom Findlay, the 27-year-old son of the company's CEO. Tom was handsome, came from a wealthy family, and was considered quite a catch in town. Susan was immediately taken with him. The two began an affair in January 1994, despite Susan still being married to David. For a few months, Susan secretly dated Tom, sleeping with him "around 10 times" by Tom's later account. In March 1994, David discovered the affair, causing a confrontation that briefly halted Susan's fling with Tom. But by the fall of 1994, Susan and David were separated again, and Susan had told Tom she was going to divorce her husband. They rekindled their romance in September 1994. Susan became infatuated with Tom Findlay and dreamed of a future with him.

However, Tom's feelings were not nearly as strong. He enjoyed Susan's company but was disturbed by some of her behavior and ultimately had no interest in becoming a stepfather to her two little boys.

In mid-October 1994, Tom ended the relationship in a very direct way: he wrote Susan a candid two-page letter explaining why they should part ways. This now-infamous "break-up letter" (dated October 17, 1994) would later be entered as evidence in court. In the letter, Tom praised Susan for being "a great mom" in some ways and even said he was proud of her for taking night classes, but he listed major concerns. First, he "did not want children," and Susan, of course, had two. He said he wasn't ready for the responsibility of being a father. Second, he admonished Susan for what he called her "boy-crazy tendencies" citing an incident in which Susan allegedly kissed and groped a married man (the husband of another Conso employee) while they were nude in a hot tub at the Findlay family's estate. "To be a nice girl, you must act like a nice girl, and that doesn't include sleeping with married men," Tom scolded in the letter. Essentially, he called her out for her flirtations and affairs, and made clear she did not fit the image of the demure, child-free partner he wanted. The breakup letter was brutally honest. Tom Findlay later testified that he thought he'd made his position clear to Susan well before the letter, and that the letter was merely continuing an ongoing discussion about why their relationship wouldn't work. But regardless, Susan was crushed. The love and stability she yearned for with Tom were slipping away, and it sent her into an emotional tailspin.

The weeks following Tom's breakup letter showed Susan's fragile emotional state deteriorating further. She became desperate to win Tom back or at least to figure out how everything had gone so wrong. Co-workers later recounted that in the days before the murders, Susan seemed extremely distraught and upset about personal matters. She was arguing on the phone and crying at work. In late October 1994, about a week after receiving the letter, Susan and Tom had a series of tense conversations. Susan grew paranoid that her estranged husband, David, might reveal embarrassing secrets about her to Tom, possibly referring to the long-term sexual abuse by her stepfather or her other affairs. She was terrified that Tom would hear more "bad things" about her. In one particularly bizarre and self-destructive move, Susan lied to Tom that she had been sleeping with his own father (Tom's dad, Mr. Findlay Sr.). It was a shocking claim and completely untrue. Susan seemingly blurted it out to hurt Tom or test his commitment in some twisted way. Naturally, it backfired. Tom was horrified and angry at the accusation. Shortly after, Susan admitted she made it up "just to see how he would react". Tom was not amused; he told her to leave him alone and said they'd talk later by phone.

On Tuesday, October 25, 1994, everything came to a head. Earlier that day, Susan had a final confrontation with Tom Findlay at the Conso office. That evening, around the end of the workday, Susan met up with a friend, Janet (per later accounts), at a local bar called Hickory Nuts. Susan had her children with her, 3-year-old Michael and 14-month-old Alex, but she was still fixated on seeing Tom one more time that night. She actually drove back to Conso with baby Alex in tow (leaving Michael in her friend's care outside) under the pretext of needing to talk to Tom again. During this encounter, Susan recanted her lie about having an affair with Tom's father and pleaded for Tom's attention, but Tom was "frustrated" and asked her to please leave; he promised he'd call her later, then walked away. A distraught Susan left Tom's workplace for the last time. As she walked out, she told her friend waiting outside, "I've just lost the best friend I ever had."

By all accounts, Susan was overwhelmed with grief, rejection, and a sense of abandonment that evening. She would later describe that night, saying "I had never felt so lonely and sad in my entire life." Those were her own words from her confession. Whether Susan's mental anguish can fully explain what she did next is debatable. Her thoughts turned dark and suicidal. She later told investigators that as she drove around with her two boys that night, she contemplated taking all of their lives in a sort of murder-suicide scenario born out of despair.

As darkness fell on October 25, 1994, Susan Smith set in motion an unthinkable plan. Sometime after 8:00 PM, Susan strapped Michael and Alex into their car seats in her 1990 Mazda Protegé and drove to the outskirts of Union, South Carolina. She later said she was initially heading toward her mother's house, seeking help, but changed course, feeling that even her mother couldn't save her from her misery. Instead, she ended up at John D. Long Lake, a quiet fishing and boating spot just outside of town. There, at a boat ramp leading into the dark water, Susan decided to end her life and the lives of her children.

According to Susan's subsequent confession, she truly intended to kill herself along with her sons at first. She described being in a hysterical, suicidal state as she arrived at the lake. It was pitch black and completely deserted. She sat in the car with the boys and prayed, cried, and agonized. Then she put the Mazda in neutral at the top of the boat ramp. The car began to roll toward the water. At the last moment, Susan slammed the brakes. She couldn't go through with it...not yet. She tried again, letting the car inch closer to the lake, then hit the brake again. She later said she did this "three times," starting to let the car roll then stopping it. Finally, on the third attempt, Susan got out of the car, stood on the driver's side, and released the parking brake while no one was inside to stop it. The Mazda lurched forward down the ramp. In a matter of seconds, with the transmission in neutral, the weight of the car carried it into the lake. Susan watched as the car, with Michael and Alex strapped in their car seats, plunged into the dark water and slowly sank out of sight.

Michael and Alex were trapped, buckled into their seats as water flooded the car. One can hardly imagine the terror and confusion those little boys must have experienced. (Divers later found the Mazda submerged about 18 feet deep, roughly 100 feet from shore, with the children's tiny bodies still strapped in their car seats.) As the car disappeared under the still surface of

John D. Long Lake, Susan allegedly immediately regretted what she'd done but it was far too late. In a panic, she ran up the road. In those frantic moments, her survival instinct kicked in and so did her capacity for deception. She concocted a false story to explain the sudden absence of her car and children. Susan decided she would claim to be the victim of a violent carjacking.

Around 9:00 PM, a nearby resident named Shirley McCloud heard frantic knocking and screams at her front door, not far from the lake. When Mrs. McCloud opened the door, she found a soaking wet and hysterical Susan Smith on the porch. "Please help me! He's got my kids and he's got my car!" Susan screamed. Gasping for breath and appearing distraught, Susan told Shirley McCloud an incredible tale: "A Black man has got my kids and my car," she cried. Mrs. McCloud immediately called 911.

Within minutes, local law enforcement arrived and Susan repeated her story to Union County Sheriff Howard Wells and other officers. She claimed that at around 8:00 PM, she had been stopped at a red light at a deserted intersection (the Monarch Mills intersection in Union) when an African American man with a gun approached her car. According to Susan, the stranger forced his way into her Mazda and ordered her to drive. She said she drove a few miles, with the gunman in the passenger seat threatening her, and her two sons crying in the back. Then, on a lonely stretch of road, the man forced her to stop the car. "I asked him to let me take the kids out," Susan recounted, "but he said no, he didn't have time." She claimed the assailant then pushed her out of the car and sped off with little Michael and Alex still inside. The car and her children were gone. In her story, Susan emphasized that she had never seen the man before, and she described him in detail: a Black male around 40 years old, wearing a dark shirt, jeans, a plaid jacket, and a knit cap. It was a horrifying account, a stranger abduction at gunpoint. And in those initial moments, everyone believed Susan. The petite 23-year-old mother appeared genuinely traumatized and concerned for her babies.

Susan's report of a violent carjacking and child abduction set off a massive search and media frenzy. That very night, law enforcement in Union County mobilized every resource to find Michael and Alex. Sheriff Howard Wells treated the case with urgency. The FBI and the South Carolina Law Enforcement Division (SLED) were called in early the next morning, October 26. Immediately, authorities focused on the area around John D. Long Lake. After all, that's where Susan had turned up claiming to have been dumped by the carjacker. On the morning of Oct. 26, divers were sent into the lake to search below the surface, and a SLED helicopter equipped with heat-sensing technology flew over the water and surrounding woods, hoping to detect the missing car or the children. However, the initial search of the lake found nothing; divers saw no sign of a vehicle in the shallow areas they checked. (Unbeknownst to them, the car was actually further from shore and deeper than they anticipated, due to the way Susan let it roll in.) Meanwhile, officers canvassed roads and highways, and roadblocks were set up to stop and inspect cars matching Susan's Mazda. A composite sketch of the supposed carjacker, based on Susan's detailed description, was drawn and circulated. The sketch showed a bearded African American man in a watch cap and jacket, and it was broadcast on news stations across the country.

Within a day, the story of the missing Smith boys had captured national attention. Here was a young mother making tearful pleas on television for her children's safe return, and a community and nation rallying behind her. Susan, along with her estranged husband David Smith, appeared in front of TV cameras multiple times in the ensuing days. On October 27, just two days after the alleged abduction, Susan and David stood on the steps of the Union County Sheriff's Office and spoke to reporters, weeping and begging for their sons to be brought home. Their anguish was broadcast on programs like NBC's Today and CBS's This Morning. In one interview, when directly asked if she had anything to do with the boys' disappearance, Susan emphatically replied, "I did not have anything to do with the abduction of my children. Whoever did this is a sick and emotionally unstable person." David, holding Susan's hand tightly on camera, said he believed his wife "totally". The sight of the grief-stricken parents moved millions. Ordinary people offered prayers and tips. The FBI tip line was inundated with calls from all over the country with possible sightings or leads.

Behind the scenes, however, investigators were growing suspicious. Susan's story had inconsistencies from the start. For one, she claimed the carjacking happened at a red light at an otherwise empty intersection but officers realized that particular traffic light (at Monarch Mills) stayed green unless another car approached on the cross street. Susan herself mentioned that no other cars were around, so why would she be stopped at a red? It didn't add up. Additionally, law enforcement noted that no witnesses saw any such carjacking that night, despite the area not being completely remote. Susan's demeanor also raised eyebrows. An FBI agent who administered a polygraph test to Susan on October 27 observed that Susan made "fake sounds of crying with no tears in her eyes." In contrast, David's polygraph was clean. He truly seemed to know nothing of the kids' whereabouts. Susan's polygraph results were inconclusive, indicating deception especially when she was asked, "Do you know where your children are?" Her physiological response went off the charts at that question. After the polygraph, Susan admitted to David that she "did not do very well" on the test and expressed worry that authorities might start doubting her. She was right.

Investigators began gently but firmly pressing Susan with the inconsistencies. Over the course of October 27 and 28, she was interviewed repeatedly, sometimes for hours, by SLED and FBI agents. During one interview, Susan mentioned that on the evening of Oct. 25, she had taken the kids out driving to Walmart because her son Michael wanted to go (a claim that seemed odd for a 3-year-old at that hour). When investigators checked Susan's story, they found no one who remembered seeing Susan or the children at Walmart that night. Confronted with that, Susan changed her narrative: she said actually she never went into Walmart, she was just driving around aimlessly for hours to soothe the kids, and she only pulled into the Walmart parking lot briefly to search for Alex's dropped bottle under the bright lights. Again, witnesses and surveillance didn't corroborate even that. With each retelling, Susan's timeline shifted in small ways, raising more red flags.

By October 30 (five days in), law enforcement was openly acknowledging that Susan was a person of interest. Sheriff Wells requested a profile from the FBI's Behavioral Science Unit on the kind of offender who might harm her own children. The profile that came back matched Susan Smith almost exactly, which further bolstered investigators' suspicions. Still, they had to prove the children were not kidnapped by someone else, so they continued running down leads. On October 31, a possible breakthrough call came: police in Seattle, Washington reported finding an abandoned toddler who loosely matched Alex's description, with a man driving a car with South Carolina plates seen in the area. For a moment, hope soared. Could someone have taken the boys across the country? But by that afternoon, it was confirmed the child was not Alex. With that false lead dispelled, investigators in Union were more convinced than ever that Susan's story was a lie and that she knew exactly where her sons were.

During this time, racial tensions were simmering in Union. Susan's lie about a Black assailant had effectively cast suspicion on every Black man in the community. Many African American residents felt unfairly scrutinized and feared vigilantism. As one local said later, "I'm a Black man...why would I want to jack a car and take two white children? For what?" The accusation struck a nerve, recalling ugly, historic stereotypes. Sheriff Wells was keenly aware of this and felt pressure to resolve the case quickly, before tensions worsened. By the start of November, he and lead investigators were essentially certain Susan was lying and that she had likely harmed her own kids. They just needed her to confess, or physical evidence.

Authorities decided to increase the pressure on Susan methodically. They continued playing "good cop" with her in interviews. Agents like Pete Logan from the FBI showed sympathy and tried to build trust, hoping Susan would let her guard down. Meanwhile, Sheriff Wells made calculated public statements. On November 1, one week into the search, Wells held a press conference and pointedly said, "There are no more clues, and no one has been ruled out as a suspect, including Susan and David Smith." This subtle announcement signaled to Susan that law enforcement was onto her, and it laid the groundwork for what came next.

On the ninth day of the ordeal, Susan finally cracked. That morning, Susan and David were scheduled for another round of national TV appearances to keep the story in the news. They appeared live on CBS This Morning, with Susan insisting she had no knowledge of what happened and David professing his trust in her. Immediately afterward, under the pretense of "running errands," Sheriff Wells quietly separated Susan from her family and brought her to a secure location for another interview.

They chose the empty Family Life Center at the local First Baptist Church, perhaps thinking the setting might bring Susan some solace or at least no distractions.

Around 1:40 PM on Nov. 3, Sheriff Wells and Susan sat down privately. This time, Wells did away with any pretense. He looked Susan straight in the eye and told her he knew she was lying about the carjacking. He laid out the evidence calmly: The traffic light couldn't have been red as she said. Undercover officers were surveilling the intersection she switched her story to (the Carlisle intersection) at the exact time she claimed, and they saw no carjacking. And most poignantly, Wells told Susan that if she continued the lie, he would have to go public and reveal that the "Black man" story was false, because it was unfairly stirring racial strife in their community. At this, Susan's facade crumbled. She bowed her head and simply asked Sheriff Wells to pray with her. The two knelt and prayed together in that quiet room. When the prayer ended, Wells looked at her and gently said, "Susan, it is time." Susan Smith responded, "I am so ashamed." And then, at long last, she confessed the horrifying truth.

Susan revealed that her children were not coming home alive. She admitted that on Oct. 25, she had driven to John D. Long Lake and let her car roll into the water with Michael and Alex trapped inside. She spoke of her suicidal intent, how she felt she wanted to die and thought her boys were better off in heaven with her than growing up without a mother. She described the harrowing details: the car in neutral, her pulling the brake at first, then finally letting it go. "They were my life," Susan said of her sons, insisting she loved them deeply and "never meant to harm them." It was a chilling and tragic confession of filicide. Susan acted as though she was emotionally shattered as she spoke, but as prosecutor Tommy Pope later noted, even in her confession she seemed self-focused talking about her feelings and her despair more than the suffering of her children.

Sheriff Wells asked Susan where exactly the car went in. Susan pointed out the boat ramp. Wells then gently had her compose a written confession for the record. Meanwhile, he immediately summoned dive teams back to John D. Long Lake for a final search, this time knowing exactly where to look. That afternoon, divers from SLED and the South Carolina Department of Natural Resources returned to the lake. At 4:00 PM, just as daylight was fading, diver Steve Morrow discovered an object under about 18 feet of water. It was the underside of an upside-down Mazda. The divers marked the spot and confirmed there were bodies inside, then radioed Sheriff Wells. At 5:40 PM on November 3, 1994, Sheriff Wells held a somber press conference and delivered the news everyone dreaded: "We have found the car…and there are bodies inside. We believe they are Michael and Alex Smith." Shortly after, Susan Smith was arrested, charged with two counts of murder in the drowning deaths of her children. The nine-day search had ended in the most tragic way imaginable.

The community of Union (and the entire nation) was in shock. People struggled to comprehend how a mother could do this to her own babies. Adding to the outrage was the fact that Susan had lied so elaborately, manipulating everyone's sympathy and wrongfully blaming an imaginary Black suspect. Crowds gathered outside the courthouse, some screaming for Susan's blood. Death threats were made; the anger was palpable. On the day of her bond hearing, Susan had to be hidden from public view for her safety; an angry mob was outside, and many shouted that they wanted her to face the death penalty. The case was already infamous, and now it took on an even more heated tone. In Union, the racial wounds from the false accusation left many in the Black community enraged, and in the white community, there was a sense of betrayal that this young mother they had all cried with had been the murderer all along.

David Smith was beyond heartbroken. He had truly believed Susan's innocence during those nine days. Now he learned that the person he had once loved and defended had killed their sons. David later recounted that when Susan finally told him the truth (in a brief conversation after her confession), she said, "I'm sorry," in a disturbingly casual way. David asked her "Why? Why did you do this?" and her only answer was, "I don't know why, but I'm sorry." It was nowhere near the kind of explanation or remorse one would hope for. The gulf between them was impossible to cross after that.

Susan Smith's trial would become one of the most high-profile cases of the 1990s. The notion of a mother deliberately killing her own young children was (and still is) beyond comprehension, and the media descended on Union, South Carolina for the legal saga in the summer of 1995. Prosecutor Tommy Pope announced he would seek the death penalty for Susan, given the heinous nature of the crime. The charges were two counts of first-degree murder. Susan was appointed two experienced defense attorneys for capital cases, David Bruck and Judy Clarke, whose primary goal was to save her life from execution.

The trial began on July 18, 1995, at the Union County Courthouse, Judge William Howard presiding. Cameras were banned in the courtroom (Judge Howard was determined to avoid an O.J. Simpson-style circus), but that didn't dampen coverage. Reporters filled the seats and relayed every detail to the outside world. Jury selection delved into sensitive topics; potential jurors were even asked if they had personal knowledge of incest or extramarital affairs, signaling that both Susan's sexual history and her abuse by Bev Russell might feature in testimony.

In his opening statements, Solicitor Tommy Pope painted Susan as a selfish, cold-blooded murderer who saw her innocent children as nothing more than obstacles to her romantic life. He told the jury that Susan invented the carjacking to hide the fact that "she had murdered her children simply because they were obstacles to an affair she was conducting." Pope walked the jury through the timeline of Susan's lies and the eventual confession. He introduced Tom Findlay's breakup letter as a key piece of evidence and it was read aloud in court, making clear to jurors that Susan believed her kids stood in the way of a relationship with Tom. The dramatic reading of Tom's words ("I do not want children," etc.) showed a possible motive. The prosecution also called witnesses to establish how meticulously Susan had lied: law enforcement testified about the fake polygraph tears, the impossible red light scenario, and Susan's own angry reaction when first accused of harming her kids (she had dramatically pounded a table and yelled, "I can't believe you think I did it!" during an interrogation). One especially harrowing moment was when diver Steve Morrow took the stand and described finding the Mazda submerged in the lake, with little Michael and Alex still buckled in their seats underwater. That testimony brought many in the courtroom to tears and highlighted the horror of the crime.

The defense did not contest that Susan let her car roll into the lake. She had confessed, after all. But they argued the act was born of mental illness and extreme emotional disturbance, not malice. David Bruck portrayed Susan as a "deeply troubled, mentally ill young woman" who had intended a murder-suicide but wasn't in her right mind. The defense's opening statement claimed this was a "botched suicide attempt" by someone "unstable" after being rejected by the man she loved. Essentially, they wanted the jury to see Susan not as a calculating killer but as a tragic figure driven by depression and trauma. Bruck reminded jurors of Susan's "lifetime of betrayals," emphasizing her father's suicide, the long-term sexual abuse by her stepfather, her husband David's infidelity, and Tom Findlay's rejection. He argued these cumulative traumas impaired Susan's sanity and judgment. The defense brought in mental health experts who diagnosed Susan with disorders like dependent personality disorder and severe depression (these details came out in the sentencing phase). They also had Susan's mother, Linda, testify tearfully about the sexual abuse by Bev Russell and how it devastated Susan. In essence, the defense plea was: Yes, Susan did this horrible thing, but she was mentally ill, and it was an act of extreme desperation, not a cold plan to get rid of her kids.

The trial lasted only about nine days. Susan herself did not testify, which is common in such cases, especially since cross-examination could have been brutal. The evidence was overwhelming, given her confession, so the real battle was over her punishment. After closing arguments, the jury deliberated for only 2½ hours before returning a verdict: Guilty on two counts of murder. There was little doubt or hesitation. It was July 22, 1995, and Susan Smith, 23 years old, now faced either the death penalty or life in prison.

In South Carolina, the jury decides on death or life in the sentencing phase for capital murder. Tommy Pope urged the jurors to choose death. He stressed that Susan had multiple opportunities to stop on the night of Oct. 25 and chose to send her boys to their deaths, and then chose to lie about it for over a week. He argued that the aggravating factors, the victims being two defenseless children and the calculated deception afterward, warranted execution. In a powerful closing, Pope said the case's theme was choice: "She made the choice to send her boys down that ramp," and then she chose to betray everyone's trust.

The defense, on the other hand, pleaded for mercy. David Bruck walked the jury back through Susan's troubled life, essentially asking them to see the wounded human being behind the monster image. In an unusual flourish, Bruck pulled out a Bible and read the story of Jesus and the woman accused of adultery, quoting "He that is without sin among you, let him cast the first stone." It was a dramatic appeal for compassion, implying that society should not simply execute Susan for her terrible deed, and that she would be haunted by her "choice" for the rest of her days. Susan herself declined to speak to the jury when given a final chance, likely because she was too overwhelmed or advised not to. (My money is on the latter.)

In the end, the jury spared Susan Smith's life. After a few hours of deliberation, on July 28, 1995, they returned with a unanimous decision to sentence her to life in prison instead of death. Several jurors later said that while they were horrified by Susan's actions, they believed she was "really disturbed" and that executing her would not bring justice. One female juror told reporters, "giving her the death penalty wouldn't serve justice." The formal sentence handed down by Judge Howard was life imprisonment with the possibility of parole after 30 years (the maximum penalty short of death, since at that time life without parole was not an option). This meant Susan would be eligible for parole in November 2024, when she would be 53 years old.

Reactions to the sentence were mixed. Many people were relieved that the "state didn't take another life," while others were angry that Susan had escaped death. Outside the courthouse, David Smith expressed bitter disappointment. "Me and my family of course are disappointed that the death penalty wasn't the verdict," he told the press. "I'll never forget what Susan has done and I'll never forget Michael and Alex." David felt justice had not been fully served. In truth, he wanted Susan dead for what she did. He later admitted that for him, execution would have been preferable so he wouldn't have to worry about her potentially getting out of prison someday.

The broader public and media response to the trial was intense. The Susan Smith case became synonymous with maternal filicide and betrayal. It sparked difficult conversations about mental health, the effects of childhood abuse, and the societal expectations of motherhood. It also unfortunately became entangled with issues of race, given Susan's false allegation. Many Black Americans saw her case as an example of how readily a white woman's lie about a Black assailant was believed (echoing historical events). The case was featured on virtually every major news network and true crime show; Oprah Winfrey did episodes on it, and it was dissected in print media from Time magazine to local newspapers. Within a year, multiple books had been written, including one by David Smith himself (Beyond All Reason: My Life with Susan Smith), and true crime TV documentaries examined the case in detail. Susan's double murder of her boys stood out as one of the most tragic and perplexing crimes of the decade.

After the trial, Susan Smith began serving her life sentence in the South Carolina Department of Corrections. On July 28, 1995, the day after sentencing, the 23-year-old was transferred to the Camille Griffin Graham Correctional Institution in Columbia, South Carolina. Graham is the state's main prison for female inmates (also where death row for women was, at the time). Susan was inmate #221487, and for a while, she kept a low profile. But it didn't take long for Susan to make headlines again... this time for her misconduct behind bars.

In the year 2000, about five years into her sentence, rumors swirled that Susan was involved in sexual activity with prison staff. Those rumors turned out to be true. In August 2000, Susan confessed to prison administrators that she had engaged in sex acts with a corrections officer named Houston Cagle on four occasions within the prison grounds. At the time, Susan was 28 and Officer Cagle was 50. An investigation revealed that Cagle, a married father of two, had indeed carried on a sexual relationship with Susan, which is a serious crime (inmates cannot legally consent to sex with staff). Cagle ultimately pleaded guilty to misconduct in office for having sex with Susan, was fired, and actually spent 3 months in prison himself as punishment. Susan received a disciplinary write-up for the illicit relationship.

Shockingly, that was not an isolated incident. Mere weeks after Cagle's actions came to light, another prison employee, Captain Alfred Rowe, was implicated in a sexual relationship with Susan. It turned out Susan had also slept with Capt. Rowe, a supervisory officer. In September 2000, Rowe was arrested after Susan revealed the affair to investigators (reportedly, she decided to tell it all during the investigation into Cagle). Rowe confessed and, in 2001, pleaded guilty. He received five years of probation (no jail time) for his crime. The back-to-back scandals of two guards having sex with the infamous Susan Smith rocked the Department of Corrections. It also reinforced a perception that Susan was adept at manipulating men, even in a prison environment. As one prison source told People, after these incidents Susan was considered such a risk that "No one trusts her to be alone with a guard...when she's being transported, there are always two guards with her, preferably a male and a female."

As a direct result of the guard scandals, in September 2000 officials moved Susan to a different prison, away from Columbia. She was transferred to the Leath Correctional Institution in Greenwood County, South Carolina. Leath is a smaller, maximum-security women's prison. There, staff took special precautions given Susan's history: she was never left alone with a single officer, and any time she was moved, multiple inmates or a female guard would accompany to ensure no further inappropriate contact. Essentially, Susan's reputation in prison was that she would seek out male attention if given the chance, and indeed one of the men (Alfred Rowe) later suggested that losing access to male attention was like Susan losing a "drug" she craved.

But sex with guards wasn't the only trouble Susan got into at Leath. Over the years, she amassed a disciplinary record including infractions for drug use and self-harm. Prison records show that starting in 2010, Susan was written up multiple times. In March and April 2010, she was caught with marijuana or other narcotics on two occasions. In April 2010, she was also written up for "mutilation" (prison jargon for self-injury) after she had harmed herself in a way that left marks or scars. On the same day as that self-harm incident, Susan was sent for outside medical treatment, indicating it was serious enough to need hospital attention. In February 2012, she was disciplined for an innocuous-sounding but still rule-breaking act: using another inmate's PIN number to make phone calls. And in March 2015, she again tested positive for or was found with marijuana. Each infraction resulted in punishments like loss of visitation, telephone, and canteen privileges for months at a time, and occasionally short stints in solitary confinement. For example, the drug offenses cost her up to a year of phone and visitation rights, and the phone-PIN misuse got her 240 days with no privileges.

It's worth noting that after 2015, Susan's disciplinary record improved significantly. Perhaps as her parole date inched closer, she realized good behavior was crucial. In the last decade, she has stayed mostly out of trouble (no major infractions on record post-2015). A prison source in 2020 noted, "She's behaving herself these days. She knows her parole date is coming and she can't get parole if she isn't being good." Indeed, Susan seemed to shift focus to self-improvement programs in prison. She earned several vocational and educational certificates: a WorkKeys Silver certificate (for workplace readiness) and completed Level I Horticulture and Custodial Maintenance programs with on-the-job training. In 2014, she received a certificate in horticulture after 200 hours of training, learning gardening and greenhouse skills. She held various prison jobs over the years, laundry, janitorial, etc., and by 2024 she was reportedly working as a ward keeper's assistant (an inmate aide role). All these efforts were likely aimed at demonstrating rehabilitation.

While in prison, Susan made a few attempts to appeal her conviction and also to explain her actions to the public. In January 2010, Susan filed a handwritten motion from prison requesting a new trial. She argued that her attorney (Bruck) had not represented her adequately and alleged prosecutorial misconduct and even a Miranda rights violation. Essentially, she was claiming her original trial was unfair. However, this was seen as a long-shot and was quickly dismissed. A Union County prosecutor pointed out that any such motion was about 14 years too late (motions for new trial must be made within a year of conviction in SC). Circuit Judge Lee Alford rejected Susan's request, noting she hadn't presented any new credible evidence or legal basis. In his denial, Judge Alford specifically mentioned that Susan's reference to "battered woman's syndrome" didn't apply here and that syndrome might explain a woman killing an abusive spouse in self-defense, but "not killing her children," he wrote bluntly. Thus, Susan's conviction stood.

Susan also attempted to reach out publicly to tell her side of the story or at least to push back against her villainous image. In 2014, a reporter from The State (a Columbia, SC newspaper) wrote Susan a letter asking if she'd share her experiences of the crime and trial. To the reporter's surprise, Susan wrote back.

Because all inmate mail is monitored, her reply wasn't delivered until early 2015 (it had to be approved by prison officials). In that letter, Susan complained, "It has been hard to listen to lie after lie and not be able to defend myself." She insisted, "I'm not the monster society thinks I am. I am far from it. I was a good mother and I loved my boys.". These words did not garner much sympathy. To many, it felt like Susan was still making it about herself, not acknowledging the unimaginable pain she caused. Tommy Pope, the former prosecutor, publicly responded that Susan's letter "has always taken a self-centered focus over the years". "If you look at the letter, it's still more about her. Not about Michael and Alex, not about regrets of the crime," Pope said, noting that Susan seemed more concerned with "the way she's perceived." Indeed, nowhere in Susan's letter did she directly say "I'm sorry for what I did" to her children. It only reinforced the public's negative view of her.

On the other hand, David Smith spent years processing his grief and trying to build a new life. David and Susan's divorce was finalized in May 1995, while Susan was in jail awaiting trial. In the late 90s, David admitted he was initially terrified to try having a family again, but eventually he did find love and hope. He had a daughter in 2000 with a woman named Tiffany (the same Tiffany Moss he'd dated years before), and a son in 2003 with another partner. David stated he would always love Michael and Alex and that no new children could replace them, but holding his baby daughter in 2000 helped him promise himself "not to be afraid to love her" and always protect her. Over time, David publicly said he forgave Susan, not for her sake, but so that bitterness wouldn't consume him and so he could find peace. However, forgiving did not mean forgetting or ever wanting her free. As Susan's potential parole drew nearer, David became vocal that he would fight her release. "I will do everything in my power to make sure you stay behind bars," he said in 2024. He insisted that 30 years behind bars was "just not enough" for what Susan did and that he had never sensed genuine remorse from her.

In South Carolina, a life sentence with parole eligibility meant that in late 2024, Susan Smith's case would go before the parole board. As that date approached, the case re-entered the headlines. By this time, Susan had served nearly 30 years. Some wondered if the now-middle-aged woman had changed, or if any compassion was warranted. Most, however, firmly believed that freeing Susan Smith would be an injustice.

On November 4, 2024, Susan Smith had her first parole hearing. She was 53 years old. Leading up to it, reports emerged that Susan had been on her best behavior in prison in recent years, trying to "better her chances". And indeed, at the parole hearing, Susan spoke in her own behalf. In a trembling voice, she told the board, "I know what I did was horrible, and I would give anything if I could go back and change it." She talked about how she had found God in prison, saying, "I am a Christian and God is a big part of my life and I know He has forgiven me... I just ask that you show that same kind of mercy as well." It was the most the public had heard from Susan directly in decades.

The two-member parole panel (it was a small hearing) did not take long to deliberate. Parole was denied. After a brief recess, the board announced that Susan's release would not be granted. In fact, it was a unanimous rejection by all three parole board members (in SC, the full board must review violent offender paroles). The news came as a relief to many who had been anxiously following the hearing. Outside, a crowd including David Smith and other family members rejoiced quietly. David had delivered an impassioned statement to the parole board, urging them to keep Susan locked up. "This wasn't a 'tragic mistake,'" he said. "She purposely meant to end their life...Thirty years is not enough." He reminded the board of the pure terror Michael and Alex experienced and that Susan's actions were conscious and deliberate. David vowed, "I will be here every two years going forward to ensure that their death doesn't go in vain." Under state law, now that she has passed the 30-year mark, Susan can seek parole every two years. David has promised to oppose her each time, and it's likely the public outcry will as well. (Notably, when 2024 came, over 80,000 people signed a petition against her parole.)

Even some who might feel sympathy for Susan's past mental health struggles believe that her freedom would be an affront to justice. As one of the prosecutors said, the community has the right to "put this behind them and forget about Susan Smith", and every parole hearing reopens old wounds. At her 2024 hearing, one board member bluntly told Susan that her disciplinary issues (drugs, sex, etc.) indicated she hadn't exactly been a model inmate. All those factors weighed against her. And so, Susan Smith remains incarcerated at Leath Correctional Institution, where she works her job and lives out her days largely quietly. Her next chance at parole will come in November 2026, but given the continued public sentiment, it's unlikely to succeed any more than the last.

True crime shows continue to revisit Susan Smith's case. In fact, NBC's Dateline aired a two-hour special "Return to the Lake" in 2025, featuring interviews with investigators and with David Smith. In that special, Susan's voice was heard via a recording from the parole hearing, marking one of the very few times the public has heard from her since 1995. Yet, even as time passes, sympathy lies firmly with the victims, Michael and Alex, whose lives were cut short. The prevailing feeling is encapsulated by something David Smith said years ago: "You don't kill your children for what happened to you."

THOU SHALT NOT KILL

Cindy Reese

Cindy Kaye Henderson was born and raised in a devout Baptist family in Alabama. Her father served as an associate pastor at Springville Baptist Church, and Cindy grew up deeply involved in church activities. By all accounts she was a "good girl." She didn't party, didn't drink, and lived a conservative lifestyle shaped by her faith. After earning a degree in accounting, Cindy married her college sweetheart, Mike Tillery, in 1995. Family pressure played a role in this early marriage, and Cindy may have wed before she was truly ready, hoping to please her strict upbringing.

The marriage to Mike Tillery was troubled. Friends recall that Mike had a difficult personality and that Cindy often seemed unhappy. She became moodier and more withdrawn over the years. Then in 2007, after 12 years of marriage, tragedy struck. One day Cindy came home from work and found Mike's vehicle in the driveway, but he didn't greet her. She went looking for him and discovered him in a downstairs room of their home, dead from a self-inflicted gunshot wound to the head. Her first husband had committed suicide with a shotgun, a horrifying scene that Cindy stumbled upon. This trauma devastated Cindy. She spiraled into a deep depression for months, barely getting out of bed. The emotional scars from finding her husband's body would stay with her, and Cindy later said she developed symptoms of PTSD after this event.

Slowly, with the support of family, Cindy tried to rebuild her life. In 2008, a cousin thought Cindy might be ready to meet someone new and introduced her to a local man named Michael Reese. Cindy was hesitant at first. After all, she was a grieving widow. But she agreed to give Michael a chance. From their very first date, Michael Reese impressed her. He was courteous, kind, and even old-fashioned in his manners, opening doors for her and treating her with genuine chivalry. As Cindy later told her friends, "I had no idea that it could be like this," referring to how caring Michael was compared to what she'd known before. Michael was equally smitten. Friends recall that he was head over heels for Cindy from day one. He acted almost like a different person, excited and hopeful about the future. After about a year and a half of dating, the couple married on September 5, 2009 in a small country church in their hometown. For Cindy, this marriage to Michael was a second chance at happiness after so much heartbreak.

Despite the darkness in her past, those who knew Cindy before 2015 describe her as a quiet, church-going woman who loved music and her faith. She served as the Minister of

Music at her church and worked as an accountant for Jefferson County. There were no red flags in Cindy's history that foreshadowed violence. No criminal record, no known erratic behavior. If anything, people thought of her as resilient for overcoming her first husband's suicide. Cindy herself would later emphasize how that trauma affected her: for instance, it made her fearful of discovering another loved one hurt or dead. This context would become important on the night of Michael's death, when Cindy claimed that her past trauma influenced her actions. But in 2009, as she walked down the aisle with Michael Reese, Cindy seemed ready to leave the pain behind and build a happy life.

Michael Earl Reese was a lifelong Alabama country boy, born and raised just outside the small town of Morris. He loved the slower pace of a rural community and wasn't interested in the hustle and bustle of big-city life. Friends and family describe Michael as an easy-going, friendly man who enjoyed simple pleasures. One of his favorite hobbies was fishing on quiet lakes, but his true passion was computers. Michael was a self-taught "computer whiz" and if anyone in town had a tech problem, they'd call Michael, and he'd fix in minutes what might have stumped others for hours. His family was proud of how he turned that passion into a career: Michael went to college to study computer technology and landed a job in IT at St. Vincent's Hospital in Birmingham after graduation. His mother once remarked how proud she was that Michael got to do exactly what he loved for a living.

By his early 30s, Michael had already been through one marriage. He had married a hometown sweetheart in his twenties, but after five years his first wife filed for divorce. The split was rough on Michael. He was the type of person who hated being alone. He deeply wanted a family, children, and a stable home life. As one friend put it, "he wasn't getting any younger" and he yearned to meet "the woman that would make his life complete… and a good Christian home". After his divorce around 2008, Michael let friends know he was ready to date again in hopes of finding that lasting love. He even asked a close friend, Jennifer, to introduce him to any nice single women she knew. Jennifer thought of a woman she'd met at her child's birthday party, Cindy Henderson. Jennifer remembered Cindy as sweet and deeply rooted in faith, much like Michael. Sensing they could be a good match, she arranged for Michael and Cindy to meet.

Those who knew Michael say he was the quintessential "good guy." He was funny, kind, and the type of friend you knew you could count on. When Michael fell in love with Cindy, he fell hard. His friends noticed a positive change in him when he began dating her. He seemed happier and more optimistic, acting "a little different" but in the best way. Michael embraced Cindy's world quickly. After they married, he joined her church and became an active member of Sardis Baptist Church in Morris, where Cindy served as choir director. He made fast friends in the congregation and was always willing to volunteer for church activities. In fact, when Sardis got a new pastor a few years later, Michael developed a friendship with him too. Michael was the kind of person who could get along with everyone.

Friends and family universally described Michael as gentle and good-natured. He had no known enemies and no dark secrets. Detectives later noted that Michael "wasn't the type of person that anybody would want to hurt for any reason". When rumors of marital trouble surfaced in 2014 (as Cindy and Pastor Jeff grew closer), Michael's relatives were skeptical that Michael was to blame for any conflict. In fact, when someone later alleged that Michael might have mistreated Cindy, his family flatly rejected the idea, saying they "don't think he had it in him... I don't even think he could be cruel". By all accounts, Michael dearly loved Cindy and was committed to making the marriage work, even when they hit bumps in the road. Tragically, Michael's devotion and forgiving nature may have put him at risk when he found himself caught in a deadly love triangle.

Morris, Alabama, with a population of about 2,000, is a place where church is at the center of community life. In fact, Morris has been called one of the most conservative towns in Alabama. Faith is woven into daily life, and small-town gossip often spreads through church social circles. Michael and Cindy attended Sardis Baptist Church, a modest local church that Cindy had been part of for years (first with her family, and later as the music minister). In 2013, Sardis Baptist decided to shake things up by hiring a new young pastor to lead the flock. The church elders hoped a younger minister would energize the congregation and appeal to youth and young families. That's how Pastor Jeffery David Brown arrived in their lives.

Jeffrey "Jeff" Brown came on as Sardis

Baptist's senior pastor in 2013. He was in his mid-30s at the time and arrived with his wife, Noel (sometimes spelled Noelle), and their two young children. At first, many in the congregation welcomed the change. A longtime member recalled thinking that Jeff's youth and enthusiasm might be a great fit: "being young… it would appeal to [the younger members] more", she said. Michael Reese himself was touched by Pastor Jeff's ministry. In fact, Jeff Brown even baptized Michael at Sardis Baptist not long after becoming pastor. Jeff was charismatic and outgoing, and he quickly formed a close bond with Michael and Cindy. The two couples (the Browns and the Reeses) started spending a lot of time together throughout 2013 and 2014. They would socialize outside of church as Cindy and Michael would babysit Jeff and Noel's kids, and in return the Browns might come over for dinner or help the Reeses with favors. On the surface, it looked like a warm friendship between a pastor's family and a devoted parishioner couple.

However, small churches in small towns can also be hotbeds of gossip, and the arrival of Pastor Jeff eventually stirred up more than just fellowship. Some older church members found Jeff's style to be a bit off-putting. The "honeymoon" phase of his tenure didn't last long. For example, there was a minor clash over something as simple as the church bulletin. Jeff made changes that upset the traditionalists, leading to what one member called the "bulletin blow-up" and creating tension between Jeff and some deacons. Beneath Jeff's friendly exterior, a few sensed that something was "beneath the surface." One congregant later said, "I could tell that he wasn't as forthcoming... there was something beneath the surface there." In a town like Morris, even subtle personal drama doesn't stay secret for long.

By early 2014, rumors spread like wildfire around Sardis Baptist that Pastor Jeff Brown and Cindy Reese were more than just friends. Whispers circulated that the married choir director and the married pastor were carrying on an affair. At first it was just church gossip with stolen glances noticed by parishioners, or Jeff and Cindy spending perhaps a little too much time together. Then a particularly scandalous rumor emerged: allegedly, someone spotted Cindy in a compromising situation with a man in a pest-control truck in a parking garage. Since Jeff Brown had a side job working for a pest control company at the time, tongues wagged that the man in the truck must have been Pastor Jeff. It's the kind of salacious small-town story that spreads fast, and it reached the ears of Sardis's leadership. When confronted, Cindy initially downplayed things. She even admitted to friends that she had begun working out regularly and that Pastor Jeff was one of her workout partners... a piece of news that only made her friends more uncomfortable given the swirling rumors.

Inside the Reese household, things had begun to change as well. Cindy later claimed that around this time, Michael had become distant at home, spending more time on his computer and less time with her, and allegedly losing interest in intimacy. Whether this was true or merely Cindy's perception, she found a sympathetic ear in Pastor Jeff. The two grew closer under the guise of "counseling" or friendship. As one observer quipped, "If she cries to him, she'll lie with him," suggesting that Cindy's venting about her marital woes to Jeff led to an emotional and physical affair. In the spring of 2014, Jeff Brown and Cindy Reese's relationship did indeed turn sexual, according to later testimony. Both were still married, Cindy to Michael, and Jeff to Noel, so they took great pains to keep the affair secret. But in a tiny community, such secrets are hard to keep.

By mid-2014, the affair was essentially an open secret in the church. Sardis Baptist's elders learned of the inappropriate relationship and were preparing to take action. Rather than face a disciplinary meeting with the deacons, Pastor Jeff suddenly resigned one Sunday morning and left the church. His departure was abrupt; he gave a sermon and stepped down, shocking many congregants. The Browns moved out of the parsonage and Jeff no longer led services. Cindy, for her part, also left Sardis Baptist shortly thereafter. Understandably, it was a tense environment for her. The scandal rocked the little church, costing it several members who were disillusioned by the turn of events. Still, the church community pressed on with interim leadership, trying to heal from the breach of trust. No one at the time could have predicted just how much worse this situation would get.

In the aftermath of the resignation, Jeff Brown's life went into flux. He had been a jack-of-all-trades before and his résumé was unusually varied. Over the years Jeff had worked as a police officer, a hairdresser, a moving company employee, and a pastor. After leaving Sardis Baptist in 2014, Jeff found work with a local moving company and also reportedly did pest control work on the side. He and his wife Noel initiated divorce proceedings, and Cindy even helped Jeff with the paperwork for that divorce. Jeff's wife and children moved away, effectively ending the Brown family friendship with the Reeses. But Jeff and Cindy's connection was far from over.

Jeff Brown and Cindy Reese's affair began in spring 2014 and burned hot through that summer. During those months, they seized any chance to be together in secret. They met at off-site locations (as the pest-control truck rumor attests), and even used Cindy's workplace parking garage for rendezvous according to town gossip. Under the pressure of potential scandal, Pastor Jeff resigned from the church by late summer 2014, effectively ending their day-to-day interactions at Sardis. Allegedly, the physical affair "ended" in the fall of 2014, around the time the Reeses took a planned trip to Disney World for their 5th anniversary. Michael had arranged this vacation as a way for him and Cindy to reconnect and mend their marriage. By then Michael was aware, at least generally, that something inappropriate had happened between Cindy and Jeff. According to Michael's family, he had learned of the affair and was deeply hurt, but he loved Cindy dearly and wanted to save the marriage. He believed, as did Cindy for a time, that a fresh start was possible if they recommitted to each other. So in December 2014, Michael surprised Cindy with a trip to Walt Disney World, hoping "the happiest place on Earth" could rekindle their bond.

By all accounts, the Disney trip did help Michael and Cindy. They rebuilt their relationship during that vacation, enjoying each other's company, laughing and bonding like they hadn't in a long time. But one person was not happy about this turn of events: Jeff Brown. Even while Cindy was on her anniversary trip, Jeff repeatedly called her cell phone. Cindy complained to friends that Jeff "wouldn't leave her alone" and kept interrupting what was supposed to be a romantic getaway. Jeff was growing increasingly possessive. In fact, when Michael and Cindy returned home from Disney in late 2014, Jeff was allegedly sitting on their doorstep waiting for them to get back. He was furious that Cindy hadn't told him they were coming home and, as Michael later recounted to a friend, Jeff got "really aggressive" with Cindy that day. Michael stepped in and told Pastor Jeff to leave his wife alone, firmly drawing a line now that he and Cindy were reconciling. This confrontation marked a major shift... Cindy now had to fully choose between her husband and her lover.

Publicly, Cindy appeared to recommit to Michael after the trip. She and Michael started attending church together again (at a different congregation, since Sardis was no longer comfortable). They spent more time with Cindy's family and tried to return to normal life. Privately, however, Cindy did not completely cut ties with Jeff. On the contrary, the two continued to talk every single day, multiple times a day. Despite promising to Michael that the affair was over, Cindy kept Jeff in her life. They had, in many ways, become entwined not just emotionally but financially. Investigators later discovered that during late 2014, Cindy and Jeff had intertwined their finances and assets in preparation for a possible future together. They opened a joint savings account at a local credit union, listing both their names. Cindy used her good credit to purchase a car for Jeff, putting his name and her name on the vehicle title. She even co-signed the lease on the apartment Jeff moved into after leaving his wife, since Jeff's own credit history was poor. In other words, even after the affair was supposedly "over," Cindy was quietly funding Jeff's lifestyle and laying groundwork to build a life with him. It's unclear if Michael knew about these financial arrangements but detectives strongly believe he did not know.

The communications between Cindy and Jeff also remained intense. Phone records would later show dozens of calls or texts between them on a daily basis. Jeff was still fixated on Cindy, and Cindy, whether out of love, lust, or fear, kept stringing him along while still playing the role of dutiful wife at home. Around this time, according to Jeff's later statements, Cindy began voicing dark fantasies about permanently removing the obstacle to their happiness: Michael. Jeff claimed that Cindy frequently said she wanted her husband dead. She allegedly mentioned multiple times that she could shoot Michael or poison him, and then "plead insanity" to avoid punishment. At one point, Cindy asked Jeff if he could arrange for someone to "do the dirty work" for her and essentially, hire a hitman. Jeff later admitted that he actually attempted this: while working at the moving company, he approached at least two co-workers and offered money (and even his car) if they would kill Michael Reese. He concocted a story to justify the hit, telling the would-be henchmen that Michael was abusive and had raped his wife, so "he needed to be handled". Jeff described the target in detail as an IT worker at St. Vincent's Hospital who drove a white Honda Accord, effectively giving away that he meant Michael Reese. The co-workers were appalled; they refused and later said they were offended that Jeff even asked. In January 2015, this incident got Jeff fired from the moving company and was even reported to police, though at the time there wasn't enough evidence for authorities to act immediately. Still, a disturbing picture was forming: Jeff Brown was desperate enough to talk about murder for hire, and Cindy, by Jeff's account, was encouraging it.

Cindy, for her part, denies that she was plotting to kill Michael during this period. She would later claim that all the murder plans were Jeff's doing alone. But what's clear is that by early 2015, even after the affair had apparently ended, Cindy Reese was deeply entangled with Jeff Brown. They had shared finances, constant covert communication, and at least one of them (if not both) was contemplating murder as a solution to their love triangle. All of this set the stage for the night of February 18, 2015, the night Michael Reese was killed in cold blood.

February 18, 2015 was a Wednesday, and it began ordinarily enough for the Reeses. Michael, 40, went to work as usual at the hospital. Cindy, 38, went to her accounting job at the Jefferson County Courthouse in Birmingham. Nothing seemed amiss to coworkers that morning. But by lunchtime,

Cindy was already in contact with Jeff. She later admitted that during her lunch break that day, she met up with Jeff Brown under the pretense of helping him with some divorce paperwork. Sometime around noon, Jeff picked Cindy up and they spent part of the lunch hour together finalizing forms related to Jeff's split from Noel. When their errand was done, Jeff drove Cindy back to her office. If any coworkers noticed, they might have thought nothing of it. After all, Jeff and Cindy were openly friends.

That afternoon, Michael had made plans to spend the evening with Cindy. It was Wednesday night church night, a routine they kept. Around 5:00 PM, Michael picked Cindy up from work (she often rode with him when they had mutual plans). On the drive home, the couple stopped by the house of Cindy's mother. Each week Michael and Cindy helped Cindy's elderly mom by taking out her trash, and February 18 was no exception. They did this small chore and visited briefly, then headed to Sardis Baptist Church for the mid-week evening service.

Approximately 6:00 – 7:00 PM: Cindy and Michael attended the Wednesday night church service. Even though Jeff was no longer pastor, the Reeses were still active in church life. Jeff himself was not present (he had no role at Sardis after his resignation). According to phone records, at 6:57 PM as the church service was wrapping up, Cindy received a text on her phone from Jeff Brown. The message was brief and telling. It said: "keep me posted." Investigators believe this was an explicit coordination signal and a clue that Jeff and Cindy had a plan underway for later that night.

Shortly after 7:00 PM, the service concluded and people filtered out of church. Michael and Cindy left together in Michael's white Honda Accord. As they pulled away, Cindy did something highly unusual. She placed a call to Jeff on her cell phone at 7:03 PM, just minutes after leaving church. The call connected, but Cindy didn't have an obvious conversation. In fact, it appears she simply kept the line open for 29 minutes, remaining connected to Jeff all the way during the drive after church. Investigators later noted this as extremely odd behavior: essentially, Cindy had an open line in the car with Jeff listening in while she was with her husband. Why would someone do that? Police theorized it was so Jeff could eavesdrop and track the couple's movements in real time knowing exactly when they would arrive home. It was the modern equivalent of keeping someone on speakerphone to hear what's happening.

After church, Michael and Cindy decided to grab a quick dinner. They stopped at Milo's Hamburgers, a local fast-food joint, to pick up some takeout. They ordered burgers and a side of french fries to share. By roughly 7:30 PM, the couple was headed home with their takeout. As they neared home, Cindy casually mentioned that she needed to pick up a few groceries from the Piggly Wiggly supermarket before the night was over. Specifically, she said they were low on some items for upcoming church events. As Cindy later testified, the only things she actually needed were a ham and some orange juice. Michael agreed to let her do a quick grocery run. They pulled into their neighborhood on Banks

Street in Morris around 7:45 PM or so. Michael parked in the driveway of their modest white house. Ironically enough, their home was just a stone's throw from the town's police station.

Cindy's story is that both of them entered the house briefly with their Milo's food. Michael, ever the gentleman, helped carry the bags inside for her. The plan was that Cindy would head right back out to the store, while Michael stayed home and started eating dinner. According to Cindy, she left the house around 7:50 PM to go shopping, leaving Michael alive and well in their home. From this point, we rely on phone records, surveillance, and later testimony to reconstruct what really happened:

Around 7:50 PM: Cindy drove toward the Piggly Wiggly. At some point very soon after leaving, she met up with Jeff Brown at a pre-arranged location. Cindy later admitted that she met Jeff at a gas station about 10 minutes from the house to give him some cash. She handed Jeff $15 for gas money, claiming it was just a friendly gesture because he was low on cash. This meetup was likely part of their coordinated plan, possibly to ensure Jeff had fuel if he needed to drive somewhere quickly that night. It also placed Jeff very close to the Reese residence at exactly the critical time. (Cell tower records later confirmed Jeff's phone was pinging near the Reese home, not an hour away in another town like he would later claim.)

8:00 PM: About ten minutes after leaving home, Cindy arrived at the Piggly Wiggly grocery store. Surveillance footage and receipts would later confirm that she purchased exactly two items: a ham and a jug of orange juice. She checked out quickly. Around this same time, just after 8 o'clock, a 911 call was placed from the Reeses' home phone.

What happened back at the house between 7:50 and 8:00 PM is the crux of the case. The prosecution's theory, supported by evidence, is that Cindy never actually left Michael alive. Instead, they argue that as soon as Michael carried the food inside and turned his back, Cindy shot her husband in the back of the head at close range, execution-style. The gun used was a .38 caliber revolver that the Reeses owned. It usually sat on a gun rack in the bedroom. (In fact, Cindy would later point out to investigators that this revolver was mysteriously missing after the murder.) The shot struck Michael in the head, killing him almost instantly and dropping him near the doorway to their kitchen at the rear of the house. Michael likely never even saw it coming.

The Reese home on Banks Street was cordoned off by police on the night of February 18, 2015. Investigators found the scene suspiciously staged: furniture was overturned, but there were no signs of forced entry or theft.

According to prosecutors, Cindy immediately set about staging the scene to look like a burglary gone wrong. She overturned a coffee table in the living room, scattered some belongings, and took off some of her own jewelry to make it appear items had been stolen. She placed a couple of her jewelry pieces in a bag (these would later be given to Jeff to dispose of). Importantly, there was no sign of forced entry. There was no door pried open or window smashed. This suggested that whoever killed Michael either had a key or was let inside willingly. By staging a messy living room,

Cindy may have hoped officers would assume an intruder slipped in and surprised Michael.

After creating a superficial ransacking, Cindy then did something chilling: evidence suggests she used the landline phone in the house to call Jeff (or at least keep an open line with him) during the immediate aftermath. Phone company records later showed an outgoing call from the Reese home phone that lasted roughly 30 minutes during the time Michael was killed. Investigators believe Cindy may have dialed Jeff and left the phone off the hook so that Jeff could listen live as the plan unfolded. In fact, when the recorded 911 call was later analyzed, the tapes revealed that Cindy was speaking to someone else in the moments before the dispatcher picked up and she could be heard saying, "My phone's about to die," as if warning an accomplice on another call. This strongly implied she was on a cell phone with Jeff while simultaneously calling 911 on the landline.

When the dispatcher answered, Cindy sounded frantic and out-of-breath. "I just got home and... stuff has been kind of... a doctor down in the house, and I can't find my husband," she exclaimed (the 911 recording is jumbled in parts, but she conveyed that her house was a wreck and Michael was missing). Cindy suggested that they might have been burglarized, telling the operator that furniture was overturned and it looked like someone broke in. Importantly, Cindy did not say anything about her husband being shot. She didn't mention finding Michael at all. In fact, she told the dispatcher she couldn't find Michael, which implied she hadn't laid eyes on him yet. She also indicated she was afraid to go inside the house further, given the unknown situation. Cindy stayed on the phone only briefly, then hung up as officers were dispatched.

Police arrived within minutes (one advantage of living so close to the station). They found Cindy outside in the front yard, appearing shaken and upset, as she had described on the phone. Officers with guns drawn swept through the Reese home, uncertain if a burglar might still be on the premises. The living room did show signs of a struggle. The coffee table was on its side and some furniture was askew. But nothing of obvious value seemed to be missing at first glance. Then, towards the back of the house, officers made the grisly discovery: Michael Reese's body in a pool of blood by the kitchen door at the rear entrance. He was face-down, slumped on the floor with a fatal gunshot wound to the back of his head. There were no signs of life. It was immediately clear to the responding deputies that this was not just a simple burglary. It was a homicide.

Detectives noted several things that made them suspicious of Cindy's account from the very start. For one, when they found Michael, his car keys were still in the door lock, as if he'd been caught off guard the moment he unlocked the house. There was no forced entry, no broken locks. And oddly, nothing appeared to be stolen. Cindy's purse was still there, electronics were untouched, even Cindy's jewelry left in plain sight hadn't actually been taken (besides the pieces Cindy herself removed). In the kitchen, investigators found the Milo's takeout meal completely uneaten, down to the French fries that were still warm in their bag. This was a big red flag. Why would Cindy have rushed out to get groceries before the couple even sat down to eat their hot food? The presence of a Piggly Wiggly shopping bag on the counter containing ham and orange juice confirmed Cindy had indeed gone to the store, but it seemed staged to establish an alibi. All signs pointed to the likelihood that Michael had been shot immediately upon returning home, and that the grocery trip was concocted after the fact to distance Cindy from the moment of Michael's death.

Cindy appeared genuinely distraught when police told her that Michael was dead, sobbing and screaming on the lawn, according to witnesses. She insisted to officers that she had walked in, seen the mess, and backed out to call 911 without ever knowing Michael was lying there. Given what we know about her past trauma, Cindy even cited her first husband's suicide as a reason she didn't venture further into the house: the sight of the overturned furniture had allegedly "flooded back memories of finding her first husband deceased," making her too scared to search for Michael herself. Whether this was truth or a calculated excuse, it momentarily explained to police why she hadn't found Michael's body herself. Still, investigators were not entirely convinced. The scene looked too "perfectly" wrong. The lack of forced entry, the untouched valuables, the timing of the 911 call...it all pointed to an inside job. And soon, their attention turned to the most likely suspects in a case like this: the spouse and her secret lover.

From the very outset of the investigation, detectives in Morris/Jefferson County sensed that something was off with the burglary-gone-wrong narrative. Veteran officers knew that in cases like this, the spouse is statistically often involved. And in this small town, Cindy's name was already familiar to law enforcement not from criminal activity, but from gossip. The lead detective immediately remembered hearing months earlier about a possible affair between Cindy Reese and Pastor Jeff Brown. In fact, when the 911 dispatch first came in and officers realized the victim was Michael Reese, some on the scene recalled, "Isn't that the woman who was rumored to be fooling around with the preacher?" Small town connections run deep, and this prior knowledge meant investigators were instantly looking at Cindy with raised eyebrows.

That night, Cindy was taken to the sheriff's office for questioning. She was still in a state of apparent shock. In her initial interview, Cindy stuck to her story: She said she and Michael came home from church, he stayed while she ran out, and when she returned she found a ransacked house and called 911. She claimed she had no idea what happened to Michael in the interim. When detectives carefully asked if there were any problems in her marriage, Cindy hesitantly admitted something she couldn't really hide. She admitted she had been having an affair with Jeff Brown, the former pastor. But Cindy downplayed it, making it seem like a past mistake that was over. She portrayed Jeff as a friend and confidant, but denied any notion that either of them would harm Michael. Who on earth would want to kill her husband? Cindy said she couldn't imagine anyone who had it out for Michael.

Simultaneously, police brought Jeffrey Brown in for questioning that very night or the next day. Jeff's demeanor was markedly different from Cindy's. He was cool, calm, and collected, almost unnervingly so for a pastor caught in an affair whose lover's husband had just been murdered. When confronted with the fact that Michael Reese had been shot, Jeff didn't even flinch. He acknowledged to detectives, in a pious tone, that he had sinned by being involved with Cindy. "Hate the sin, not the sinner," Jeff said, trotting out a classic line when asked about the affair. He claimed that yes, he and Cindy had been emotionally involved and "made mistakes," but he denied it was a sexual relationship (a claim that would later be proven false by evidence of their intimacy). Importantly, Jeff had an alibi ready for the night of the murder: he told investigators that on the evening of February 18, he was 50 miles away in the town of Oneonta, driving to his storage unit and then stopping by a buddy's house. He insisted he was nowhere near Morris when Michael was killed. At first glance, detectives had no proof otherwise, so they had to let Jeff go that night after taking his statement. But their suspicions were mounting.

Within a day, the case was being worked hard by the Jefferson County Sheriff's Office. Given the high-profile nature of a beloved church member's murder, they pulled phone records, attempted to gather surveillance video, and interviewed witnesses. A critical tip came in shortly after Michael's death, likely from

Carla Serhan, one of Jeff's former co-workers at the moving company. Carla contacted investigators and revealed the startling conversation she had overheard back in January 2015: Jeff Brown had approached two guys at work and asked if they'd be interested in killing someone. Carla recounted how Jeff had described the target (an IT worker husband supposedly abusing his wife) in a way that clearly matched Michael Reese. The co-workers had taken offense and later even filed a police report about Jeff's solicitation. At the time, no action was taken against Jeff beyond firing him, but now that Michael had ended up dead, this tip was pure gold for investigators. It gave them probable cause to suspect Jeff's involvement in a murder plot.

Armed with this information, detectives obtained search warrants for Jeff Brown's apartment and car. The searches, conducted within days of the murder, yielded damning evidence. In Jeff's car and home, they found documents tying Cindy to Jeff. Investigators recovered the title for Jeff's vehicle showing Cindy's name, bank statements for the shared account, and the lease paperwork listing Cindy as guarantor. This confirmed beyond any doubt that Cindy was actively supporting Jeff. One detective later remarked, "That is how we learned Cindy Reese was funding Jeff's lifestyle. Cindy was building a life for Jeff Brown." It was now clear that Cindy had a powerful incentive to eliminate her husband. She had one foot out the door building a new life, but Michael stood in the way.

Forensic examination of the crime scene also bolstered the case. The bullet that killed

Michael was a.38 caliber. Police noticed that a.38 revolver was missing from the Reese home's gun rack (Cindy herself pointed this out, as if an intruder must have stolen it). To detectives, it looked more likely the murder weapon was that very gun, removed by the killer. They didn't find the gun during initial searches, which suggested it had been taken from the scene. (Much later, Jeff would claim he tossed this revolver off of Highway 75 in Pinson after Cindy gave it to him.) Also, the lack of shell casings at the scene hinted a revolver was used (revolvers don't eject shells like semi-automatic guns do). So, the forensic and physical evidence lined up with an inside job scenario: Michael shot with his own gun, scene staged, weapon taken.

But the most incriminating evidence came from the digital trail left by Cindy and Jeff. Investigators subpoenaed phone records for both Cindy and Jeff, covering calls and texts on February 18, 2015. The data, once compiled, was a smoking gun in its own right. It showed "something over a dozen" calls, voicemails, or texts between Cindy and Jeff throughout that day. Far from cooling off, the lovers were in near-constant communication in the hours leading up to Michael's death. Key highlights from the phone records included multiple findings:

- The 29-minute phone call at 7:03 PM that night from Cindy to Jeff. Investigators immediately flagged this as highly suspicious as Cindy was literally on the phone with Jeff during her drive home with Michael. The call lasted until around 7:32 PM, likely staying connected as they arrived home. Detectives concluded this was an "open line" situation to keep Jeff in the know of Michael's exact whereabouts. Also included were the text message from Jeff at 6:57 PM that said, "Keep me posted." This text, arriving minutes before the long call, strongly suggested Jeff and Cindy had a coordinated plan for that evening. It was as if Jeff was saying: let me know when it's done or when it's happening. In hindsight, it's an eerie precursor to murder and the timing (right as church ended) fit perfectly.

- Cell tower pings from Jeff's phone contradicted his alibi. Jeff had told police he was out in Oneonta (roughly 50 miles away) around the time of the murder. But phone records showed Jeff's phone connecting to a tower only a few hundred yards from the Reese house around that time. In other words, Jeff was in Morris, near the scene, not an hour away as he claimed. This blew apart his "I wasn't there" defense.

- Cindy's 911 call quirk: When prosecutors later synced the timelines, they noted that by 8:00 PM Cindy was on with 911, and by then Michael was already dead. Jeff's phone records show he called Cindy seven times the next morning (Feb 19), presumably in panic or to iron out their stories. And the 911 recording itself (as mentioned) caught Cindy speaking to someone else (Jeff) about her dying phone battery.

As this evidence stacked up, detectives zeroed in on the theory that Cindy and Jeff plotted Michael's murder together. By March 11, 2015, just three weeks after the killing, police felt they had enough to make arrests. Investigators arranged to pick up Cindy and Jeff when they knew the two would be together. Sure enough, the pair met for lunch that day (despite everything, Cindy was still seeing Jeff regularly). As Cindy returned to work at the courthouse after lunch, authorities moved in and arrested both Cindy Reese and Jeff Brown in the parking lot outside her office. The alleged lovers-turned-conspirators were taken into custody simultaneously, preventing them from warning each other.

The small community of Morris was stunned by the news. A beloved church member and a pastor, both arrested for murder? It was almost unbelievable, yet many folks also had a sense of "I knew something wasn't right." The case quickly made headlines around Birmingham. The Jefferson County Sheriff's Office announced the arrests, emphasizing that under Alabama law, a person involved in a murder plot can be charged the same as the one who pulled the trigger. Even if Cindy had been the shooter, Jeff could be charged with murder as an accomplice, and vice versa. So both were charged with murder in the first degree for the death of Michael Reese.

During subsequent interrogations, Cindy and Jeff turned on each other in a classic blame game. Jeff changed his story once confronted with the mountain of evidence. Facing capital murder charges, Jeff decided to cooperate. He claimed that it was Cindy who had actually killed Michael, and that he was merely a participant after the fact. According to Jeff's later testimony, Cindy had frequently talked about killing Michael, saying she'd shoot or poison him and then feign insanity to escape punishment. Jeff admitted that he had tried to hire hitmen (confirming the Carla story) but failed. On the night of the murder, Jeff said, Cindy pulled the trigger. He testified that Cindy called him immediately after shooting Michael and asked him to help clean up the mess. Jeff claimed that when he met Cindy (either at the gas station or house), she handed him the .38 revolver used in the killing along with a bag of her jewelry that she staged as "stolen". Jeff then disposed of the evidence: he said he dumped the revolver along Highway 75 in Pinson, Alabama, and gave Cindy's jewelry to another woman to hide or pawn. (The gun was never recovered, as far as reports indicate.) Jeff also told police about an allegation Cindy had made. He said Cindy told him Michael had been abusive and even that "he had raped her," which Jeff used as partial justification for going along with the plan. Notably, Michael's family vehemently denied any abuse ever took place, and investigators found no evidence to support those claims. It appeared to be a story Cindy concocted to manipulate Jeff or rationalize the murder.

Cindy, on the other hand, maintained her innocence. After her arrest, she claimed that she did believe Jeff was involved but as the sole killer. She now said that Jeff must have snuck into the house and killed Michael while she was away at the store. In Cindy's version, Jeff was furious that she wouldn't leave Michael, so he acted on his own to eliminate him. She admitted to the affair and the continued contact, but painted herself as a woman torn between a jealous lover and a good husband. Essentially,

Cindy tried to shift all the intent and action onto Jeff, insisting she never wanted Michael dead.

Investigators, however, felt the evidence spoke for itself. By the time the case was ready for trial, the theory was clear: Cindy Reese was the mastermind and driving force behind the murder, and Jeff Brown was her willing accomplice who helped plan it and cover it up so they could be together. Prosecutor Danny Carr would later describe Michael's killing as an "execution-style" murder carried out by Cindy, with Jeff's help. With both suspects in custody, the long process of legal proceedings began.

After the arrests, both Cindy Reese and Jeff Brown were indicted on charges of murder in Michael's death. Initially, both of them pleaded not guilty, each pointing the finger at the other. The Jefferson County District Attorney's office had to decide how to proceed in a case with two co-defendants who were one-time lovers. In mid-2016, as Jeff Brown's trial date approached, a deal was struck. Jeffrey Brown agreed to plead guilty to a lesser charge of manslaughter in exchange for testifying against Cindy. In August 2016, just before his trial was set to begin, Jeff formally took the plea bargain: he admitted to participating in the crime and received a 20-year prison sentence. This was a significant reduction from a potential life sentence for murder. As part of the plea, he had to provide full, truthful testimony in Cindy's upcoming trial, laying out the whole plot. Jeff, then 37 years old, was promptly sent to state prison to begin serving his sentence even as he awaited his turn on the witness stand against Cindy. (Under Alabama law, a 20-year sentence for a violent crime like manslaughter typically requires a substantial portion to be served, though parole is possible.)

Cindy Reese, however, refused any plea deal and maintained her innocence. By late 2016, her case went to trial for the charge of murder. The trial was held in Jefferson County and garnered considerable local media attention. The salacious details of a church affair and a love-triangle murder were hard to ignore. During the trial, prosecutors laid out the narrative we have detailed: Cindy wanted Michael dead, conspired with Jeff, and pulled the trigger herself. They brought forth the evidence: phone records showing the incriminating "keep me posted" text and 7:03 call, cell tower data placing Jeff near the scene, the 911 call audio where Cindy is speaking to someone else, and the financial records proving Cindy's future plans with Jeff. Investigators and forensic experts testified about the staged burglary scene and how everything pointed to an inside job. The missing.38 revolver and the fact that Michael was shot with that caliber in the back of the head was highlighted as evidence of premeditation.

A star witness for the prosecution was, of course, Jeff Brown himself. It must have been a surreal scene: the former pastor testifying in court about his own sins. True to his plea agreement, Jeff took the stand and recounted in detail how the affair with Cindy began and how it led to murder. He testified that Cindy had often spoken of killing Michael and even pressured him to find a hitman. He admitted his role in trying to solicit co-workers (Carla and another colleague also testified to this effect, corroborating Jeff's story of the solicitation at the moving company). Jeff then described the night of the murder from his perspective: he claimed Cindy called him after shooting Michael, and that he assisted by disposing of the gun and staging items. Jeff's testimony painted Cindy as the instigator and trigger-puller. The prosecution also played Cindy's 911 call recording for the jury, and as Jeff had described, one can hear Cindy on the tape speaking to someone else before the dispatcher fully engages, specifically her statement about her phone dying, which prosecutors argued was clearly Cindy talking to Jeff on another line. They presented the phone company evidence that the other party was indeed Jeff Brown, due to the call records and timing.

Cindy's defense faced an uphill battle. They argued that Jeff was the real murderer and that he had spun a self-serving tale to get a lighter sentence. Cindy took the stand in her own defense, a risky move but perhaps deemed necessary. She testified that she loved her husband and never wanted him dead. Cindy confirmed the affair and the daily contact with Jeff, but she claimed that when she tried to end things, Jeff became enraged that she wouldn't divorce Michael. She alleged that Jeff must have snuck into the house while she was on the errand and killed Michael in a jealous fury. Essentially, Cindy tried to invert the narrative: in her telling, Jeff was the mastermind who "ambushed" Michael, and she was guilty only of adultery, not murder. The defense pointed to Jeff's history of lies (for instance, his initial claim of an "emotional affair" with no sex, which was disproven by a trove of explicit photos and sexts found on their phones). They argued Jeff had a strong motive to kill because he couldn't stand Cindy reconciling with Michael and that he had the opportunity as well.

However, Cindy struggled to explain away the hardest evidence. The prosecutors countered her claims effectively: If Jeff alone killed Michael, why were Cindy and Jeff on the phone with each other constantly during the critical time? Why did Jeff text "keep me posted" to Cindy right before the murder? Why did Cindy lie initially about the extent of the affair? And why was Cindy financially entangled with Jeff's life if she intended to stay with Michael? The physical evidence also favored the state. There were no signs of forced entry (indicating Michael likely let his killer in or knew them) and the fact that Michael was shot immediately upon getting home, before dinner was touched. If Jeff had broken in, would Michael really have set aside his food and not noticed an intruder until it was too late? The scenario was far-fetched compared to Cindy being the culprit. In closing arguments, DA Danny Carr emphasized the cold-blooded nature of the crime: Michael was shot execution-style by someone he trusted, and then Cindy tried to cover it up with a phony burglary.

It took the jury less than two hours (approximately 90 minutes) to reach a verdict. In December 2016, Cindy Kaye Henderson Reese was found guilty of the murder of her husband Michael Reese. Several of Michael's family members were in the courtroom and let out sighs of relief at the verdict. They had attended every day of the trial, resolutely hoping for justice.

On January 11, 2017, a sentencing

hearing was held before Judge Tommy Nail. Cindy, then 42, appeared in shackles, formally receiving her punishment. The judge sentenced Cindy Reese to 40 years in prison for the murder. In Alabama, a 40-year sentence for murder meant Cindy would not be eligible for parole for many years. Initially, it was reported she could first seek parole after 10 years (which would be 2027). However, updated state records later clarified her parole consideration date is September 2030, presumably based on time served and credit calculations. Either way, Cindy was facing a very long time behind bars. Michael's family expressed satisfaction and a sense of closure at the sentencing. Michael's cousin Mickey Self spoke to the press, saying "40 years is a victory for us... It's somewhat closure. It won't bring Michael back, but... we will be at every parole hearing, we will be there for Michael all the way to the end." The family also emphasized they were trying to find forgiveness because of their faith, but they would never forget what happened.

Jeff Brown had already been sentenced per his plea deal, but some formalities occurred after Cindy's trial. In December 2016, right as Cindy's trial was underway, Jeff was officially sentenced by a judge to 20 years in prison for manslaughter. The sentence was in line with the deal struck, and the judge noted it on record. Jeff was incarcerated and began serving time, with the possibility of parole on the horizon. According to Alabama Department of Corrections records, Jeff's first parole eligibility was in July 2023. If he were denied parole, he would have to serve the full 20 years (meaning his release would be in 2035). As of the latest updates, Jeffery David Brown remained in state custody as inmate records in 2020 showed him at the Staton Correctional Facility in Elmore, AL, and later reports indicated he was moved to a minimum-security work release facility as his sentence progressed. His exact status by 2023 isn't publicly clear, but the Reese family started a petition to oppose his parole when the date neared, indicating they strongly feel he should serve his full time.

Cindy Reese was sent to Julia Tutwiler Prison for Women, the state women's penitentiary in Wetumpka, Alabama, to serve her 40-year sentence. Tutwiler is an infamous maximum-security facility. In the first couple of years, Cindy likely lived the typical life of a prisoner with routine, isolation from society, and reflection on how she ended up there. She maintained her innocence publicly, and in 2017 her defense team filed an appeal of her conviction. They argued that the evidence was circumstantial and that the jury should have been instructed to consider a lesser charge (like manslaughter) since Jeff was the one who actually had a plea to that effect. However, on August 11, 2017, the Alabama Court of Criminal Appeals denied Cindy's appeal and upheld the conviction and sentence. The appellate opinion stated that the State had presented "sufficient evidence from which the jury could conclude that Reese murdered Michael," squashing her hopes of a reversal.

Cindy's case mostly fell out of headlines for a few years until 2020, when NBC's Dateline featured the story in an episode titled "Even the Devil Went to Church." The true crime community took renewed interest in the case, and so did Michael's family when they discovered something alarming that year. In April 2019, less than three years into her four-decade sentence, Cindy Reese had been quietly moved into a work-release program in Birmingham. This means Cindy was reclassified as a "minimum-out" custody inmate and transferred from Tutwiler to a Birmingham facility where prisoners are allowed to work jobs in the community during the day and return to a center at night. Such a status is usually reserved for inmates deemed low-risk. The news of Cindy's transfer was not well-communicated to the victim's family or even the prosecutors of her case. When word finally reached them (reportedly through an AL.com news inquiry in late 2020), it sparked outrage.

Michael's father, Earl Reese, was horrified to learn that the woman convicted of killing his son was being allowed to live outside prison walls so soon. "It makes me sick, to be honest with you," Earl said, reacting to Cindy's work-release status. The Jefferson County DA, Danny Carr, also publicly criticized the Department of Corrections' decision. He said, "The jury and judge heard evidence of this woman planning a murder of her husband and then she carried out the plan in an execution-style killing… It's a travesty of justice that this woman would be allowed to serve the remainder of her sentence outside a prison… after only serving less than three years of her sentence." Carr called it a "disgrace" and urged the DOC to reconsider. Indeed, not only was Cindy out in the community during the day, but the Birmingham work-release center was alarmingly close to where Michael's family lived and where the investigators and prosecutors of her case worked.

Facing mounting pressure, the Alabama Department of Corrections did clarify that Cindy had not been granted full freedom and she was still under supervision and had not actually been sent out to a job yet. They indicated her placement there was temporary and no community assignment had started. Ultimately, in response to the uproar, the DOC transferred Cindy Reese back to Tutwiler Prison and out of the Birmingham work-release center. As of the latest information, she remains incarcerated at Tutwiler, albeit her classification on paper still lists "minimum-out" (which the DOC explains doesn't guarantee an inmate is in a minimum facility). Cindy will be eligible to formally apply for parole in 2030, and you can be sure Michael's family will be there at that hearing, just as they promised. If she is not paroled, her sentence runs until 2055, when Cindy would be in her seventies.

The community of Morris had mixed emotions in the aftermath. Sardis Baptist Church survived the scandal but had lost members and trust. One church member lamented, "This whole situation has been sad, tragic... we lost several members because of it, but we're still strong," indicating the church's resolve to move forward despite the dark chapter. Many locals felt deep sympathy for Michael Reese's family. A good man had been lost due to senseless greed and lust. At the same time, there was a sense of betrayal and shock that a former pastor was involved in such a crime. The case served as a cautionary tale that even in the most outwardly pious circles, human frailty and evil can lurk.

In the end, the Reese family achieved justice through the legal system, but it's a hollow victory in many ways. Michael Reese lost his life simply because he loved the wrong person. His relatives have had to relive the pain through trials and TV shows, but they keep Michael's memory alive. They describe him as a man of faith, humor, and kindness who didn't deserve what happened. One can only hope that with passing years, the community remembers Michael for how he lived, not just how he died. As for Cindy Reese, she will spend many more years reflecting on her actions from a prison cell: a far cry from the church pews and family home she once occupied. It's a tragic story all around: a devoted husband betrayed in the worst way and a small-town church community that learned even the devil can go to church, hiding in plain sight.

FATAL ATTRACTION

Katherine Knight

Katherine Mary Knight was born on October 24, 1955, in rural New South Wales, Australia. Her family situation was anything but conventional. Katherine's mother, Barbara Roughan, had four sons with her first husband Jack Roughan before entering into a scandalous affair with Ken Knight, one of Jack's co-workers. The affair caused such an uproar in their conservative town of Aberdeen that Barbara and Ken fled to start a new life together in a different town. Barbara's four boys were split up among relatives. Two stayed with their father and two were sent to an aunt in Sydney while she and Ken went on to have four additional children of their own. In 1955 Barbara gave birth to twin girls, one of whom was Katherine. Katherine was the younger of the twins, and would ultimately grow up in a blended, often tumultuous household of half-siblings and step-siblings. By age four, Katherine saw two older brothers (from Barbara's first marriage) move into the Knight household after their father Jack's death in 1959.

It was a crowded home and by all accounts a deeply dysfunctional environment.

From a young age, Katherine's world was marked by violence and trauma. Ken Knight, her father, was an alcoholic who regularly terrorized Barbara with domestic violence. Family lore holds that Ken would rape Barbara up to ten times a day, and Barbara in turn did not hide the abuse from her children. In fact, Barbara often told her daughters graphic details of her sex life and expressed a deep hatred of men. This warped family dynamic left an imprint on Katherine. She later claimed that several members of her family sexually abused her throughout childhood (though notably not her father) until about age 11. Psychiatric evaluations would later accept these claims as likely true, corroborated in part by other family members. Such experiences undoubtedly contributed to Katherine's deep psychological scars and volatile temperament in her youth.

Katherine was especially close with her twin sister and with an uncle named Oscar Knight. Tragically, Uncle Oscar, whom Katherine adored, died by suicide in 1969 when Katherine was 14. His death devastated her, eliminating one of the few positive adult figures in her life. Meanwhile, chaos reigned at home. Barbara and Ken's relationship was wrought with brutal violence, with Barbara often on the receiving end. Barbara's way of coping, sharing her bitterness toward men and advising her daughters to "put up with it" when they complained about boyfriends, modeled deeply unhealthy attitudes about abuse and relationships. This was the cauldron in which Katherine's own identity and views on relationships were being shaped.

In school, Katherine's behavior could swing between extremes. Some classmates later remembered a friendly, well-behaved girl; others saw a loner with a hair-trigger temper. She reportedly bullied smaller children and even attacked at least one classmate with a weapon. In one incident, a teacher fought back against Katherine's aggression, and Katherine was injured; the teacher claimed self-defense for what happened. These episodes suggest that even as an adolescent Katherine had violent outbursts and lacked impulse control... early red flags of the brutality to come. By her early teens she was known for uncontrollable rages in response to minor provocations. Outsiders might have seen two sides of Katherine Knight. One moment a polite, ordinary schoolgirl; the next, a fury-driven aggressor.

Unsurprisingly, academics were not her focus. Katherine dropped out of school at the age of 15, barely literate by that time. She immediately entered the workforce, first taking a job as a cutter in a clothing factory. But the following year she landed what she considered her "dream job": working at the local slaughterhouse (abattoir) in Aberdeen. For a young woman who had endured so much violence, the abattoir may have been oddly fitting. Katherine likely saw it as a place to wield power, quite literally, over life and death. Naturally, Katherine thrived there. She was quickly promoted to boning and given her own set of butcher's knives, which she treated like prized possessions. At home, she hung her razor-sharp knives above her bed, a morbid decor choice she maintained wherever she lived. She said she kept them there "just in case anything happened," as if ready to defend herself (*or attack*) at a moment's notice. This peculiar habit of displaying her knives would later take on a darker significance, but at the time it was simply a point of pride for the skilled meat worker. Co-workers recalled Katherine as exceptionally adept at her job of slicing and skinning animal carcasses. In a grim foreshadowing, she was literally honing the tools and techniques that would make her infamous.

By age 18, Katherine Knight sought the kind of love she never saw at home. What she knew of relationships, however, was twisted by her upbringing. In 1973 she started dating David Stanford Kellett, a coworker at the slaughterhouse. David Kellett was 22, a hard-drinking rail worker-turned-bar-brawler with trauma in his past. He had been present at several horrific accidents on the railroad. Once, seeing a close friend killed in front of him, and another time heroically rescuing injured children from a school bus hit by a train. Those experiences haunted him, and David often drowned his sorrows in alcohol. Katherine, physically imposing and tough herself, had no problem handling David's pub fights. In fact, if David got into a scuffle, Katherine would jump in and back him up with her fists. An early sign that she was not really the demure, peacekeeping type.

Katherine and David married in 1974, when she was 18 and he 22. The wedding day itself came with a warning sign that few could forget. As the story goes, the couple arrived at the ceremony on Katherine's motorcycle with

David blind drunk on the back. Barbara, Katherine's mother, pulled the groom aside and, in her typical crude manner, warned him about her daughter's volatile nature. "You better watch this one or she'll fucking kill you," Barbara reportedly told David, adding that Katherine had "a screw loose somewhere". It might have sounded like an inappropriate joke or a scorned wife projecting her own anger at men, but it was deadly serious advice. And David Kellett would soon find out just how serious.

The marriage proved nightmarish from day one. On their wedding night, Katherine tried to strangle David because he fell asleep after they'd had intercourse only three times. (Apparently, the new bride was dissatisfied with her groom's exhaustion.) That incident was an omen of the violent dominance Katherine would exert. Over the next few years, David Kellett was often on the receiving end of Katherine's sudden rages. In one particularly brutal episode, when Katherine was heavily pregnant, David came home late from a darts competition where he had made the finals. Enraged that he'd spent the evening out, Katherine burned all of his clothing and shoes and then cracked his skull with a frying pan when he returned. David fled the house, collapsing bloodied at a neighbor's before being treated for a badly fractured skull. Remarkably (or perhaps predictably, given the cycle of abuse) Katherine was able to sweet-talk David into dropping the charges when he recovered. Her pattern of alternating violence with remorse or charm was already in play.

In May 1976, shortly after the birth of

their first child (a daughter named Melissa Ann), David Kellett finally decided he'd had enough. Unable to cope with Katherine's violence, he ran off with another woman and fled to Queensland, effectively abandoning Katherine and their newborn baby. This abandonment was a major trigger for Katherine. The new mother's response went beyond the scope of ordinary heartbreak and into the realm of the deranged. Following David's abrupt exit, Katherine was seen violently pushing her infant daughter Melissa in a stroller down the street. Concerned neighbors alerted authorities, and Katherine was admitted to St. Elmo's Hospital, where she spent several weeks in the psychiatric ward for what was diagnosed as postpartum depression. One might have hoped that she'd get help and stabilize but the worst was yet to come.

A few weeks after being released from the hospital, Katherine's mental state deteriorated further. In a shocking act of revenge against her estranged husband, Katherine placed 2-month-old baby Melissa on a railway line just before a train was about to pass through. She then stole an ax and went into town, threatening to kill several people at random. Fortunately, a man scavenging near the tracks discovered the infant and rescued her minutes before a train came through, saving Melissa's life. Police were alerted and Katherine was arrested and readmitted to the psychiatric hospital. This time she was diagnosed with postnatal depression again, and spent only a brief period in care before checking herself out the next day. Astonishingly, her reign of terror continued almost immediately. Only days later,

Katherine slashed the face of a woman with one of her knives and forced the injured woman to drive her to Queensland in search of David Kellett. This hostage-taking road trip ended at a service station, where Katherine took a young boy hostage at knife-point as well. Police intervened, disarming her (reportedly by broomstick) and again had her admitted to psychiatric care at the Morisset Hospital. Katherine had intended to track down and kill both David and his mother when she reached Queensland, a plan she thankfully never got to carry out.

News of these episodes filtered back to David Kellett. In a bizarre twist, upon hearing of Katherine's violent breakdown, David left his new girlfriend and moved back home to Aberdeen with his mother to support Katherine. It appears David felt a sense of responsibility or fear for what Katherine might do next. In 1977, not long after returning, Katherine was released from psychiatric care into the care of David and his mother. The couple reconciled, at least enough to cohabitate, and by 1980 they had a second daughter together, Natasha Maree. This reconciliation phase lasted a few more years, but the relationship remained volatile. In 1984, Katherine left David Kellett on her own accord. She took her two daughters and moved out, first back in with her parents in Aberdeen and then to a rented house nearby. The turbulent decade-long saga with Kellett had finally ended, leaving in its wake two children and a trail of violence and terror.

Still, Katherine's capacity for brutality did not end with her first marriage. Soon she was onto the next relationship and the next unfortunate man. In 1986, Katherine began dating David Saunders, a 38-year-old local miner. Saunders moved in with Katherine and her girls not long after they met, but notably he kept his own apartment in the town of Scone as a refuge. He would need it. Katherine was intensely jealous and suspicious about what David Saunders did when she wasn't around. If he wasn't home, she would imagine he was with other women or living a separate life. They argued frequently, and whenever Katherine threw David out of the house, he would retreat to his Scone apartment until she inevitably convinced him to return. The cycle of possessiveness and contrition was turning again.

Katherine's violence toward Saunders escalated in truly horrific fashion. At one point in early 1987, to "teach him a lesson" about what would happen if he ever cheated, Katherine grabbed Saunders' two-month-old dingo pup (his little pet dog) and slashed its throat right in front of him. She slaughtered the innocent puppy essentially as a threat, a demonstration of what she could do to him. As if that weren't enough, immediately after killing his dog she knocked Saunders unconscious with a frying pan to the back of the head. It was a scene of outrageous cruelty and sadism, even by Katherine's standards. One can only imagine the mix of terror and heartbreak that David Saunders felt. In June 1988, Katherine gave birth to her third child, a daughter named Sarah (fathered by Saunders). Hoping to solidify their family, Saunders put a down payment on a house. Katherine delighted in decorating this new home in her own unique style. That is, decorating it with animal skins, skulls, horns, old machetes, leather jackets, rusty animal traps, and even taxidermy. Every available surface was adorned with some kind of deathly object; it was as if no space was left undecorated by a skull or hide. This macabre interior design was noted later as essentially a shrine to her obsession with knives and butchery.

The new baby did not curb Katherine's violence. In one incident in 1989, an argument between Katherine and Saunders culminated with her hitting him in the face with a hot iron and then stabbing him in the stomach with a pair of scissors. Saunders survived the wound and fled back to his apartment in Scone. When he eventually returned to their shared house, he discovered that Katherine had cut up all of his clothing as a final message of contempt. That was the last straw. Saunders went into hiding, understandably fearing for his life. He wanted nothing more to do with Katherine Knight. Katherine, for her part, reported to police that she felt afraid of him. Ever manipulative, she played the victim and successfully obtained an Apprehended Violence Order (AVO), Australia's version of a restraining order, against Saunders. The audacity was stunning: Katherine was the abuser, yet she managed to convince authorities she was the one in danger.

By the early 1990s, Katherine had acquired a fearsome reputation in the region. But that didn't stop her from finding another partner. In 1991, she hooked up with John Chillingworth, a former butcher (perhaps an old colleague from the abattoir). With Chillingworth, Katherine had a son in 1992, her fourth and last child, a boy named Eric. Surprisingly, this relationship was reportedly less violent than the previous ones, or at least there are no well-documented assaults like before. However, it didn't last. After three years, Katherine left John Chillingworth for yet another man. One she'd been having an affair with on the side. This new lover would soon become her final victim: John Charles Thomas Price.

John "Pricey" Price was a 43-year-old father of three when Katherine Knight entered his life in 1994. Price was a native of Aberdeen, described as a personable, hard-working Aussie bloke. He worked as a miner and had two of his children (a boy and a girl) living with him; he was divorced but on decent terms with his ex. By all accounts, Price was well-liked in town. He enjoyed socializing at the local Royal Australian Legion (RSL) club, where he and Katherine likely first crossed paths. When Katherine and John Price began their relationship, things were rosy at first. Price's kids genuinely liked Katherine, and Price himself seemed to enjoy the companionship of this outgoing, robust woman. Knowing her past, Price allowed Katherine and her children to move into his home around 1995, and for a time, life resembled a "bunch of roses," as Price would later say. Katherine was helping look after Price's kids, cooking meals, and the arrangement felt much like a blended family.

However, it didn't take long for Katherine's demons to resurface. She had a long history of violent jealousy and a pathological need for control. Soon the couple's arguments became the stuff of local gossip. They would fight viciously, sometimes even physically. Price's friends began to distance themselves when Katherine was around, wary of her explosive temper. Still, Price tolerated a lot. Perhaps more than any reasonable person would because he loved Katherine in his way and she had integrated herself into his family. One thing Price steadfastly refused, however, was Katherine's desire to marry. He already had a failed marriage behind him and apparently saw no need to legally marry Katherine. This refusal became a major sore point. To Katherine, it was an unbearable rejection.

In early 1998, Katherine decided to retaliate in a calculated way. Price worked in the local mines and, like many miners, occasionally brought home odds and ends from work. Among these were some out-of-date medical kits that he had salvaged from the company trash. In a malicious move, Katherine videotaped these first aid kits and sent the tape to Price's employer, essentially reporting him for theft. It was an outrageous betrayal of trust, sabotaging her own partner's livelihood. When Price's bosses saw the footage, they terminated his employment, firing him from a job he had held for 17 years. That was finally a red line for John Price. Utterly furious at Katherine for costing him his job, he kicked her out of his house in February 1998. The whole town learned that Katherine's notorious temper had gotten Pricey sacked. Unperturbed by public opinion, Katherine moved back to her own place. Now unemployed, Price tried to make the best of things; he found work at a nearby smaller mine. And despite everything, by late 1998 he reconciled with Katherine enough to restart their relationship. But tellingly, he did not allow her to move back in. This time, they would date while living apart, a decision meant to maintain some boundary and independence for Price. Katherine did not take that lightly. She felt she deserved to live with him and that his house was her house. Being kept out, in her view, was Price's way of living a "separate life", something she grew increasingly paranoid about.

The fights escalated in frequency and intensity once they were back together but living separately. Neighbors and friends saw the storm clouds gathering; most of them refused to get involved or even associate with the couple while they were in this volatile on-again, off-again state. Katherine would fly into rages over perceived slights and throw John out of her house; then she'd seduce him back. Price confided to a friend that "life with Katherine was like a bunch of roses: Lots of thorns", indicating that while there were good moments, the bad were brutal. In February 2000, things hit a breaking point. Katherine had been assaulting Price in a series of incidents. One fight led to her stabbing him in the chest (not fatally). That attack convinced John Price that he had to end the relationship for good. He kicked Katherine out of his house again, this time determined to sever ties permanently.

On February 28, 2000, a shaken John Price went to the Scone Magistrate's Court and obtained a restraining order against Katherine Knight. The order was meant to keep her away from him and his children. It was a critical step that many domestic violence victims take, though in this case tragically it would prove too little, too late. That same afternoon, Price told colleagues at work that he had a bad feeling about what might happen now that he had served Katherine with the restraining notice. In fact, he said if he didn't show up to work the next day, it would be because Katherine Knight had killed him. This chilling prediction turned out to be entirely correct. Price's co-workers were alarmed and pleaded with him not to go home that night. They urged him to stay with friends or even go to the police. But Price felt a sense of fatalism and also concern for his children. He reportedly told his friends that he feared Katherine might harm his kids in revenge if he didn't come home. That evening, he followed his usual routine: he visited with neighbors for a bit, had some beers, and then returned to his now-empty house around 11:00 p.m. to sleep. Unbeknownst to Price, earlier that day Katherine had been busy plotting. She purchased new black lingerie, perhaps a calculated piece of stage dressing for what she intended to be a "special" night, and then went to her daughter's home to videotape her children while making strange, cryptic comments. This home video would later be interpreted as a sort of crude will, a goodbye message or at least a strange personal manifesto.

In hindsight, it seems Katherine was putting her affairs in order and possibly saying farewell in her own twisted way. After recording the video, Katherine arrived at John Price's house (where she was no longer welcome) on the late night of February 29, 2000. Finding that Price was asleep in bed, she let herself in, sat calmly on the sofa and watched

TV for a few minutes, then took a shower. Dressed in her new black negligee, Katherine then woke Price and came onto him. Despite everything, Price slept with her that night, a decision that has since haunted everyone who knew him. Perhaps he believed that satisfying her might defuse her anger. Unfortunately, it would be the last thing he ever did.

In the pre-dawn hours of March 1, 2000, Katherine Knight's simmering rage finally erupted into one of the most grotesque murders in Australia's history. Sometime after 2:00 a.m., with John Price fast asleep from their earlier lovemaking, Katherine reached for her butcher's knives, the very set she kept so proudly displayed. In a blitz attack, she began stabbing Price as he lay in bed. The first blows must have been horribly confusing and agonizing for Price, who woke to a nightmare in his own bedroom. Blood spray on the light switch later indicated that Price managed to get up and desperately tried to turn on the light as he fought off his attacker. Wounded and in panic, he stumbled from the bedroom, heading for the front door. The trail of blood proved that Price was badly bleeding from dozens of wounds as he fled through the hallway. He made it out the front door, leaving a bloody handprint, but either collapsed on the porch or, as forensic evidence suggested, was dragged back inside by Katherine. John Price, 44 years old, succumbed to his injuries inside the home he had worked so hard for, murdered by the woman he had loved and feared. The autopsy later counted 37 stab wounds across the front and back of his body, many of which punctured vital organs. The sheer ferocity of the attack showed that Katherine's fury was at a fever pitch; this was overkill in the most literal sense.

But horrifically, Katherine Knight's actions did not stop at killing. In fact, the murder itself was just the beginning of her morbid plans. With Price's lifeless body on the floor, Katherine left the scene briefly and she drove into town and withdrew $1,000 from John Price's bank account via ATM for reasons that remain unclear. Perhaps she intended it as some final financial gain or evidence of theft to support whatever story she might concoct. When she returned to the house, she set about a ghastly ritual that can only be described as post-mortem mutilation of the most depraved kind.

Drawing on her professional skills as an abattoir worker, Katherine skinned John Price's entire body with expert precision. Using her boning knives, she removed Price's skin in one continuous pelt, including his head, face, ears, nose, torso, genitals, and legs, literally peeling him. The autopsy would later marvel that the skin was removed so neatly and intact that it could be re-sewn onto the body in a mortuary, like a morbid suit. Katherine then hung this full human skin on a meat hook affixed to the beam of a doorway in the living room. When the first police officers arrived, one of them initially thought the hanging skin was a "curtain" or some kind of weird curtain-like decoration until a closer look revealed the horrifying truth. The sight was so disturbing that it reportedly continues to haunt those officers decades later; even seasoned police had "never seen anything like it".

Katherine's depravity continued. She decapitated John Price, cutting off his head and putting it in a large pot on the stove. She sliced off parts of his buttocks and other flesh and baked them in the oven, along with vegetables and gravy, to prepare a "sickening stew". In a grotesque tableau, she set the dinner table with two place settings. On each plate she arranged cooked meat slices from Price's body alongside roasted pumpkin, zucchini, cabbage, potato, and baked squash, smothered in gravy. Next to each plate she placed a note with the name of one of Price's two older children. It was abundantly clear that Katherine intended for John Price's son and daughter to eat their father's flesh, a final act of revenge and cruelty almost beyond human comprehension. On the stove, the pot containing Price's boiled head and parts of his body was found still warm, simmering away when police arrived around 8:00 a.m., indicating the cooking had been done in the early morning hours.

To add another layer of gruesome symbolism, Katherine placed John Price's decapitated head in the boiling pot with vegetables, as if making a soup. Investigators also found a third meal, similar meat and vegetable stew, thrown on the back lawn, untouched. Perhaps Katherine had attempted to eat some of Price's cooked flesh herself and couldn't go through with it, hurling the plate outside in disgust. This theory was later cited as possibly supporting her claim of having no memory of the crime (suggesting she might have come to her senses momentarily and recoiled). Additionally, Katherine arranged John's decapitated, skinless corpse in a deliberate manner: she positioned his left arm draped over an empty 1.25-liter soft drink bottle, and crossed his legs. In court, experts would testify that this odd positioning of the mutilated body was an act of defilement, essentially Katherine posing the victim in a humiliating, almost feminine repose to mock him. It demonstrated her utter contempt for Price even in death.

As a final touch, Katherine penned a handwritten note and left it on top of a photograph of John Price that she placed on the bloodied crime scene. The note was smeared with blood and pieces of flesh. In barely literate scrawl littered with spelling errors, it essentially accused Price of awful crimes: "Time got you back Johathon [Johnathan] for rapping [raping] my douter [daughter]... Now play with little John's d**k, John Price," it read in part. She mentioned Price's children by name, as if to implicate him in harming them or others (the note included "You to Beck for Ross – for Little John"). The rambling message made little coherent sense beyond a vile accusation that Price had sexually abused Katherine's young daughter, an accusation for which there was **zero** evidence. Investigators quickly determined the claims in Katherine's note to be baseless lies, likely an attempt by her to deflect blame or establish some twisted justification for her crimes. It was the final malicious act in her elaborate plan: after committing an act of cannibalistic butchery, she sought to frame the victim as a child rapist, perhaps to smear his memory or rationalize her savagery.

After carrying out these unthinkable acts, Katherine Knight calmly took a shower to wash off the blood. At some point in the early morning, she swallowed a large number of pills variously described as sleeping pills or anti-depressants in what appeared to be a suicide attempt or a gesture of self-pity. Then she lay down next to the mutilated remains of John Price (or perhaps in the spare room, accounts vary) and lost consciousness in a drugged stupor.

That same morning, March 1, 2000, John Price's neighbors noticed something amiss. His work truck was still in the driveway, and it was highly unlike Price to not show up for his 6 a.m. shift without any notice. Remembering Price's ominous warning, his employer sent a colleague to check on him when he didn't arrive at work. A concerned neighbor and the co-worker both tried to wake Price by knocking on his bedroom window, but saw blood on the front door and quickly alerted police. By 8:10 a.m., officers from the Aberdeen police department arrived. They forced entry through the back door and stepped into what could only be described as a house of horrors.

The first officer on the scene, Constable Scott Matthews, nearly tripped on something hanging in the doorway of the lounge. In the dim light, he thought it was a curtain or a heavy drape covering the archway. When he reached out to move it aside, his hand was covered in blood. He suddenly realized he was touching human skin. The "curtain" was John Price's flayed hide hanging from a hook. The shock of this realization is hard to overstate. Seasoned police later recounted that they'd "never seen anything so horrific" and the image would haunt them forever. Just beyond that, on the floor of the lounge, lay Price's headless, skinless body, eerily posed. In the kitchen, the stovetop pot was still warm, filled with a ghastly stew of vegetables and human remains. The prepared plates sat on the table, each labeled with the names of Price's children. A sight so macabre it sent waves of nausea through even the most hardened detectives.

Police found Katherine Knight comatose on the bed, having overdosed on pills. Remarkably, she was still alive. They woke her up, but she was incoherent, babbling, and had to be taken by ambulance to the hospital for treatment of the overdose. Investigators immediately secured the crime scene, though it was as clear-cut a case as they come. There was no doubt who had butchered John Price. The evidence of Katherine's handiwork was everywhere, from the notes in her handwriting to the very personal nature of the tableau. On the kitchen floor, they even found a bloodied knife and chunks of flesh and bone. Later forensic analysis determined that the murders and mutilation all took place in the span of a few hours before dawn. The brutality defied imagination; it was as though Katherine had choreographed her own horror movie.

News of the atrocity spread rapidly through the small community of Aberdeen and beyond. Local residents who knew Katherine and Price were utterly stunned. Rick Banyard, a neighbor who socialized with the couple at the RSL, recalled that "absolutely it was a dark day… it came out of the blue", adding that no one expected "the crime that became recorded as one of the worst pieces of history in Australia". Those who knew Katherine as a cheerful drinking buddy at the pub or a helpful neighbor struggled to reconcile that image with the monstrous acts she had now committed. Aberdeen, a tight-knit town, was suddenly infamous for a crime that sounded like a ghastly legend. Parents kept their children indoors, and rumors flew. The media descended on the town as well, reporting every gruesome detail that police sources would leak. It wasn't long before Katherine Knight was being called "Australia's own Hannibal Lecter", a reference to the fictional cannibal from The Silence of the Lambs. In fact, at the time, newspapers as far away as London splashed headlines about the "Woman Cannibal" or "Hannibal Lecter-style" murder in Australia. The combination of lurid elements, a female perpetrator, cannibalistic overtones, and the domestic setting made it a media sensation.

At the hospital, Katherine claimed to have no memory of what happened. She was charged with John Price's murder while still hospitalized on March 2, 2000. Transferred to a correctional psychiatric ward, she received a medical evaluation as investigators built the horrific case against her. Given the overwhelming forensic evidence and Katherine's history of violence, there was little question of her responsibility. The only real question was what strategy her defense would use, since insanity was an obvious consideration.

Katherine Knight's trial for the murder of John Price was set to begin in July 2001, about a year and a half after the crime. Initially, she maintained a plea of not guilty to the charge of murder. This raised the prospect of a lengthy trial where jurors would have to endure ghastly crime scene evidence. Indeed, when the proceedings were about to begin, Justice Barry O'Keefe took the unusual step of offering the jury pool an option to be excused due to the extremely graphic nature of the evidence. A number of potential jurors promptly accepted that offer and bowed out; even among hardened members of the public, few had the stomach for the photographs and testimony that were expected. As the final jury was being empaneled, several more members dropped out in shock after hearing the witness list, which included very senior and experienced forensic experts who only get involved in the worst cases.

However, before the trial could properly begin, an unexpected twist occurred. On the second day of the trial, October 15, 2001, Katherine Knight changed her plea to guilty. The day prior, her attorneys had conferred with the judge in light of some developments, and it later came out that Justice O'Keefe had been informed of Katherine's intention to plead guilty. He had ordered a psychiatric evaluation overnight to ensure that Knight was fit to make such a plea and fully understood its consequences. The psychiatrists evidently found Katherine sane and competent enough to plead guilty, so the next morning her legal team formally withdrew her not-guilty plea. This meant there would be no trial, only a sentencing hearing. It also meant the public might never hear Katherine speak in her own defense or get a clear explanation from her, since a guilty plea avoids the need for a detailed courtroom testimony or cross-examination. To this day, no official motive has been provided by Katherine for why she committed such an act.

Many believe the evidence of premeditation (sending the kids away, the new lingerie, the videotaped will) made a trial hopeless for her, and a guilty plea was a strategy to avoid the worst publicity or a strategic move to appear remorseful. Yet remorse was something Katherine Knight demonstrably lacked. Despite her guilty plea, she still refused to accept full responsibility for her actions. She told psychiatrists that she had amnesia about the night of the killing, essentially claiming she didn't remember anything, and thus implying she couldn't rationally explain it. Her defense team had originally planned to argue amnesia and dissociation, meaning Katherine might claim she was not in her right mind or even conscious of her actions during the crime. Psychiatric experts did acknowledge that Knight appeared to have dissociated at the time of the killing but they agreed this did not equate to legal insanity. In other words, even if she mentally "checked out" during the attack, she had orchestrated everything right up to that point with a clear, calculating mind. Crucially, two court-appointed psychiatrists diagnosed Katherine Knight with Borderline Personality Disorder (BPD). BPD is a mental health condition often marked by unstable personal relationships, fear of abandonment, impulsivity, and extreme emotional swings; features abundantly present in Katherine's life. However, they found her legally sane. She knew right from wrong and was capable of controlling her actions and her personality disorder did not absolve her of culpability. One psychiatrist later even commented that Katherine's personality problems were "not psychiatric disease, they are her nature," emphasizing that her violent traits were ingrained and not some temporary break from reality.

At the sentencing hearing in November 2001, gruesome details of Katherine's crime were recounted in court to ensure the record was clear on the brutality involved. It was so graphic that Katherine's lawyers requested she be excused from hearing some of it, especially the pathologist's testimony about skinning and decapitation. But Justice O'Keefe refused this request. When forensic pathologist Timothy Lyons took the stand and methodically described how Katherine dismembered Price, Katherine became hysterical and had to be sedated in the dock. It was one of the few times anyone witnessed an emotional reaction from her related to the crime but whether it was genuine horror at herself or just distress at being confronted with her actions is unclear.

On November 8, 2001, Justice O'Keefe delivered a landmark sentence. Citing the extreme nature of the crime, Katherine's apparent enjoyment in committing it, and her complete lack of remorse, he concluded that this case fell into the category of the very worst murders. In his sentencing remarks, he stated that "the last minutes of [Price's] life must have been a time of abject terror for him, as they were a time of utter enjoyment for her". He declared Katherine Knight "a very dangerous person" who would likely reoffend if released, particularly against anyone who crossed her, "especially males". Therefore, the judge spared no mercy: Katherine Knight was sentenced to life imprisonment without the possibility of parole. Moreover, he ordered that her file be marked "never to be released", making her the first woman in Australian history to receive this indelible sentence. In Australian legal terms, this was as harsh a sentence as one can get, reserved for the absolute worst of the worst. The courtroom and the public overwhelmingly supported this outcome; if ever there was someone who deserved to never walk free again, it was Katherine Knight.

Unsurprisingly, Katherine appealed the sentence. In June 2006, her lawyers petitioned the NSW Court of Criminal Appeal, arguing that life without parole was too severe a punishment for her crime. It was a long shot, to put it mildly. The appellate justices, Peter McClellan, Michael Adams, and Megan Latham, reviewed the case. In September 2006, the court unanimously dismissed her appeal, with Justice McClellan writing that Katherine's actions were "an appalling crime, almost beyond contemplation in a civilized society". McClellan's statement, drawn from his formal judgment, echoed the public sentiment: this crime tested the limits of what society could even imagine one human doing to another. With that, Katherine Knight's fate was sealed. She would spend the rest of her natural life behind bars.

From the time of her arrest and throughout the legal process, Katherine Knight underwent extensive psychological evaluation. The goal was to understand what could drive a 44-year-old mother of four to such barbarity and to determine her mental state. Three court-appointed psychiatrists examined Katherine. They did not all agree on every nuance, but a consensus emerged on key points: Katherine Knight was not insane or psychotic at the time of the murder. She did, however, suffer from a severe personality disorder. As noted, two evaluating psychiatrists diagnosed her with Borderline Personality Disorder (BPD), and a third concurred that while she had serious psychological issues, she did not meet the threshold for an insanity defense. In plain terms, Katherine knew exactly what she was doing; her actions were deliberate and goal-oriented (no matter how twisted the goal).

Reading Katherine's life story like a case study, one can see many classic BPD patterns: her relationships were volatile and marked by extremes (all love or all hate, nothing in between). She would idolize a partner one moment and then viciously attack them the next, often triggered by trivial events or paranoid suspicions. Her fear of abandonment was profound...recall how she reacted when each partner tried to leave: she chased one with a knife, took another hostage, murdered a dog in front of another, and ultimately slaughtered John Price when he sought to be done with her. Psychiatrist Peter Toohey, analyzing the case, noted that while Knight had BPD, the psychiatrists "didn't agree that she was insane". In other words, her personality disorder explained her emotional volatility but did not rob her of awareness or intent. She was responsible for her actions. Toohey also pointed out that no clear single motive was offered by the experts beyond Katherine's lifelong pattern of rage and jealousy in the face of perceived betrayal or desertion.

Katherine's childhood of abuse and

trauma was also scrutinized as a contributing factor. Growing up witnessing her father's horrific violence and her mother's dysfunctional responses likely played a role in shaping Katherine's psyche. Children who experience or observe abuse can develop disordered attachments and may come to view violence as a normal component of relationships. Katherine herself claimed sexual abuse by relatives, which, if true, adds another layer of trauma that can lead to later violent behavior or personality disorders. Psychiatrists generally accepted her account of abuse given corroboration by family members and the consistency of her behavior with someone who had been severely traumatized in youth. The suicide of her beloved uncle Oscar when she was 14 was another emotional scar. All these events potentially fed into the making of a person with little ability to regulate emotions or cope with loss.

It's worth noting that BPD often includes episodes of self-harm or suicidal gestures, and Katherine's post-murder overdose can be seen in that light. After her furious orgy of violence, when the reality of what she had done set in, she possibly swung to the other pole of her emotional spectrum, self-pity or self-destruction, and attempted to overdose on pills. It fits the profile: individuals with BPD can go from outward rage to inward collapse, especially after they "lose" the object of both their love and hate (in this case, John Price, by killing him, was now permanently gone, an abandonment of sorts that she caused). But make no mistake, this does not earn sympathy so much as it provides a framework to understand her erratic behavior.

Psychiatrists also evaluated whether Katherine had any other disorders, such as psychosis, schizophrenia, or mood disorders, and concluded she did not. She was not hallucinating or delusional during the crime. In fact, one could argue a grim rationality in her actions. She executed a perverse punishment on Price and orchestrated the aftermath to maximize the trauma (targeting his children). That pointed to a level of cunning and sadism inconsistent with any sort of insanity plea. Indeed, the sentencing judge commented on Katherine's apparent enjoyment of the crime, a hallmark of a sadistic personality. It's telling that in one psychiatric report, as quoted in a law review, the evaluator stated: "The personality problems demonstrated in Ms Knight's life are not... psychiatric disease, *they are her nature*". They deemed her essentially irredeemable.

To summarize Katherine Knight's psychological profile: she is an individual with severe borderline personality disorder traits, born from a cauldron of childhood abuse and lifelong violent behavior, who remains fully accountable for her extraordinarily cruel actions. She exhibits a pattern of domestic violence perpetration virtually unheard-of among women, leading some to label her Australia's first female serial domestic abuser even before the ultimate crime. She is not mentally ill in the sense of a break from reality; rather, she is terrifyingly sane in how she went about her brutality. This understanding of Katherine as not "mad" but "bad" was critical in ensuring she faced the full force of the law.

The Katherine Knight case shocked not

only the small town of Aberdeen but all of Australia and soon, the world. As details emerged, the media had a field day with the story's lurid elements. Here was a female, middle-aged abattoir worker who had savagely butchered her lover and cooked parts of him. It was the ultimate anti-fairy tale, a nightmare scenario that challenged gender norms and societal taboos. The press wasted no time in giving Katherine monikers befitting a horror movie villain. She was dubbed "Australia's Hannibal Lecter", the "Cannibal Killer", and even "Lady Leatherface" (after the human-skin-wearing killer in The Texas Chain Saw Massacre). The Daily Telegraph and other tabloids ran screaming headlines about the "Cannibal Mum" and "House of Horrors". Australian media, typically restrained with graphic content, issued warnings before stories due to the gruesome details, but still audiences were morbidly fascinated. At the time of her sentencing in 2001, the Sydney Morning Herald noted that Knight had been "branded an evil monster" by the public and press. The sensational nature of her crime invited comparisons to fictional monsters, and some felt that casting her as a ghoul or a "female Hannibal Lecter" was almost a way to cope with the reality as if a normal human couldn't have done this, only a monster could.

In popular culture, Katherine Knight unfortunately became a macabre legend. True crime TV shows featured her story; the case was dramatized in an episode of Crimes That Shook Australia, and she's frequently listed in "Top 10 Most Gruesome Murderers" lists on the internet. Podcasters and YouTubers recount her crime with a mix of fascination and horror. The dark humor that often accompanies discussions of Katherine Knight is a reflection of how over-the-top the case is; it almost invites nervous jokes as a coping mechanism. For instance, one might sardonically comment that Katherine Knight "took the phrase 'take-away dinner' to a horrific new level," though such humor belies the real pain behind the case.

Amid the sensationalism, it's easy to forget that at the center of it all were innocent victims: John Price, a likable father and friend, was brutally slain. His kids, who mercifully were kept out of harm's way that night, nonetheless had their lives shattered. Their father was gruesomely taken from them and nearly desecrated in the worst possible way. The community's outpouring of support for Price's family was considerable. Media outlets noted that locals were "unable to forget the day the news broke", and even twenty years on, the crime was still spoken of with hushed horror in the Hunter Valley. It remains a cautionary tale that even in a peaceful small town, unimaginable violence can erupt from within a home.

Katherine Knight today remains behind bars, serving out her life sentence in Silverwater Women's Correctional Centre in New South Wales. As per the judge's order, her paperwork is marked "never to be released", meaning she will die in prison. In the years since her incarceration (now 20+ years), a portrait has emerged of Katherine's life on the "inside." Surprisingly (or perhaps not, given her history of dominating those around her) Katherine has managed to carve out a role for herself among the inmate population. According to journalist James Phelps, who wrote a 2017 exposé on women in Australian prisons, Katherine is treated with a mix of fear and respect by other prisoners. In Silverwater, fellow inmates refer to her by the unsettling cozy nickname "Nanna", owing to her older age (she's now in her late 60s) and white hair and grandmotherly appearance. She's also been called the "Queen Bee" of the prison, a matriarch who settles disputes and keeps the other inmates in line. Indeed, reports say that Katherine uses her notoriety and imposing personality to act as a peacemaker or referee among the "girls" (as she calls them) when tempers flare over trivial matters like phone usage or chores. It seems in the controlled environment of prison, Katherine has found a way to reassert some degree of control and significance.

Over the years, Katherine has reportedly found religion and become a regular attendee of the prison chapel services. She also occupies her time with painting and knitting, hobbies that present a much gentler side than the one for which she is infamous. One can only imagine fellow inmates receiving a knitted scarf or painting from Katherine Knight and the morbid curiosity it might evoke. Despite her seemingly benign routine, prison officers are never complacent about who Katherine is. Guards "never take their eyes off her" when she's out of her cell. Infamously, she's not allowed access to certain standard privileges: for example, unlike other inmates, Katherine is never permitted near a knife. Not even a plastic one. The prison kitchen is strictly off-limits to her for obvious reasons. It's said that she once half-jokingly told an officer she can't have a cellmate because she might kill again. Whether dark humor on her part or a genuine warning, nobody is taking chances.

To this day, she is housed *alone* in her cell.

MOMMY DEADLIEST

Diane Downs

Late on a spring night in 1983, a red Nissan sports car screeched into the emergency bay of McKenzie-Willamette Hospital in Springfield, Oregon. The driver, a 27-year-old mother named Diane Downs, stumbled out, screaming for help: **"Someone killed my kids!"** Inside the car were her three children, Christie (8), Cheryl (7), and Danny (3), all soaked in blood. Little Cheryl had no pulse, and the other two were barely clinging to life. Diane herself had a single gunshot wound in her left forearm, bleeding but far from life-threatening. As doctors and nurses frantically worked on the children, Diane spun a bizarre tale for authorities that would kick off one of the most disturbing true crime cases in Oregon's history.

To understand how that chaotic night came to be, we have to rewind and get to know who Diane was before she became infamous. Elizabeth Diane Frederickson was born on August 7, 1955, in Phoenix, Arizona. She grew up in a strict conservative household with parents who enforced rigid rules and traditional values. Diane would later describe her father as overly disciplinarian and claimed he even sexually abused her as a child, an accusation she eventually recanted, and which her parents adamantly denied. True or not, it's clear Diane felt stifled and unheard in her family. She once complained that her father demanded all of her mother's attention, leaving none for Diane. This strict upbringing (her parents even prohibited trendy clothes and makeup) made Diane an outsider among her peers and a target for bullying. By her mid-teens, she was ready to rebel.

Diane's rebellion began around age 14. Tired of being the "good Baptist girl," she started breaking her parents' rules and seeking freedom. In high school at Moon Valley High in Phoenix, she met a boy across the street named Steve Downs. Steve was two years older, and Diane's parents didn't approve of him which only made the romance more appealing. When Steve went into the Navy after high school and Diane enrolled at a Bible college in California, they kept up a long-distance relationship. But college didn't last long for Diane. She was expelled after one year for "promiscuous behavior," essentially for disobeying the strict moral code. So, at 18, she returned to her parents' home, only to run away not long after to be with Steve.

In November 1973, 18-year-old Diane defied her parents and married Steve Downs. She would later admit, "I did not marry Steve for love... I married Steve to get out of the family". The marriage was rocky from day one. The young couple fought often about money, about Diane's suspected infidelities, about basically everything. Diane had a habit of leaving Steve and retreating to her parents when things got rough, but they'd patch up and start the cycle again. Despite the turmoil, Diane and Steve soon became parents. Their first daughter, Christie Ann, was born in 1974, and a second girl, Cheryl Lynn, followed in 1976. By Diane's account, she hadn't exactly planned these pregnancies with Steve. She just went ahead and got pregnant, seemingly for her own reasons. Steve later remarked that Diane was "the only woman I know who gets pregnant to cheer herself up", suggesting that while Diane loved the idea of having babies, she didn't much enjoy the day-to-day reality of caring for them.

Indeed, Diane's maternal instincts were virtually non-existent, according to those who knew the young family. Steve said "She treated the kids like crap", recalling that Diane would harshly punish or completely ignore the children when they misbehaved or needed attention. Neighbors in Arizona later reported troubling signs of neglect: Christie and Cheryl often appeared hungry, even begging neighbors for food, and were inadequately dressed in cold weather. Diane would leave little Christie, at only six years old, to babysit her younger siblings alone for hours if she couldn't find a sitter. One neighbor said young Cheryl confided that she was afraid of her mother. In one heartbreaking story, Steve once found Cheryl, around age 5 or 6, saying she "wanted to kill herself" because "My mom says I'm bad". These glimpses into the Downs home life paint a chilling picture: long before the crime, Diane seemed dangerously detached from her children's well-being.

By the late 1970s, Steve decided he didn't want any more children, having witnessed Diane's poor parenting and suspecting her serial cheating. He got a vasectomy to prevent further pregnancies. But Diane had her own plans. She became pregnant again in 1978, this time by another man during an affair; a fact she didn't hide. In December 1979, she gave birth to a son, Stephen Daniel (Danny). Despite knowing he wasn't Danny's biological father, Steve initially tried to accept the boy. The marriage, however, couldn't survive Diane's behavior. Within a year of Danny's birth, Steve and Diane divorced in 1980, finally ending their volatile union.

Newly single in her mid-20s, Diane drifted aimlessly. She moved in with various men one after another, carrying her three young kids along like baggage. She even attempted to become a surrogate mother for extra money, despite her own kids being in unstable condition. Notably, she failed two psychiatric evaluations required for surrogacy with one test indicating signs of psychosis. Instead of being concerned, Diane found this hilarious and would brag about it to her friends. It seems she either didn't grasp or didn't care that a professional found her psychologically unfit. Eventually, though, Diane did manage to become a paid surrogate. In late 1981, she was accepted into a program, and in May 1982 she gave birth to a baby girl for another couple, earning around $10,000 for the surrogacy. For a brief time, this was a bright spot. She got money and the satisfaction of pregnancy (which she oddly enjoyed) without the responsibility of another child.

Around this same period, Diane found a new love interest. Working as a postal carrier in Chandler, Arizona, she met Robert "Nick" Knickerbocker, a charming co-worker. Nick was married, but that didn't stop Diane. She fell deeply in love and started a passionate affair with him. This affair would soon set the stage for everything that followed.

By early 1983, Diane Downs' life had become a complicated mess of her own making. She had three small children from a broken marriage, a string of ex-lovers, and was obsessively infatuated with Nick Knickerbocker, the married man back in Arizona. Diane had moved to Oregon in 1983 (transferring to the postal service in a rural route near Springfield, Oregon). On the surface, it looked like she was starting fresh. In reality, Diane was still utterly fixated on Nick. She wrote to him constantly, phoned him, and refused to accept that their affair was over. Nick, for his part, was trying to repair his marriage and had told Diane in no uncertain terms that he did not want her children in his life. In fact, Nick had made it clear he didn't want to play daddy to anyone's kids. To him, Diane's kids were a deal-breaker.

This was the crux of Diane's growing desperation: she believed her children stood between her and the man she wanted. According to her later-discovered diaries, she fantasized extensively about Nick and fretted that her kids were an obstacle to winning him back. Friends and family would later note that Diane seemed remarkably unconcerned about her children's welfare, except as it related to her own love life.

In April 1983, about a month before the shooting, Diane made a trip back to Arizona, supposedly to visit friends, but really, it was to see Nick one more time. During this visit, Nick firmly broke things off with her. He told Diane that he loved his wife and was going to reconcile, and that he had zero interest in raising her kids. It was the ultimate rejection. Diane returned to Oregon heartbroken, angry, and, it appears, plotting her next move.

We can't know exactly what was going through her mind, but prosecutors later argued that Diane decided if her children were the only thing keeping her from Nick, then they had to be eliminated. It's a chilling thought, a mother considering murder as a solution to her romantic problems. But sadly, that's where all the evidence points. Her personal writings at the time were consumed with Nick. Investigators who read Diane's diary entries said she had an "obsession with a married man" and was pressuring him to leave his wife. Nick himself later told police that Diane had begun stalking him and even suggested she might kill his wife so that she could have him to herself. In Nick's words, he was "relieved when she left for Oregon", figuring some distance would cool things off. He gravely underestimated Diane's determination.

As we approach that fateful night in May, the pieces of Diane's life were arranged in a dangerous way. She was a single mom who didn't enjoy mothering, infatuated with a man who didn't want kids, and desperate enough to do something drastic. Sadly, that desperation would soon turn into a night of violence that left one child dead and two others grievously wounded.

On the night of May 19, 1983, Diane decided to take the kids out for a drive. According to her, it was meant to be a fun outing. She claimed they had visited a friend's house and, even though it was after dark, she impulsively took a "scenic route" on the way home for some sightseeing...in the dark. Nonetheless, Diane later described this drive in almost casual terms. She said her three children had dozed off in the car, and she was driving along a quiet country road listening to music. In fact, she noted that Duran Duran's hit song "Hungry Like the Wolf" was playing on the cassette deck as they rolled through the darkness. It's a detail that would become infamous, symbolic of Diane's strangely lighthearted attitude amid horror.

According to Diane's original story, as she recounted it to police and later to reporters, the following unfolded: While driving on that isolated road around 10 p.m., she spotted a shaggy-haired man standing by the side of the road, flagging her down. Concerned, she stopped the car to see if he needed help. She even turned off the engine and took the keys out...an unusual level of trust with a stranger, but that's what she claimed. Diane said the man demanded, "I want your car." She responded flippantly, "You gotta be kidding me!", refusing to hand over her keys. At that moment, she said, the man pulled out a gun. He shoved her aside, leaned into the car, and opened fire on the sleeping children. In the chaos, Diane herself got shot in the left arm during an apparent scuffle with the man.

Diane claimed she thought fast. Even as

she was wounded, she pretended to throw her car keys into the bushes, shouting "Go fetch!" (or something to that effect) to distract the shooter. The trick worked as the bushy-haired stranger turned away momentarily to look for the keys. Seizing that instant, Diane pushed him away, jumped back into the driver's seat, and sped off "like a lunatic" towards the nearest hospital. She said she drove at breakneck speed, racing to save her kids' lives. This, in essence, was Diane's account: a random violent carjacking by a stranger on a dark road, a mother who survived by her wits, and her frantic effort to get help for her children.

Police initially treated Diane as a victim and even put out an APB (all-points bulletin) for the described "bushy-haired stranger" who might be on the loose. The community was shook. Was some psychopath roaming the area, targeting mothers and kids? But almost immediately, red flags started popping up. The details of Diane's story just didn't make sense. Detectives on the scene and hospital staff noted several oddities that very first night.

For one, Diane's demeanor was strangely calm and emotionless given the situation. Detective Doug Welch, one of the first investigators, was struck by how "emotionally flat" Diane seemed. Here was a mother whose children had just been shot, one was dead, the other two at death's door, and yet she wasn't behaving like you'd expect. Nurses and the ER doctor, Dr. Steven Wilhite, later reported that Diane did not appear upset or panicked at the hospital. In fact, her priorities seemed off: right after arriving, rather than desperately asking about her kids' condition, Diane was urgently trying to call her boyfriend, Nick, from the hospital phone. It was as if contacting Nick was more pressing to her than checking on Christie, Cheryl, and Danny.

Diane's own wound also raised eyebrows. She had a neat, bandaged bullet wound on her left forearm. A relatively minor injury and oddly, her right (dominant) arm had no blood on it, even though the car was soaked with blood from the children. How could a mother who supposedly tried to staunch her kids' bleeding or hold them in her arms have one arm completely clean? It looked as if she hadn't even tried to render first aid or hug her children in their last moments, which was deeply suspicious to the medical staff.

Then there were the bizarre comments Diane made that night. At one point, upon hearing Danny was paralyzed from a bullet to his spine, she reportedly expressed surprise the bullet didn't hit his heart. A weird thing to wonder aloud. She also said things like, "Boy, this really ruined my new car. I got blood all over the back of it," and "This has spoiled my vacation". These offhand remarks about her car and vacation, with zero concern for her children, absolutely stunned those around her. Who says that in such a moment?

By the time dawn broke on May 20, detectives strongly suspected that the real danger to the Downs children hadn't come from a shaggy stranger at all. It had come from their own mother. The official investigation into Diane began in earnest, and over the next several months an increasingly damning case would be built.

From the start, investigators saw inconsistencies and holes in Diane's account. As Det. Welch later recounted, "There were a number of things which didn't make sense, even that first night". For instance, Diane said she went "sightseeing" on a deserted road when it was pitch black outside. That defies common sense. Who takes three sleepy kids out in the dark just to enjoy the scenery? She also was right-handed, yet conveniently her only injury was to her left arm. If a stranger with a gun saw Diane as a threat, wouldn't he shoot her more seriously than a little arm wound? And why would an armed carjacker waste time shooting three children at close range, killing one, while leaving the adult who could identify him relatively unharmed? None of it added up logically.

Police began to quietly investigate Diane herself, even as they publicly said they were looking for the mysterious assailant. Forensic evidence from the scene soon flat-out contradicted Diane's story. Crime scene analysts found no traces you'd expect if her version were true. For example, no blood spatter on the driver's side of the car where the alleged stranger would have leaned in to shoot. Also, no gunpowder residue on the driver's door or interior, which there likely would have been if someone fired multiple shots from that position. These forensic clues suggested the shots were actually fired from inside the car or very close to the victims, not by someone standing outside reaching in.

Then came a break. Investigators recovered .22 caliber shell casings at the roadside where Diane said the shooting happened. However, no gun was found at that time. When they asked Diane if she owned a gun, she insisted she did not. That was a lie. Both her ex-husband Steve and her ex-lover Nick independently informed police that Diane did own a.22 caliber handgun, specifically, a Ruger pistol. Armed with that info, police dug up a record of her gun purchase, proving she had bought a.22 Ruger. A search of her home turned up unfired.22 bullets whose markings matched the casings at the crime scene. The actual gun itself was never recovered, but these unfired cartridges had unique extractor markings that linked them to the same weapon that ejected the shells found by the road. In essence, it was as good as finding the smoking gun. It tied Diane's ammunition to the bullets that struck her children.

Eyewitness evidence further undermined Diane's claims. A man came forward to report he had been driving on that lonely road on the same night and had actually overtaken Diane's Nissan. Why? Because she was driving extremely slowly, around 5 to 7 mph, towards the hospital. This directly contradicted Diane's dramatic narrative of racing at high speed to save her kids. If your children have just been shot and you're trying to get them to the ER, you'd floor it. The witness's account suggested Diane was in no rush at all, perhaps to allow more bleeding (a horrifying thought), or simply because her story about a panicked drive was fabricated.

Perhaps most damning of all were Diane's own words and behavior during the investigation. Just four days after the shooting, while her two surviving kids lay in the hospital, police brought Diane back out to the scene to reenact the incident on camera. If Diane were innocent, this reenactment might have been her chance to show genuine emotion or help find the killer. Instead, what happened was truly disturbing: Diane treated it like a joke. Footage shows her before the cameras, first primping her hair and checking her makeup in the rear-view mirror, then launching into an energetic demonstration of the struggle with the "stranger." She was smiling and laughing, even giggling as she pretended to grapple with an invisible attacker. At one point she accidentally bumped her still-bandaged arm on the car door and cracked a joke that it "almost hurts worse than when it happened", followed by more laughter. The detectives watching this were stunned. Diane's affect was completely inconsistent with a traumatized mother. She acted more like a giddy actress in a bad reenactment skit. Sgt. Welch and others later said this tape was when their early suspicions hardened...Diane Downs wasn't a victim, she was the prime suspect.

During this time, investigators also dug into Diane's personal background and relationships, uncovering the troubling patterns we've already discussed; her history of manipulative behavior, neglect of her kids, and the intense affair with Nick. They soon learned about the diaries she kept. Sure enough, when police got a warrant and searched Diane's home, they found her journals and letters, which laid bare her obsession with Nick Knickerbocker. Entry after entry yearned for Nick and complained about how her children made everything harder. There were even indications she had contemplated running away with him or doing something drastic to remove obstacles. At that point, detectives felt they had a clear motive: Diane wanted to be free of her kids so she could have a relationship with the man she "loved".

Meanwhile, Nick was questioned back in Arizona and he did not mince words. He told police he believed Diane was capable of hurting her kids. Nick recounted how Diane had stalked him after their breakup, and mentioned, chillingly, that he thought she might "kill [his] wife" to eliminate competition. Nick also confirmed that Diane had expressed that her children were a burden to her romantic life. To him, Diane seemed frighteningly fixated and unhinged by the time she left Arizona.

All of this evidence was piling up, yet prosecutors were cautious. They had built a circumstantial case, but there was still no confession or eyewitness to the actual shooting. And crucially, there were two little victims who did survive the attack, Christie and Danny. But at first, neither could speak to what happened. Danny, being only 3 and having been asleep when shot, likely remembered nothing and due to his age, he wasn't a viable witness. Christie, however, almost certainly remembered the night but she had suffered a stroke that night from massive blood loss and was left temporarily unable to speak. As she recovered in the hospital, hooked to machines, Christie was literally the only other witness to the crime besides Diane herself. Detectives noticed something telling: whenever Diane came to visit Christie in the hospital, the little girl's vital signs would spike. Her heart rate and blood pressure would abruptly rise as if she were terrified. The nurses noted that reaction and subtly informed investigators. It seemed Christie was afraid of her mother. On one occasion, according to Dr. Wilhite, Diane coldly suggested they "pull the plug" on Christie if she remained in a coma, insisting the girl was "brain dead". This was not true. Christie had good chances of recovery. Dr. Wilhite was horrified; it appeared to him that Diane might actually *want* her daughter to die. All these signs further convinced police that Christie likely knew her mom was the shooter.

So, investigators waited. They gave Christie time to heal and undergo therapy, hoping she'd eventually be able to tell them what really happened on that road. Behind the scenes, the case against Diane was more or less ready. By early 1984, about nine months after the incident, prosecutors felt they had enough to move forward even if Christie couldn't testify. On February 28, 1984, they made their move: Diane Downs was arrested and charged with one count of murder (for Cheryl's death) and two counts each of attempted murder and assault (for the attacks on Christie and Danny).

The arrest made headlines and shocked the community. The grieving mother from the nightly news was now accused of being the perpetrator. But as details trickled out about the evidence, public sympathy swiftly shifted to outrage. Many who had initially felt sorry for Diane began to wonder what kind of person could harm her own kids in cold blood.

Once Diane was charged, there was intense interest in her mental state and personality. How could a mother do something so unthinkable? Over the course of the investigation and trial, forensic psychologists and psychiatrists evaluated Diane, and their conclusions were disturbing. Diane Downs was diagnosed with a cluster of personality disorders: narcissistic, histrionic, and antisocial personality disorders. In lay terms, these labels suggested she had a profoundly egocentric, attention-seeking, and remorseless character. One psychiatric expert even labeled her a "deviant sociopath," noting that she showed no genuine remorse or empathy for her children.

In court testimony, a psychiatrist described Diane's attitude toward her kids in chilling terms: "She shows no remorse. She regards her children with no empathy and as objects or possessions. Any feelings she has for them are superficial and only extend to how they are part of her and her life." In other words, Diane viewed her children not as independent human beings to love and protect, but as belongings or tools and when they became inconvenient to her, they were disposable. This psychological profile fit with so much of what investigators had observed: her flat affect after the shooting, her self-centered TV interviews, and her prioritizing of her love affair over her kids' lives.

Looking back at her history, you can see hints of these traits even before the crime. Narcissistic personality disorder would explain Diane's need to make everything about herself. For example, the way she spoke about the shooting as something that happened to her, rather than to her children. Histrionic personality might explain her dramatic, attention-craving behavior on camera as the kind of person who loves being in the spotlight (even if that spotlight comes from tragedy). And antisocial personality (which is akin to sociopathy) explains her lack of empathy, deceitfulness, and willingness to break social norms (like, say, shooting your kids) to get what she wants.

It's worth noting that Diane failed those psychiatric tests back when she tried to become a surrogate, with one exam indicating possible psychosis. At the time, she shrugged it off and joked about it, but in hindsight it was a glaring red flag. Additionally, those close to her often saw signs that Diane wasn't mentally well. She seemed to live in a fantasy world at times, laughing off serious issues and centering her own desires above all. After she was jailed, Diane apparently continued to concoct new versions of the story to explain her innocence. She varied between blaming two men in ski masks, or drug dealers, or corrupt officials, instead of the lone "bushy-haired stranger" she originally described. This tendency to constantly fabricate and shift blame was noted by the parole board years later as evidence that Diane lacked any insight into her actions. In their words, even decades after conviction, "she continues to fabricate new versions of events" and refuses to truly accept responsibility.

The psychological picture of Diane Downs that emerged was that of a profoundly self-centered individual with a callous disregard for others, even her own flesh and blood. She craved attention and sympathy, yet couldn't genuinely connect with or care for her children. This context, while not excusing her, at least helps us comprehend how she was capable of such an atrocity. As one reporter who covered the case said, "For her to take such aggressive action, holding a gun point-blank to her children and shooting it repeatedly...that's unheard of...We still don't hear of it."

Throughout the investigation and trial, Diane couldn't resist sharing her side of the story again and again. In fact, even before she was arrested, Diane eagerly spoke with the media, granting interviews that left viewers uneasy. Just a month after the shooting, while her guilt was not yet proven, Diane appeared impeccably groomed on camera, at times sporting a stylish new haircut, to recount the night of the attack. In these interviews, she talked at length about what a terrible ordeal she had been through and how hard it all was on her. Observers noted that she frequently used the words "I" and "me". "I suffered this, I went through that", and shockingly little about the actual suffering of Christie, Cheryl, and Danny. She smiled and even laughed during parts of her retelling, as if oblivious to the gravity of what had happened. Most striking: Diane never shed a tear in these interviews, nor did she express any real grief for her children's pain.

One particular interview exchange has gone down in infamy. A reporter asked Diane if she felt lucky that she only got a minor wound, considering one of her kids died and the others were badly hurt. Diane's response was chillingly narcissistic. She snapped that in fact it was her children who were "the lucky ones", because she had been stuck unable to use her arm for a while and "couldn't tie [her] shoes for two months". Imagine that: calling the kids "lucky" because her arm injury inconvenienced her. This quote laid bare Diane's mindset for the public, and it turned many people's stomachs. Any remaining public sympathy evaporated after that. As news outlets replayed Diane's bizarre interviews, the audience reaction turned from concern to anger and disgust. The consensus became that Diane Downs was not the innocent, grieving mother she pretended to be. She was a liar and quite possibly a murderer.

Besides media interviews, Diane also communicated through letters and statements. She wrote to friends, family, and even near-strangers, always asserting her innocence with dramatic flair. Notably, she struck up correspondence with a local reporter, Anne Jaeger, who had covered the case. From prison, Diane sent Jaeger multiple letters proclaiming that she was the victim of injustice. In one such letter, Diane wrote, "The only people who will rail against the truth are the lovers of lies." In typical fashion, she was implying that anyone who doubted her was simply in love with lies and that she alone spoke "the truth." This kind of self-righteous, grandiose statement is classic for someone with her psychological profile (narcissistic/sociopathic). Jaeger, who kept these letters, was struck by Diane's consistency. She always maintained her innocence, and always in this melodramatic way, painting herself as a martyr to others' lies.

We also have Diane's own words from police interviews and the trial. While she never outright confessed, bits of her accounts are revealing. At one point, in an interview tape played for the jury, Diane described the moment in the car, saying, "I can see Christie reaching her hand out to me while I'm driving, and the blood just keeps coming out of her mouth… That haunts me the most." On the surface, that sounds like a mother tormented by her child's suffering. However, even that statement raised eyebrows because if Christie was reaching out while Diane was driving, it suggests the shooting had already happened before Diane started driving to the hospital. Why, then, did Diane claim she sped off immediately during the struggle? Little slips like this made investigators suspect that Diane's recounting of the timeline was off. Additionally, it's hard to know if that vivid description of Christie bleeding was even real or another bid for sympathy. Given Diane's penchant for dramatization, many thought it was exaggerated or fabricated for effect.

One thing Diane did not do in any interview or letter was express genuine sorrow or ask for forgiveness regarding Cheryl's death or Christie and Danny's injuries. She maintained a sort of breezy confidence that she would be proven innocent. Even decades later, in parole hearings, Diane would continue spinning new versions of the events and insisting she was blameless. Her communications over the years are consistent in that sense: a refusal to acknowledge any wrongdoing and a tendency to cast herself as the unjustly persecuted hero of the story.

As the case unfolded in 1983–84, the media swarmed around the Diane Downs story. It had all the elements of a sensational and disturbing true crime: a young attractive mother, accusations of an unimaginable betrayal of maternal duty, and innocent children as victims. Early on, news reports showed Diane as a grieving mom in tears (footage from Cheryl's funeral, for instance) and ran with the initial story of a "shaggy-haired gunman." But the tone shifted dramatically once Diane was arrested and revelations about her behavior came out. The media began portraying Diane as a real-life "evil mother", often mentioning her alongside the most infamous cases of mothers killing children. In fact, she became one of the first modern cases of a mother committing filicide that got wall-to-wall national coverage, preceding later cases like Susan Smith or Andrea Yates that also shocked the nation.

During Diane's trial in 1984, the public was riveted. The courtroom in Eugene, Oregon, was packed, and national TV and newspapers covered every twist. People just could not fathom why a mother would shoot her kids, so there was intense focus on her possible motive (the affair) and her psyche. The media highlighted her odd affect. For example, reports noted how Diane sometimes smiled or chuckled in court, even as gruesome evidence was presented. One vivid media moment was when the prosecution played "Hungry Like the Wolf" in the courtroom, since Diane had mentioned that song. Astonishingly, Diane reportedly started tapping her feet and bobbing her head to the catchy tune, right there at the defense table. Journalists seized on that detail, painting her as callous and alarmingly nonchalant. It made headlines like "Mother Bobs Her Head to Pop Song as Jury Hears of Children's Shooting."

The public reaction was overwhelmingly one of outrage and morbid fascination. Talk shows and newspaper op-eds debated how someone like Diane could exist. Many viewers wrote angry letters or called into radio shows expressing hatred for Diane Downs. Remember, in 1984 the concept of a mom killing (or attempting to kill) her kids was especially taboo. To be fair, it still is, but back then it was almost unthinkable. The public and press dubbed Diane with dark nicknames, and she became, as one ABC News piece later put it, one of the "Most Infamous" mothers accused of murdering her children. When details of her motive emerged, that only intensified public revulsion. The story became almost archetypal: the "selfish seductress" who would sacrifice her own children for a man.

At the same time, the public was deeply sympathetic toward Christie and Danny. Updates on the children's conditions and eventual new life with an adoptive family were covered positively (more on that soon). People essentially saw the kids as the real victims twice over. First of the shooting, and secondly of having a mother like Diane. When little Christie testified in court, the nation was moved by her courage and heartbroken at what she had endured.

After the trial, Diane's infamy only grew. True crime author Ann Rule wrote a best-selling book about the case in 1987 titled "Small Sacrifices," which many in the public read to get the full, lurid story. Ann Rule's book portrayed Diane as a narcissistic, cold-blooded woman and included interviews with people who knew Diane, reinforcing the media image of an uncaring mother. The book was then adapted into a popular made-for-TV movie, also called "Small Sacrifices," in 1989, with actress Farrah

Fawcett starring as Diane. Millions tuned in to watch, further cementing Diane Downs as a household name in true crime lore. The media, through these portrayals, etched Diane's story into public memory for decades to come.

In Oregon, the community reacted with particular bitterness because Diane had been living in their midst. There was relief that she was convicted and off the streets, especially among those who initially feared a random shooter on the loose. Law enforcement officers and prosecutors involved were lauded as heroes for bringing justice for the children.

Over the years, Diane's name would resurface in news stories whenever she attempted parole or when one of her children spoke out. Each time, the public sentiment reignited. People would recall the shock of the case and often express that she should never be released. In many ways, Diane Downs became a byword for the ultimate violation of motherhood, and the media has consistently treated her as such: a fascinatingly horrifying figure, to be remembered as a cautionary tale.

While Diane Downs commanded the media spotlight, the true heart of this tragedy lies with her children.

Cheryl Lynn Downs, age 7, was the middle child and the one who did not survive the shooting. She was fatally shot that night, with the bullet wounds killing her almost immediately or certainly by the time she reached the hospital. Cheryl was described as a sweet, energetic girl who, heartbreakingly, likely trusted her mom until her last moment. We know from the forensic evidence that at least one of the children (likely Cheryl) was actually outside the car when a shot was fired as there was evidence one child may have been shot while trying to escape. It's believed Cheryl might have been awake and got out of the car in terror, only for her mother to shoot her down on that roadside. That detail was mentioned in court and drives home the horror that Cheryl may have been literally running for her life from her own mom. Cheryl died before she could receive any treatment, and all that's left of her story is the memory her siblings carry and the legacy of the case. She was laid to rest in 1983, mourned by her father Steve and others. Notably, Diane did attend the funeral, weeping dramatically in front of cameras, which some saw as only an act.

Christie Ann Downs, 8 years old at the time, is nothing short of a survivor. She was the oldest child and was extremely close with her little siblings, often more of a caretaker than their mother was. On the night of the shooting, Christie was hit by a bullet that caused a severe stroke, incapacitating her. She nearly died. Doctors had to work heroically to stabilize her. She lost so much blood that oxygen deprivation caused temporary brain damage affecting her speech. It took months of speech therapy and physical therapy for Christie to recover enough to communicate effectively. And when she did, it was monumental. By early 1984, Christie was placed in protective foster care (separate from her mother) and was working with therapists not only to regain speech but also to feel safe enough to talk about the trauma. Eventually, Christie confirmed to prosecutors what they suspected: her mother had shot them. When

Christie was strong enough, authorities asked her the crucial question: "Who shot you?" In response, Christie simply said, "My mom.". It was the confirmation everyone had been waiting for.

During the trial in May 1984, 9-year-old Christie bravely took the stand as the star witness for the prosecution. Imagine the courage it took facing the courtroom, and even facing her mother, to recount the worst night of her life. Due to her stroke, Christie spoke softly and with some difficulty (she was left with a permanent mild speech impairment), but her testimony was clear. In her own words, she described how her mother parked the car, went to the trunk (possibly to retrieve the gun), then came around and shot all three children. Christie's voice broke as she recounted how her mom then shot herself in the arm. There was a particularly dramatic moment when the prosecutor gently asked Christie to identify who had harmed them, and she pointed at Diane, saying, "She did." The courtroom was reportedly silent, many in tears, and Diane notably showed little emotion even as her daughter effectively condemned her. Christie's testimony was absolutely key in securing the conviction. The jurors later said that looking at this little girl and hearing her say her mother shot her was something they could never forget.

After the trial, Christie's life began a new chapter. She and her brother Danny were adopted in 1986 by Fred Hugi, the Lane County prosecutor who put Diane in prison, and his wife Joanne. The Hugis had grown very protective of the children during the legal process, and when Diane was convicted, they stepped up to give Christie and Danny a stable, loving home. By all accounts, the children thrived with the Hugi family. Christie slowly recovered from her trauma, though she has a lasting speech disability from the stroke. She eventually went on to lead a relatively private life. As an adult, Christie got married and even named her daughter Cheryl in honor of her late sister. That small detail speaks volumes about her love for her siblings and the memory she carries. She has largely stayed out of the public eye and, according to those who know her, wants nothing to do with her biological mother. In fact, when her half-sister Becky (more on her in a moment) once tried to reach out, Christie and Danny conveyed through intermediaries that they want to live their lives "without the stigma of being Diane Downs' children." It's hard to blame them for that.

Stephen "Danny" Downs, who was just 3 years old, survived but paid a heavy price. He was shot in the back, the bullet shattering his spine, which left him paralyzed from the chest down. Danny was so young that he likely doesn't remember the event itself. He, too, was adopted by the Hugis and grew up in their care, using a wheelchair for mobility. Despite his disability, reports indicate Danny grew into a well-adjusted young man, thanks to the supportive upbringing by his adoptive parents. Like Christie, Danny has kept a low profile in adulthood. The siblings have occasionally been mentioned in media. For example, we know from an ABC News interview with their half-sister that Danny and Christie prefer not to be publicly identified or involved in Diane-related publicity. They truly started life over as part of the Hugi family, even presumably taking the Hugi last name (though that detail is private).

Finally, there is the fifth child of Diane Downs...the baby girl born while Diane was in custody and on trial. In a strange turn of events, Diane became pregnant again after the shootings but before her arrest. She later claimed she did this intentionally by seducing a man on her mail route, saying "I got pregnant because I miss Christie and I miss Danny and I miss Cheryl so much... You can't replace children, but you can replace the effect they give you". It was an outrageous rationale to conceive another baby essentially as an emotional Band-Aid. Many believe she also did it to gain sympathy during her trial (a pregnant woman might appear more sympathetic to a jury). Whatever the reason, in late 1983 Diane was indeed pregnant, and in June 1984, just a month after her conviction, she gave birth to a healthy girl. Diane named the baby Amy Elizabeth before the state swiftly took the newborn away. The infant was adopted by a loving couple, Chris and Jackie Babcock, and was renamed Rebecca "Becky" Babcock.

Becky Babcock grew up knowing she was adopted, but she learned the shocking truth of her origins only later. At age 11, Becky cleverly tricked her babysitter into revealing her birth mother's name. Imagine being a middle-schooler and discovering that your biological mother is a notorious convicted child killer splashed all over true crime books. It rocked Becky's world. In her teens and early adulthood, Becky struggled with that knowledge. She even reached out and wrote to Diane in prison at one point, searching for answers. Diane wrote back, but whatever she said did not give Becky peace; Becky has since said she regrets contacting Diane, whom she bluntly calls "a monster." As an adult, Becky decided to share her story publicly, partly to reclaim it on her own terms. She appeared on The Oprah Winfrey Show in 2010 and on ABC's 20/20 in 2019, talking about how she came to terms with her biological mother's identity. Becky emphasizes that while she carries Diane's genes, "that's not who I am inside", and she credits her wonderful adoptive parents and supportive upbringing for that. Becky today works in behavioral health and is a mom herself, determined to be nothing like Diane. Her journey is actually an inspiring subplot to this saga. One of resilience and the classic debate of nature vs. nurture. "When I was young, I worried I would be like Diane Downs," Becky said, "But as I grew up, I realized nature is not gonna win over nurture."

After a trial that lasted about six weeks, the verdict came in June 1984: Diane Downs was found guilty on all counts: one count of murder, two counts of attempted murder, and criminal assault. She was later sentenced to life in prison plus 50 years. The judge made it clear he intended for Diane to serve the maximum time and remarked that he did not want to ever see her free again. Under Oregon law of the time, she'd have to serve at least 25 years before being eligible for parole on the life sentence.

Between the conviction and sentencing, Diane gave birth to the baby girl (Becky). Ten days before formal sentencing, the infant was seized by the state and placed for adoption, as mentioned. Diane then headed off to begin serving her time at the Oregon Women's Correctional Center in Salem.

For most criminals, that would be the end of the story until a parole date decades later. But Diane being Diane, she just couldn't stay out of the headlines. In July 1987, a few years into her sentence, she managed to escape from prison, albeit briefly. It was like a scene from a movie: Diane scaled a 15-foot chain-link fence topped with razor wire (she padded her clothes around the wire to avoid being cut) and she climbed over. An alarm went off, but by the time guards responded, she was gone into the night.

For the next 10 days, Diane Downs was a fugitive and the subject of a massive manhunt. Authorities were extremely concerned, especially prosecutor Fred Hugi, who feared Diane might try to find Christie and Danny (who were in his care) to harm or kidnap them. Hugi actually moved his family to an undisclosed location temporarily. The search for Diane spanned 14 states, and tips poured in from everywhere, some claiming sightings as far as Wisconsin.

So where did Diane actually go? It turned out she had a plan of sorts. Investigators later found a hand-drawn map in her cell that basically showed the route from the prison to a certain house nearby, with "You are here" written on it. That clue led them to the home of a man named Wayne Seifer, who lived just a few blocks from the prison. In a bizarre twist, Seifer was the husband of a fellow inmate (they were estranged) so Diane had learned about him through prison connections. When Diane escaped, she apparently went straight to Seifer's house, knocked on his door in the middle of the night and basically said "Can I stay here?". Wayne Seifer, who later admitted he was drunk and high at the time, bizarrely agreed. According to Seifer, Diane introduced herself simply as "a girl with no clothes on" (indeed she wasn't wearing much after the escape) and then the two began a sexual relationship that lasted the duration of her time on the run. She hid in his upstairs bedroom for over a week while he provided food and clothes. Seifer said he foolishly fell in love with her in those 10 days.

Police finally got a solid lead and raided Seifer's home on July 21, 1987. They found Diane upstairs, wearing Seifer's t-shirt and boxer shorts, but she surrendered peacefully when caught. Reportedly, Seifer claimed that Diane had talked about trying "suicide by cop", essentially planning to provoke the police into shooting her, and he had talked her out of it before they arrived. Seifer was later charged for aiding her (he got probation and some community service). Diane's escape attempt added five extra years to her sentence. More significantly, it prompted Oregon officials to take no more chances with her: at the request of Fred Hugi and others, Diane was transferred out of state to maximum security prisons far from her children. First, she was moved to the Clinton Correctional Facility for Women in New Jersey, to put a continent between her and Oregon. Eventually, in 1994, she was transferred to California's prison system. As of the latest information, Diane is incarcerated at the Central California Women's Facility in Chowchilla, California, which houses many notorious female offenders. The state of Oregon keeps her there under an interstate compact, considering her too high-risk to house locally (because of the potential threat to Christie and Danny if she were ever to escape again).

After being recaptured, Diane largely faded into the background of prison life, but she pops up in the news whenever she becomes eligible for parole. Under her sentence, her first shot at parole came after serving 25 years, which was around 2008-2009. The Oregon parole board scheduled a hearing, and true to form, Diane maintained her innocence throughout the process. At her 2008 parole hearing (she also had a hearing in 2010 and again in 2020), Diane continued to insist she never harmed her kids and even put forward new versions of the events at one point blaming a supposed conspiracy of drug dealers. The parole board was unmoved. They noted in their denial that Diane showed zero remorse and had not taken responsibility in any way. The Lane County District Attorney wrote a letter to the board stating that Diane "continues to fail to demonstrate any honest insight into her criminal behavior", and highlighted how she keeps changing her story and deflecting blame. After a hearing of three hours, the board deliberated for only thirty minutes before denying her parole.

Diane Downs had subsequent parole hearings in 2010 and 2020, both of which likewise resulted in denial. Victims' advocates and the families of Christie and Danny have consistently argued against her release, and Diane's own bizarre parole statements haven't helped her cause. For example, in one hearing, she suggested that in the years since the trial, maybe her children had been "brainwashed" into believing she did it. An assertion that the board found absurd and offensive. As of now, she will not be eligible for another parole consideration until 2030 (parole reviews in Oregon for such cases are typically at 10-year intervals after denial). The consensus is that Diane will likely never be freed; her notoriety and lack of rehabilitation make it politically and practically unlikely that any parole board would let her out. In fact, her earliest possible release date is listed as 2025, but as that year arrives, there is no indication she'll actually get out as it would require a parole board reversal that no one anticipates.

To this day, Diane Downs continues to proclaim her innocence from behind bars. In occasional interviews or writings, she has hinted at conspiracy theories and insists the real killer is out there. But to almost everyone else, investigators, jurors, the public, the truth was decided back in 1984: Diane herself committed these crimes, and she's where she belongs. The trial and its aftermath ensured that she would never have access to her children again, and indeed her parental rights were terminated after her conviction. Christie and Danny were legally and emotionally freed from being her kids, which was undoubtedly for the best.

It has been over four decades since the night of the shooting, yet the Diane Downs case remains firmly in the public eye. Why does this story endure? For one, it's a stark and shocking example of maternal filicide which is among the most taboo and compelling of crimes. The case has been studied in criminology courses and psychology journals as an example of extreme narcissism and sociopathic behavior in a parent. The profile of Diane that emerged (narcissistic, attention-hungry, violent, manipulative) has been used as a reference point in analyzing other cases of mothers who kill. In a broader sense, the case challenges our assumptions about innate motherly love, making it both disturbing and fascinating to the public even years later.

KILLER CATFISH

Liz Golyar

Dave Kroupa was a 35-year-old single father from Omaha, Nebraska, trying his hand at online dating in 2012. Fresh out of a long-term relationship with his children's mother, Amy Flora, he made it clear to any new date that he wasn't looking for commitment. That spring, he met Shanna "Liz" Golyar through a dating site. Their relationship was casual, and Dave made his intentions known. They had a great time together, going out to bars, playing pool, riding bulls, and partying together. However, unbeknownst to Liz, by late October, Dave also began seeing another woman, 37-year-old Cari Farver, a vivacious single mom and computer programmer he met at the auto repair shop where he worked. Sparks flew, but they didn't exchange phone numbers on that first encounter. Soon after, as Dave was scrolling on the dating sites, he stumbled upon none other than Cari Farver's profile. So, he reached out and asked her on a date. On October 29, 2012, they went on their first date at an Omaha restaurant.

Partway through the evening, that first date took an awkward turn. Dave's phone kept buzzing with texts and calls from Liz, which he ignored. After dinner, Dave brought Cari back to his nearby apartment. Moments later, someone began relentlessly ringing the building's security door. It was Liz, in tears, insisting she needed to grab some belongings from Dave's place. Caught off guard, Dave stepped out to talk to Liz, while Cari waited upstairs. Cari ultimately decided to call it a night and headed out, passing by a distraught Liz in the hallway as she left. It was a brief but tense encounter. Dave recalled that moment, saying "they only made eye contact for all of three seconds, maybe."

Despite the rocky interruption, Dave was able to smooth things over with Cari. Later that night he called her to explain, and even drove to Cari's home in Macedonia, Iowa, to spend the night. In the following weeks, Dave continued casually dating both women, honest with both of them that he wasn't exclusive. He and Cari grew closer, seeing each other frequently, but he hadn't entirely cut ties with Liz just yet.

Then, on November 9, 2012, someone vandalized Cari's Ford Explorer with spray paint while it was parked outside her home in Iowa. At the time, Cari was undertaking a big project at work in Omaha that required long hours. Nervous after the vandalization, Cari arranged for her 15-year-old son Max to stay with her parents that week, and Dave agreed that Cari could crash at his Omaha apartment so she wouldn't have a long commute. On the night of November 12, 2012, Cari came to Dave's place after work as planned. The next morning, November 13, Dave gave her a kiss goodbye and headed to work around 6:20 AM while Cari stayed on his couch using her laptop.

Later that morning, Dave received an abrupt text from Cari's phone. "We should move in together," she said. Her tone was surprising as they'd only been dating two weeks and both had agreed to keep it casual. Confused, Dave texted back that no, moving in together wasn't a good idea. Almost instantly, a barrage of angry messages flooded in. "As soon as I text her back, I get a text that says, 'Fine! I don't ever want to see you again… I hate you…' on and on," Dave recalled of Cari's strangely furious reaction. The sudden 180°, from proposing living together to viciously breaking up with him, left Dave perplexed. She threatened him, called him names, and clearly didn't handle the rejection well. When he returned home that day, Cari was gone. She had left behind the key to his apartment and taken all her belongings as if she'd abruptly moved out.

Over the next few days, unsettling messages from Cari continued. She texted Dave cruel insults and inexplicably hateful words while also telling him to leave *her* alone. On November 15, Dave was stunned to learn that Cari's boss received a text apparently from Cari quitting her job. In that text, Cari oddly said she was recommending Liz Golyar to fill her position. Sure enough, Liz promptly submitted an online job application to Cari's company that same day.

Cari's family was also getting bizarre updates. Her mother, Nancy Raney, received a text from Cari's number saying she had taken a new job in Kansas and would be out of touch for a while. This made no sense to Nancy. Cari lived for her son and would never just run off. Nancy grew increasingly alarmed when Cari failed to show up for her half-brother's wedding on November 16. By that date, Nancy hadn't heard her daughter's voice in days as Cari only responded with texts that never answered direct questions. Then, Cari started posting bizarre updates on social media. One post read, "I am not missing, I just don't want to come home right now." Knowing something was very wrong, Nancy filed a missing person report with the Pottawattamie County Sheriff's Office on November 16, 2012.

Police initially had little to go on. When Nancy mentioned that Cari had been diagnosed with bipolar disorder and occasionally took medication, officers wondered if perhaps Cari had left on her own during a mental health episode. They attempted to contact Cari, but when they, too, received a text reply telling them to essentially back off, it appeared to confirm that Cari didn't want to be found. As one investigator later put it, the early evidence was inconclusive. Without signs of foul play, they had to consider that Cari chose to disappear. Heartbroken, Nancy was not convinced; her gut told her this wasn't really her daughter texting. In fact, she noticed the messages were full of typos and lacked Cari's usual perfect punctuation. This was very unlike the real Cari, who was a stickler for spelling.

In the meantime, Cari kept busy harassing not only Dave, but Liz as well. One night, Liz showed up at Dave's apartment to let him know that Cari had not only been sending her a hateful barrage of messages but she also went as far as to deeply key the side of Liz's car.

Meanwhile, on November 16, Cari's debit card was used at two Omaha stores to buy over $300 worth of goods. Among the items purchased was a distinctive black-and-white floral-patterned shower curtain. Family members also received a photo emailed from Cari's account with an image of a $5,000 check made out to Cari and signed by Liz Golyar. Alongside the image was a message saying Liz had bought Cari's furniture for $5,000 and someone should let Liz into Cari's house to pick it up. This was beyond strange: why would Cari sell her belongings to the very woman who was her romantic rival? And why would Liz purchase the items from someone who was viciously harassing her? Suspicious, Nancy alerted police about the check and refused to let anyone into Cari's home. Investigators traced the phone signal from which that text was sent and it pinged in the early hours of November 18 near Liz Golyar's home in Omaha. But when officers canvassed the area, they couldn't find Cari's phone or any sign of her.

As days turned to weeks, Cari Farver remained elusive. She missed her own birthday, her son Max's birthday, and even her father's funeral in December. Important and tragic events that no loving mother would ignore. Yet texts and Facebook posts from Cari continued to insist she was fine, though wanting nothing to do with her old life.

What began as a perplexing breakup text quickly escalated into a full-blown nightmare for Dave and those around him. In the weeks after Cari dumped him, Dave began receiving a barrage of messages from accounts, all claiming to be Cari Farver. Dave would receive texts, block the number, and Cari would just text him from a new number. These texts and emails poured in constantly. Dave would get as many as 50–60 emails per day, plus countless texts and even messages left as drafts in his phone that he never saw her send. The sender tormented Dave with statements like "I'm going to destroy the things you care about" and "Your life will be ruined". Another message chillingly warned, "I will do what I can to make you suffer."

Much of the hostility in the messages was also directed at Liz Golyar. Cari called Liz awful slurs, frequently referring to her as a "whore," and seemed obsessed with breaking up any relationship between Dave and Liz. Liz told Dave that she, too, was getting harassing texts and emails from Cari. This bizarre situation oddly drew Dave and Liz closer; they bonded in their shared fear of Cari's wrath. As Dave later observed, every time he drifted apart from Liz, some new scare would pull them back together like a cruel puppetry designed to keep them both on edge.

The harassment soon moved beyond words on a screen. Liz reported that someone vandalized her property on multiple occasions. In late November 2012, she called Dave in a panic after discovering graffiti spray-painted inside her garage. The words "WHORE FROM DAVE" scrawled menacingly on the wall. She was certain Cari was behind it. A couple months later, in February 2013, and again on April 1, 2013, Liz said her property was vandalized with similar hateful messages. Each time, either Dave or Liz (or both) would promptly get an email or text from Cari taking credit for the damage. Dave himself wasn't spared. His apartment and car were also targeted with keying and graffiti that referenced Liz in vile terms. It truly felt like a vindictive stalker was lurking in the shadows, lashing out at anything and anyone close to Dave.

Some of the creepiest moments came when Cari claimed to be watching Dave. One night, Dave was relaxing in his recliner at home when an incoming text made his blood run cold. "I see you. You're sitting in your chair with your feet propped up, wearing a blue shirt," it read. Dave looked down...he was wearing a blue shirt, exactly as described. How could Cari be seeing him in real time? On several occasions, messages described Dave's activities or outfits with eerie accuracy. Sometimes these messages arrived when Liz was right there in the same room with him. Dave could see that Liz wasn't on her phone at that moment, so he never suspected she was sending them. In fact, he often turned to Liz for comfort, marveling together at how Cari seemed to know their every move.

The digital onslaught continued for years. By early 2013, Omaha police were involved, but every lead was a dead end. In January 2013, about two months into the harassment, Dave spotted a familiar vehicle parked near his apartment: a black Ford Explorer that looked just like Cari's. He knew that SUV well (he'd even done maintenance on it before). Dave immediately snapped a photo of the license plate and alerted police. When officers searched the vehicle, they found it wiped immaculately clean with no obvious blood or signs of struggle, just an empty, vacuumed car. The only clue was a single latent fingerprint on a mint candy container in the cup holder. Oddly, the print didn't match Cari or anyone in law enforcement databases at the time. With nothing else to go on, the discovery only deepened the mystery: Cari's car had turned up, but Cari herself was still nowhere to be found.

Meanwhile, unbeknownst to Dave, during these same years Liz had an entirely separate boyfriend, a man named Todd Butterbaugh whom she'd been dating exclusively since 2010. Todd claimed he had no clue about the Cari drama. So, when Cari randomly emailed Todd in early 2013 claiming to be a friend of Liz's, Liz played it off as if Cari really was an old friend so as not to give away her infidelity. For nearly three years, Liz lived with Todd and her children, never once mentioning that she was being "stalked" or harassed by anyone. It's baffling to realize that while Liz cowered in fear of Cari to Dave, she maintained total normalcy with Todd. She had compartmentalized her life so well that even the man she lived with didn't know about the chaos consuming her.

For Dave and Liz, life in 2013 was dominated by fear of the "crazy ex" who wouldn't let them be. By summer, the harassment hit a new level of cruelty. Dave and Liz had broken up yet again in early August 2013 (the strain was constant), but on the morning of August 17, 2013, Liz phoned Dave in hysterics: her house was on fire. Flames had engulfed the Omaha home she was renting, tragically killing her four pets inside, two dogs, a cat, and a pet snake. Liz said she had been out of the house when it happened and that she'd left the day before and returned that morning to find everything destroyed. Fire investigators quickly determined it was arson; there were multiple separate ignition points and signs of accelerant use. Not even an hour after the blaze was reported, both Liz and Dave received emails from the ever-present Cari. One message to Dave read, "I am not lying. I set that nasty whore's house on fire. I hope the whore and her kids die in it." Another email sent to Liz around 12:56 AM that day said she "hoped Liz and her children burned to death." All signs pointed yet again to Cari Farver as the diabolical stalker. Terrified and traumatized, Dave and Liz rekindled their relationship in the aftermath of the fire, bound tighter than ever by the menace that seemed determined to destroy them. If Cari's intent was to scare off Liz, she was only pushing her further into Dave's arms.

Meanwhile, Cari's family was still desperately searching for answers. In late 2013, Nancy Raney received what seemed like a promising tip: a man called claiming he'd seen Cari at a homeless shelter and that Cari wanted her mom to come get her. Nancy's heart leapt. Could her daughter be alive after all, lost and wanting to come home? She raced to the shelter with investigators, only to learn that no one matching Cari's description had been there. The call was a cruel hoax. "I was shaking... then devastated," Nancy said. "I knew somebody was playing games here."

Over time, Dave tried to reclaim some normalcy. In February 2015, more than two years into the nightmare, he changed his phone number and even moved from Omaha across the river to Council Bluffs, Iowa. For a while, the harassing messages subsided. He also began distancing himself from Liz; the constant drama had taken its toll. In mid-November 2015, Dave definitively broke things off with Liz, telling her he was going to pursue a more serious relationship with another woman. Liz did not take the rejection well. And right on cue, a new twist emerged...

On December 4, 2015, Liz contacted the Omaha police with a surprising new theory: she claimed the person who'd been terrorizing them might not be Cari Farver after all. Liz now accused Dave's ex, Amy Flora, of being the culprit. Amy (remember, the mother of Dave's kids) had always had a cordial relationship with Dave, and aside from a brief meeting, Amy barely knew Liz. Nonetheless, Liz told police that Amy had been sending her threatening messages and that Amy must have been impersonating Cari this whole time. To bolster her claim, Liz showed officers a series of recent Facebook messages and texts she said were from Amy. Willing to investigate any lead, police asked Liz to turn over her phone yet again so they could download these new messages. She agreed, and her phone data was copied on December 4. Investigators told Liz they'd follow up with Amy in a few days.

Less than 24 hours later, events took a dramatic turn. On December 5, 2015, at 6:40 PM, a 911 call came in from Big Lake Park in Council Bluffs. Officers arrived to find Liz Golyar on the ground by her car, bleeding from a gunshot wound to her left thigh. She had been shot, but thankfully the injury was not life-threatening.

Liz claimed she had gone to the park to meet a friend when an assailant came up and shot her out of the blue. Over the next days, her story shifted. Initially she said the shooter was a mysterious woman in a car, later she blamed a man, then ultimately, she stuck to accusing Amy Flora. According to Liz, Amy had ambushed her and pulled the trigger.

Police were skeptical, especially Detective Jim Doty and Deputy Ryan Avis of the Pottawattamie County Sheriff's Office, who had quietly started re-examining the Cari Farver case earlier that year. They immediately checked on Amy Flora's whereabouts. Amy was at home with her toddler that evening, and her car engine was cold when officers arrived. She clearly hadn't been out shooting anyone. In fact, Amy was stunned by the accusation. She cooperated fully, handing over her phone for analysis on December 7, 2015. Detectives increasingly suspected that Liz had shot herself in a desperate ploy to frame Amy.

Detectives Ryan Avis and Jim Doty had joined the case in early 2015 after it languished for years. By now, they had a strong hunch that Cari Farver was not alive. They realized they were likely dealing with a long-term homicide investigation, not just a stalking. But how could they prove it? They began meticulously combing through old case files and digital records, essentially starting from scratch. In the wake of the December 2015 shooting incident, the focus narrowed squarely on Liz Golyar. As Sgt. Doty later put it, "the big break in the case" came when they re-analyzed the phone data dumps from 2013. With the help of digital forensics expert Tony Kava, they uncovered damning evidence hiding in plain sight on Liz's old cell phone.

First, they found a photograph of Cari's Ford Explorer on Liz's phone. It was a photo taken on December 24, 2012, a full month before police recovered the vehicle in that Omaha parking lot. "Somehow Liz knew where Cari's vehicle was before law enforcement even did," Det. Doty noted incredulously. There was no innocent explanation for Liz having that picture. Investigators also noticed that Liz's phone had made six calls to Cari's home phone in the days just before Cari disappeared (using the *67 feature to mask her number). This directly contradicted Liz's claim that she only met Cari once in passing. It appeared Liz had been actively trying to contact or track Cari in early November 2012, before Cari went missing. Piece by piece, a picture was forming of Liz as the predator rather than the prey.

Dave Kroupa also allowed detectives to download his current phone and comb through years of messages. One crucial finding was that many of the threatening emails Dave received from Cari had originated from an IP address associated with Todd Butterbaugh's Wi-Fi network. In other words, the emails from Cari were often sent from Liz's own home internet while she lived with Todd. Liz had tried to cover her tracks by using disposable phones, fake email addresses (over 30 of them), and anonymizing software. But forensic analysts traced it all back: the patterns of IP addresses, device identifiers, and timing all pointed to Liz as the author of every message from Cari and from the supposed "Amy Flora" accounts.

Investigators weren't limited to

cyberspace. They revisited physical evidence, too. In September 2015, they had quietly re-run the fingerprint from Cari's SUV through updated databases and finally got a match: **it was Liz Golyar's fingerprint**. Armed with new warrants, they impounded Cari's Ford Explorer once more in late 2015 for a deeper forensic search. On the second inspection, they found nothing, but refusing to give up, crime scene techs literally peeled back the upholstery on the seats of her car. On February 18, 2016, under the fabric of the front passenger seat, they discovered a large blood stain soaked into the foam padding. This time, DNA tests yielded the match they'd been expecting. The blood was Cari Farver's. The interior of the vehicle had been scrubbed impressively clean, but not even Liz could erase every trace of what happened. The car had been the murder scene.

The noose was tightening. In February 2016, police executed search warrants at Liz Golyar's apartment and also at her former residence with Todd. The results were telling. Among Liz's possessions, they found a black-and-white floral shower curtain, the exact pattern matching the one bought with Cari's credit card on November 16, 2012. They also found a pile of electronics and camcorder equipment that seemed out of place. In fact, receipts stored by Cari's family proved those electronics (a Sony camcorder and Nikon camera) had belonged to Cari. She'd purchased them just a month before her death. Finding Cari's property in Liz's home was a smoking gun: Liz had kept trophies of her victim.

At this point, detectives employed one more savvy tactic to solidify their case. They had already suspected that the supposed "confession" emails from "Amy Flora" were actually written by Liz. These emails, which started hitting Liz's inbox in late December 2015 after police hinted Amy was a suspect, were practically a killer's journal. In them, "Amy" (really Liz) confessed to murdering Cari Farver and to burning down Liz's house, even to shooting Liz herself. The writer rambled about how "she" (as Amy) stabbed Cari in her car, wrapped the body in a tarp, burned the remains, and disposed of them in garbage bags. One message included chilling detail: the killer described a yin-yang tattoo on Cari's hip as she was destroying the body. That information had never been made public; only someone who had seen Cari's body would know. (Cari did indeed have a yin-yang tattoo on her left hip, a matching one to her ex-husband's, which her family confirmed to police.) By feeding Liz's ego and paranoia, letting her believe they bought her frame-up of Amy, investigators got Liz to effectively write her own confession. She had unwittingly provided details only the true murderer could know, all under the guise of implicating Amy.

To leave no stone unturned, authorities did one more deep dive into Liz's digital devices. In February 2017, they recovered an old tablet that Dave Kroupa still had, which Liz had used back when they were dating. Inside the tablet was a memory card, and though all files had been deleted, forensic techs managed to retrieve thousands of erased images and texts. What they found defied belief: among over 13,000 recovered photos were several images of a human corpse. Specifically, the photos showed what looked like body parts wrapped in a blue tarp, and close-ups of flesh with distinctive tattoos... a Chinese character for "mother," which Cari had on her foot and a yin-yang symbol on the hip. A forensic pathologist examined one photo and confirmed it showed the decomposing foot of a human female, with the "mother" Chinese-character tattoo exactly like Cari's. In another, the yin-yang on what appeared to be a slab of skin matched Cari's unique tattoo. It was a horrific but crucial discovery: Liz Golyar had kept photos of Cari Farver's dead body. The woman who had so long pretended that Cari was still alive had, in fact, documented her gruesome handiwork as a morbid keepsake. Investigators had finally uncovered virtual remains to accompany all the virtual lies.

By the end of 2016, detectives had built an ironclad case. All evidence indicated that back on November 13, 2012, Liz Golyar ambushed Cari Farver in Dave's apartment or in her car, stabbed her to death, and disposed of her body, then spent the next three years masquerading as Cari via text and email to cover up the crime. Liz went to extraordinary lengths, including self-harm and arson that effectively killed her four pets, to perpetuate the illusion that Cari was a deranged stalker, when in reality, the only deranged person was Liz herself. With the truth in hand, police finally moved to make an arrest.

On December 22, 2016, Shanna "Liz" Golyar was arrested and charged with first-degree murder in the death of Cari Farver. After four long years of twists and turmoil, the real culprit was unmasked. When the news broke, those who knew the case were stunned. The whole time, the supposed victim of stalking was the stalker and killer all along. Dave Kroupa had truly been in a relationship with his girlfriend's murderer, all while being fooled into thinking the threat came from someone else.

Liz Golyar went to trial in May 2017 in Omaha, Nebraska. In a final bid to control the narrative, she waived her right to a jury, opting for a bench trial (perhaps hoping a judge might be more swayed by legal arguments given the largely circumstantial case). The prosecution laid out the incredible tale of deceit, backed by the trove of digital forensics. They presented over 20,000 emails and texts showing Liz's elaborate impersonation of Cari. They showed the photos of the blood-soaked car seat and even more gruesome images from Liz's recovered memory card. Liz's own words, the faux confessions, the threats, all became evidence against her. Tellingly, Liz did not take the stand in her own defense. In fact, her defense team offered no witnesses and barely challenged the evidence. One of Liz's attorneys had even accidentally referred to Liz as Cari during trial! It was a moment that underscored how thoroughly Liz had tried to assume her victim's identity. The outcome was inevitable.

On August 15, 2017, Judge Timothy Burns found Liz Golyar guilty of first-degree murder and second-degree arson. The evidence, though largely digital, was overwhelming and corroborative. Cari's body has never been recovered, but it didn't matter when it came to finding Liz guilty. Liz's trail of emails, photos, and stolen items told the story of a murder in stark detail. At sentencing, the judge did not mince words: "Cari Farver did not voluntarily disappear," he said, affirming that Liz's actions proved a premeditated killing. Liz Golyar received life in prison for the murder, plus an additional 18–20 years for arson. The sentences were to run consecutively. In the end, the woman who spun a web of lies was caught fast in the web of justice.

Outside the courtroom, Dave Kroupa and Cari's family finally had clarity, though it was a bitter victory. Cari Farver's name was cleared. For years she had been painted as an unstable, possibly violent missing woman; now everyone knew she had been an innocent victim all along. Dave was stunned at how the investigation turned out. "She [Liz] ruined my life as much as you can without actually killing me," Dave told reporters, reflecting on the toll the ordeal took on him. He felt a heavy weight of guilt knowing that his connection to these two women had set the tragedy in motion. "I don't feel blameless in all of this... A lot of bad things happened to good people, all because of a series of events that I'm at the center of," he said quietly. Dave could not have foreseen the madness that would unfold from a simple online date, but the "what-ifs" still haunt him. "If I hadn't met Cari, she wouldn't have met Liz and this all wouldn't have happened," he lamented. "If I'd have known the choice was this craziness or [just] tell Cari I'm not interested, I would've told Cari I'm not interested. But you don't get that choice."

Cari's mother Nancy and her son Max finally learned what became of their beloved Cari. Though they never got to bury Cari's body, they at least got the truth and some measure of justice. Dave made a point to acknowledge their suffering: "Nancy and Cari's son were foremost in my mind... They're the ones that have to live with the repercussions," he said, relieved that Liz would never hurt anyone else's family.

In the aftermath, Liz Golyar appealed her conviction, arguing that without a body, the evidence was insufficient. But in 2018 the Nebraska Supreme Court upheld the verdict. The court noted that this case was a landmark example of how powerful digital evidence can be in modern investigations. Indeed, the detectives' persistence in following the electronic footprints ensured a killer didn't get away with murder.

Today, Liz Golyar sits in the Nebraska Correctional Center for Women, serving life behind bars. She will never be eligible for parole. Dave Kroupa has tried to move on, keeping a low profile and guarding his privacy closely. He still checks over his shoulder out of habit, but with Liz locked away, he's slowly learning to breathe again. The story of Cari Farver's murder stands as one of the most bizarre tales in the annals of true crime. A real-life "Single White Female" saga taken to technological extremes. For over three years, Liz Golyar impersonated the woman she had killed, tormenting everyone in that woman's life, all to hide a crime driven by jealousy. In the end, justice prevailed, but the scars linger for those involved. As Dave poignantly put it, "I don't mind watching a movie with a terrible twist but I never want that in my life again."

HELL HATH NO FURY LIKE A WOMAN SCORNED

Betty Broderick

Elisabeth "Betty" Anne Bisceglia was born on November 7, 1947, and raised in Eastchester, New York, a suburb just north of New York City. She was the third of six children in a strict Roman Catholic family. Her father, Frank Bisceglia, was an Italian-American businessman who built a successful plastering company with his brothers, and her mother, Marita (née Curtin), was Irish-American. The Bisceglias were an "aspirational" family not born wealthy, but determined to achieve an upper-middle-class life through hard work, education, and strict adherence to proper manners and social norms. From a young age, Betty was taught that her purpose in life was to be a good wife and mother, bringing honor, never shame, to her family. As Betty later recalled, "I was being trained to be a housewife since the day I was born... Go to Catholic schools, be careful with dating until you find a Catholic man, support him while he works, be blessed in your later years with beautiful grandchildren".

Betty attended Catholic schools, including Maria Regina High School and later Eastchester High (from which she graduated in 1965). Described as a smart and personable young woman, she dutifully followed her parents' expectations. In 1965, at age 17, she enrolled at the College of Mount Saint Vincent, a small Catholic women's college in the Bronx, where she majored in early childhood education and minored in English. By all accounts, Betty was an ideal daughter in her youth. She was studious, devout, and eager to please her family. Friends from her childhood noted that Betty and her peers were brought up in a similar fashion, giving them "little chance to rebel" against their parents' traditional values. This sheltered upbringing and desire to fulfill a predetermined role would later shape Betty's identity and her reactions when life veered from the expected script.

In the fall of 1965, during her freshman year of college, Betty's life took a turn when she met a charming young man named Daniel "Dan" Broderick III. The two crossed paths at a University of Notre Dame football weekend. Betty had traveled to South Bend, Indiana, with a friend for the game, which is where Dan, then 21 and a senior at Notre Dame, first introduced himself. Dan was from a large Irish Catholic family in Pittsburgh and was on a pre-med track; he confidently told Betty he was an "M.D.A." (almost a doctor) and had plans to attend Cornell University Medical College in New York the next year. At 5-foot-10 with long sideburns and nerdy glasses, Dan didn't immediately sweep 17-year-old Betty off her feet. She later quipped that she thought he was "geek city" at first glance. Still, Dan was smitten from day one. He later told friends that the first time he saw Betty, he knew she would be his wife.

After that brief meeting, Dan persistently kept in touch, sending Betty letters and telegrams while she returned to her studies in New York. His intelligence, ambition, and sense of humor grew on her. Both came from devout, disciplined Catholic families and shared similar dreams of an affluent life filled with career success (for him), social standing, and a big family. By Betty's account, "He was very ambitious, very intelligent and very funny. And I am those three things. We both wanted the same things in the future". Dan courted Betty energetically; she recalled that "the guy asked me to marry him every day for three years". Eventually, Betty agreed. On April 12, 1969, at Immaculate Conception Church in her hometown, 21-year-old Betty Bisceglia married 25-year-old Dan Broderick in a lavish Catholic ceremony. The wedding was picture-perfect. Betty was a radiant bride in lace, and Dan stood out in a sharp blue pinstripe suit (eschewing a traditional tux). The newlyweds looked like a golden couple destined for success.

Yet, cracks in their fairy tale began to show even before the honeymoon ended. Dan's vision of marriage was traditional to an extreme and for Betty, unexpectedly harsh. While honeymooning in the Caribbean, Dan abruptly dismissed the household staff at the villa, making it clear he expected Betty to do all the cooking and cleaning from then on. Betty, who had grown up with domestic help and a mother who "ruled the roost" while the father earned the income, was stunned by this immediate shift. "He had the idea that the wedding changed everything," Betty later said. Back in New York, she'd never even lived away from her parents or had to keep house on her own. Now she found herself in a tiny medical school dorm apartment in Manhattan (Dan was starting at Cornell's med school) with a pile of new domestic duties and a husband absorbed in study. The sudden loss of the comfortable life she knew and the realization that Dan's courtship charm had given way to rigid expectations left Betty feeling trapped and disillusioned within weeks of saying "I do". She even threatened to annul the marriage when it became clear what was expected of her. However, fate intervened: Betty returned from the honeymoon pregnant with their first child. Embracing the role she had been groomed for, she chose to stay and make the best of her new life.

Their daughter, Kimberly (Kim), was born in early 1970, and Betty threw herself into motherhood. Over the next decade, the Brodericks would have four more pregnancies and three more surviving children: second daughter, Lee, and two sons, Daniel IV and Rhett. Another son, born in 1973, tragically died just a few days after birth. Betty also endured two miscarriages and two abortions in those years, as Dan did not allow birth control and she became pregnant nine times in their 16-year marriage. These repeated pregnancies, the heartbreaking loss of an infant, and the strain of raising young kids with little support took a serious toll on Betty's physical and emotional health. She later revealed that after the death of their newborn son in 1973, she fell into a deep depression and even attempted suicide for the first time. "I felt totally trapped with [Dan] and cut off from my family. I just wanted to escape from it all and die," she wrote of that dark period, noting that she was only 23 years old and already felt she couldn't face "decades more of this existence". She would attempt to take her own life at least once more in the ensuing years.

During this early phase of the marriage, Dan was laser-focused on building an impressive career. After completing his M.D. degree, he surprised Betty by announcing he would not practice medicine but instead pursue a law degree so he could combine medical and legal expertise. He enrolled at Harvard Law School, and the young Broderick family relocated to Boston. Betty became the breadwinner while Dan was in law school, taking whatever jobs she could find. She taught school briefly and sold Avon cosmetics and Tupperware on the side all while caring for their growing family. Those were lean, difficult years. The couple lived in a modest apartment in Somerville, Massachusetts, barely making ends meet on Betty's income and student loans. Isolated from her relatives back in New York and exhausted by the responsibilities on her shoulders, Betty struggled emotionally. Friends later noted that the pair frequently fought during this period, and Betty would threaten to leave Dan during heated arguments. Each time, however, Dan smoothed things over or Betty relented, and she continued to play the role of the supportive wife. In her eyes, she had made a deal: she would support Dan's ambitions now, and they would enjoy the rewards together later. Indeed, Betty "backed him completely" in his quest for higher education as she joked, "I'd vote for being rich any day, wouldn't you?" She trusted Dan's promises that all the sacrifices would pay off.

By the mid-1970s, Dan Broderick's grand plan was bearing fruit. In 1975, after Dan earned his J.D. from Harvard, the Brodericks moved clear across the country to sunny San Diego, California, where Dan accepted a position at a law firm. They settled in the upscale seaside community of La Jolla (pronounced, "La Hoya"). Betty, then in her late 20s, continued to support the family in any way she could, often with part-time work or side gigs, but with Dan now working as an attorney, their finances improved dramatically. By 1978, Dan had cofounded his own law practice specializing in medical malpractice law. He quickly proved to be a brilliant attorney, and his income skyrocketed to around $1 million per year. The Brodericks' lifestyle rose along with Dan's earnings: they bought a five-bedroom house in La Jolla, installed a pool in the backyard, and started acquiring the trappings of success. They lavished in sports cars (including Dan's prized red Corvette), country club memberships, ski vacations in Colorado, and luxury trips. Betty became a prominent hostess in La Jolla's social scene, organizing dinner parties with the elite and keeping up appearances as the charming attorney's wife and devoted mother of four. To outside observers, the Brodericks appeared to have achieved the American Dream: a beautiful family, a mansion by the sea, and financial prosperity beyond what Betty had ever known growing up.

Yet behind closed doors, not everything was idyllic. The power dynamic in the marriage had shifted dramatically. Dan, who had always been strong-willed, could now be openly controlling. After all, he was the breadwinner to an extreme degree, and Betty's life revolved entirely around home and family. He managed all the finances, giving Betty little autonomy with money she technically "earned" by her earlier support. Betty later recounted that from the time they reached California, "he took charge of the bank books and my paychecks, and I more or less had to do what he said". Those who knew them observed that Dan could be dismissive of Betty, and as his legal career flourished he spent more time at work and less with his family. Betty, for her part, had by then tied her entire identity to being Dan's wife and the mother of his children. She prided herself on keeping an immaculate home and supporting Dan's every need, believing that she had fulfilled her end of their marital bargain. But the emotional distance between them was growing.

The pressures and resentments that had simmered in the lean years did not disappear with wealth. If anything, success made Dan more confident and headstrong, and Betty more anxious to maintain a picture-perfect image. She later described these times in conflicted terms: materially, she had everything she wanted, but she often felt unappreciated and insecure about her place in Dan's world. According to one of Dan's brothers, Larry Broderick, the more financially secure Dan became, the less attention he paid to Betty's emotional needs, which only increased her feelings of isolation. They would argue, sometimes viciously. Betty's friends recalled her venting about Dan's high-handed behavior. Dan's colleagues knew he referred to Betty's temper and outbursts with frustration. Still, divorce was unthinkable to Betty in those days and she was determined to "get through everything," as she believed a good Catholic wife should. In her own words, "I thought we did have the perfect marriage. I took those marriage vows, and I believe he did at the time, too".

By the early 1980s, the Broderick marriage was deeply strained, even if Betty and Dan continued to present a polished front. The breaking point came in 1983, and it arrived in the form of a 21-year-old former airline stewardess named Linda Kolkena. That year, Dan hired Linda as a receptionist and legal assistant at his law office. Young, attractive, and reportedly lacking any formal legal experience, Linda quickly became a source of marital tension. Betty immediately sensed something was going on. Dan insisted Linda was just a capable assistant, but he also began working longer hours and taking business trips more frequently. Betty noticed the classic warning signs; secretive phone calls, a change in Dan's wardrobe and fitness habits, and his increasing emotional distance from her at home. By October 1983, Betty was voicing her suspicions openly, but Dan repeatedly denied that he was having an affair. The gaslighting only infuriated Betty more. Years later she would say that Dan's constant denials and calling her "crazy" for suspecting him were a form of psychological torture, making her question her own sanity. In truth, Dan was deeply involved with Linda by then, according to later accounts, though he refused to admit it publicly.

On Dan's 39th birthday in 1983, the conflict exploded. Dan chose to spend the day with Linda rather than his wife, lying to Betty about his whereabouts. When Betty discovered that Dan and Linda had been out together (some sources say she learned they went skiing or on a day trip), she was devastated...and enraged. In a now-infamous act of retaliation, Betty piled Dan's expensive custom-tailored suits and shirts into a heap in their yard, doused the clothes with gasoline, and set them on fire. The bonfire of Dan's wardrobe was a dramatic signal: Betty was no longer suffering in silence. She later smashed a cream pie on his bed and spray-painted obscenities in the house for good measure. By this point, any façade of a functional marriage was gone. Dan moved out in early 1985, initially renting Betty a separate house to live in, and in September 1985 he filed for divorce. Betty, after 16 years of marriage, was completely gutted and unprepared for the legal onslaught that followed.

What ensued was a five-year-long divorce battle that one judge called the worst case of divorce acrimony he had ever seen. Dan Broderick, leveraging his knowledge and connections as a prominent lawyer (he had by then served as president of the San Diego Bar Association), had a distinct upper hand in the proceedings. From Betty's perspective, Dan orchestrated a campaign to "legally bully" her into submission. He obtained restraining orders to keep Betty off the property and away from him and Linda. When Betty violated those orders (as she did repeatedly) Dan pushed for contempt of court penalties. On multiple occasions, Betty was briefly jailed or fined for her behavior during the divorce. In one notable incident, Dan got a court order reducing Betty's spousal support by $100 for every vulgar word she left on his answering machine; Betty defiantly responded by flooding the machine with profane tirades, willing to incur hefty fines just to spite him. The more Dan tried to control her through legal means, the more unhinged Betty became. She vandalized the home that Dan had moved back into, the former family home in La Jolla, now occupied by Dan and, soon, Linda. Betty broke windows, spray-painted the walls with graffiti, and even attempted to set the house on fire on one occasion. In a particularly dangerous outburst in 1986, Betty rammed her Chevrolet Suburban through the front door of Dan's house, shattering the doorframe. (Terrifyingly, their children were inside at the time, though no one was injured.) Dan had her briefly committed to a psychiatric facility after that car crash, and Betty's own parents, mortified by their daughter's increasingly erratic and "unladylike" conduct, largely withdrew their support.

Through all of this, the four Broderick children were caught in the middle of a war zone. Initially, Betty had custody, but as her behavior grew more volatile, Dan maneuvered to gain full custody of Kim, Lee, Daniel, and Rhett. At one point, a desperate and depressed Betty dropped the kids off on Dan's doorstep one by one, feeling she had no means to care for them without support, a decision that Dan later used against her in court to claim she'd abandoned the children. He eventually won sole custody. He also managed to sell the family's La Jolla house against Betty's will (exploiting a legal loophole since he held the deed), further enraging her. By 1989, after years of motions, hearings, and delays, some caused by Betty firing or losing multiple divorce attorneys (she claimed Dan's influence scared off any lawyer who might represent her), the divorce was finalized. The settlement awarded Betty a sizable sum (reports say around $16,000 per month in support), but far less than what she felt she deserved from Dan's million-dollar yearly income. More painful to her, Dan had primary custody of the children and was free to marry Linda, which meant Linda would occupy the role in the family that Betty still considered rightfully hers. To Betty, this outcome was the ultimate betrayal.

During those bitter divorce years, Betty's sense of self unraveled. She fixated on Dan and Linda as the cause of every misery in her life. Her phone messages to Dan (played in court later) were "hundreds" of profanity-laced screeds, raging that he was "evil" and that she'd make him pay. Friends tried to intervene. A court-appointed therapist, Ruth Roth, attempted to mediate custody issues, but described Betty as uncooperative and singularly focused on vengeance. In Betty's view, Dan was the one abusing her: not physically, but by "using the system" and his power to strip her of everything. She often complained that Dan was "gaslighting" her, deliberately driving her to act crazy so he could justify his treatment of her.

Indeed, Dan did little to soften the blows: he wrote Betty curt letters in legalese rather than speaking to her directly, docked her support payments for any perceived misconduct, and reportedly would needle her by calling her "crazy" in front of others. One friend described their prolonged feud as mutual psychological warfare with Dan pushing Betty's buttons, and Betty reacting with escalating hysteria. "No one has the right to take the life of another," one psychologist noted, "however, Dan's consistent lies, minimizations and calling Betty crazy fueled a lot of the animus in the relationship." It was a toxic dance that neither spouse stepped away from. Betty later likened her fight to "putting a housewife in the ring with Muhammad Ali," saying the legal system was stacked in Dan's favor and left her feeling powerless.

In April 1989, Dan Broderick married Linda Kolkena in a beautiful ceremony. It was a fresh start that was, in Betty's mind, the final insult. Linda, only 28 years old, was closer in age to the Brodericks' oldest daughter than to Dan. She had become Dan's new bride and the stepmother of Betty's children. Knowing Betty's volatility, the couple took precautions: Linda urged Dan to wear a bulletproof vest at the wedding and even to hire security, fearing Betty might crash the event. Betty did not show up to disrupt the wedding (she reportedly considered it, then decided against it), and no violence occurred that day. Still, according to Betty, Linda could not resist taunting her afterward. Betty claimed that Linda mailed her things like weight-loss advertisements and wrinkle cream coupons, cruelly suggesting she was old and unwanted. (Whether Linda actually sent these is unproven, but Betty believed it.) By the fall of 1989, Betty Broderick was a 41-year-old divorcee who felt the life she'd devoted herself to building had been stolen from her. She was depressed, furious, and increasingly unmoored. In one of her last letters to her own divorce lawyer, written in late October 1989, Betty wrote, "I can't stand this anymore… them always insinuating I'm crazy". She spoke of having "no life left." It was a dire, ominous statement. Friends and family didn't know just how close Betty was to the edge but her younger kids, Danny and Rhett, later said they warned their father. "Not having her kids was driving her crazy," Rhett remembered telling Dan, "and she could do something extremely irrational if she didn't have us." In other words, even the Broderick children sensed their mother might be a danger to herself or others if the situation didn't change.

In the predawn hours of Sunday, November 5, 1989, Betty Broderick decided to put an end to her torment. About seven months had passed since Dan and Linda's wedding, and Betty's simmering anger had reached a boiling point. She had purchased a five-shot Smith & Wesson revolver eight months earlier, telling friends it was for self-protection. Now, that gun was in her purse as she drove to the upscale Hillcrest section of San Diego, toward the home that her ex-husband shared with his new wife. It was around 5:30 A.M., still dark outside. Betty later said she never intended to hurt anyone that morning and that she only wanted to force a conversation with Dan and then kill herself in front of him as the ultimate expression of despair. What happened next would be debated endlessly, but the brutal outcome was indisputable.

Betty quietly used her daughter Kim's key to unlock the side door of Dan and Linda's house on Cypress Avenue. She had stolen Kim's key earlier, knowing Dan kept the alarm system off due to the previously damaged front door that Betty had rammed with her car. Inside, the house was silent. Betty climbed the stairs to the master bedroom, where Dan, 44, and Linda, 28, lay asleep in bed. In a matter of moments, Betty burst into the room, pulled out her revolver, and started firing at the couple at close range. Chaos erupted. According to Betty, Linda screamed, "Call the police!" which startled Betty into firing reflexively again and again. Five shots rang out in total. Two bullets tore into Linda, one hitting her in the head and another in the chest. She was killed instantly. Dan was struck by one bullet that entered his chest as he was apparently trying to reach for the phone on his nightstand. One bullet missed and lodged in the wall; another hit a piece of furniture. The room was pandemonium in those seconds with shattered glass, the acrid smell of gunpowder, Linda lifeless, and Dan bleeding badly on the bed.

In the sudden quiet after the gunshots, Betty saw Dan, still alive, slumped over the phone. She ripped the phone cord out of the wall, removing the couple's means to call for help. Dan, gravely wounded but not dead, gasped at Betty, "OK, OK, you got me," by Betty's later account. She would claim that in that moment, she wanted to kill herself. That her plan had been to turn the gun on herself after confronting Dan but the gun had jammed after firing all five rounds. Instead, she says, she and Dan exchanged final words. Betty alleged that as he was dying, Dan's last words were a curse at her: "Okay, you shot me. I'm dead, bitch." (This quote is disputed and it comes only from Betty's own retelling.) Medical evidence later showed Dan did not die immediately; he likely lived for a few minutes after being shot. But without the phone, and with a fatal injury, he could not get help in time. Linda lay dead at 28 years old, and Dan soon succumbed as well, just shy of his 45th birthday.

Betty fled the scene and called her daughter Lee from a payphone soon after. In a panicked voice, she told 18-year-old Lee, "I'm in trouble... I just shot Dad". Lee, stunned and terrified, urged her mother to turn herself in. Not long after, Betty Broderick did exactly that and she drove to the police station and surrendered. She readily admitted to officers that she had pulled the trigger, but her first words to the arresting detectives were, "I didn't mean to do it!" She would maintain from that day forward that, while she had done the deed, it was not a premeditated murder but rather the act of a desperate woman driven beyond the brink.

The news of the killings of Dan and Linda Broderick sent shockwaves through San Diego and soon the nation. Dan Broderick had been a respected figure in legal circles, and Linda was so young, the case had an irresistible and tragic storyline. A successful man and his beautiful new wife gunned down in their bed by an enraged ex-wife. The tabloids dubbed it "the ultimate divorce revenge" and a media frenzy ensued. But for many who knew the Brodericks, the tragedy was not entirely a surprise. Some in La Jolla's social set had seen the drama escalating for years. In fact, not long after the murders, a grim joke made the rounds at local cocktail parties: "I guess this is 'Be Nice to the Ex-Wife Week'" one man quipped while standing next to his younger second wife. Beneath the dark humor lay an uneasy recognition... Betty's fury was an extreme manifestation of feelings shared by *many* women who felt wronged in divorce. Letters poured into the local newspapers and even to Betty in jail from people (especially middle-aged women) expressing a twisted sympathy. "While we don't condone murder, we understand the rage that prompted it," wrote one woman, saying she too had been driven nearly mad by a ruthless ex-husband and a legal system that wouldn't listen. Betty, in their eyes, had become a symbol: the spurned first wife who refused to go quietly. As one letter to the editor put it, "Isn't it time we take a good look at our courts and our system of divorce?" Betty had given new meaning to the phrase, "Hell hath no fury like a woman scorned."

Betty Broderick was charged with two counts of murder and went on trial in October 1990 in San Diego. From the outset, her case was not a simple whodunit. After all, Betty freely admitted she pulled the trigger. The trial instead centered on why she did it and what level of criminal culpability she bore. Was this cold-blooded, premeditated murder? Or a spontaneous act lacking intent, perhaps even a form of extreme "self-defense" born of years of abuse? The prosecution and defense painted starkly different pictures of Betty's motives and mental state.

On the prosecution side, Deputy District Attorney Kerry Wells cast Betty as a calculating killer fueled by vengeful rage. Wells argued that Betty had plotted the killings as the ultimate punishment for Dan and Linda's perceived wrongs. The evidence of planning was there: Betty had bought a gun months before, she had taken her daughter's house key, and she chose a time early in the morning when the victims would be most vulnerable. According to the state, Betty's claim that she was going to commit suicide was a ruse and the removed phone cord in the bedroom, for example, suggested she wanted to ensure Dan couldn't call for help after she shot them. Wells emphasized that Dan and Linda were sleeping, posing no immediate threat, which undercut any argument that Betty acted in self-defense. To drive home that Betty's behavior was deliberate, the prosecution noted how methodically Betty had harassed Dan over the years, seemingly reveling in causing misery. One neighbor testified that Betty would brag about violating court orders, and recordings of Betty's vicious voicemail messages left the jury with the impression of an unrepentant, angry woman. This, Wells contended, was not a battered woman acting out of fear. This was a woman scorned who "spiraled into a jealous, murderous rage".

Jack Earley, Betty's defense attorney, had a very different story to tell. Earley did not deny that Betty pulled the trigger, but he argued passionately that her mindset was closer to that of a victim than a villain. In legal terms, they pursued a defense of diminished capacity, essentially asking the jury to find her guilty of manslaughter (unintentional killing) rather than murder. Betty was portrayed as a devoted wife driven over the edge by years of psychological and emotional abuse at Dan's hands. Earley described Dan as a gaslighter and manipulator who had cruelly undermined Betty's sanity. He reminded jurors of how Dan lied about the affair for years, publicly humiliated Betty through the divorce, took her children, and wielded the legal system like a weapon against her. According to the defense, by the time of the shootings Betty was not a rational, cold-blooded actor but a wreck of a person. She was depressed, traumatized, and practically out of her mind with grief and rage. Earley argued that on that morning, Betty intended to confront Dan one last time and then kill herself, not them. Any actual shooting of Dan and Linda, he maintained, was in the heat of the moment, panic-triggered by Linda's scream or by Betty's own instability, but not a calculated execution.

To bolster their cases, both sides called psychological experts. The prosecution's expert witnesses, including famed forensic psychiatrist Dr. Park Dietz, diagnosed Betty with narcissistic and histrionic personality disorders. In essence, labeling her an emotionally unstable, attention-seeking narcissist. Dr. Melvin Goldzband, a psychiatrist who had evaluated Betty earlier for the court, testified similarly that she was severely narcissistic but not mentally ill in a way that would excuse her behavior. These experts emphasized that Betty showed no signs of psychosis or major depression that would impair her understanding of her actions;

instead, they said her extreme reactions stemmed from an exaggerated sense of entitlement and need for dominance. In their view, Betty wasn't out of control, she was in control and chose to murder out of ego and anger. One therapist even minimized Betty's trauma, testifying that Betty was essentially just very "angry" but not otherwise suffering from a mental disorder. The defense's mental health witness, a psychologist named Dr. Katherine DiFrancesca, actually concurred that Betty had a histrionic personality with narcissistic traits. However, she and other defense-allied experts framed those traits in a more sympathetic light: Betty had no identity outside of being Dan's wife, they explained, and when that identity was annihilated by Dan's betrayal and the divorce, she experienced an emotional breakdown. In short, Betty was depicted as a woman who had been psychologically battered into a state of desperation. She was not rational, they argued, but nor was she inherently evil. In a dramatic moment during closing arguments, Earley slammed a framed family portrait of the Brodericks onto the floor, shattering the glass, and proclaimed to the jury: "This is the family that Dan Broderick destroyed." The implication was clear. Dan's actions had figuratively "broken" Betty long before she broke into his home with a gun.

The first trial stretched on for weeks in late 1990, with Betty herself taking the stand in her own defense. Her testimony was a spectacle in itself: by turns defiant, sorrowful, and bitterly angry. She recounted the history of the marriage and divorce in excruciating detail mentioning every slight, every insult, every perceived cruelty by Dan. At times she cried; at other times her temper flared, such as when she emphatically told the prosecutor that she "was not the one who had the affair" and would "not accept the blame" for all that happened. This raw performance left the public divided on whether Betty was sincere or manipulative. The jurors, too, were split. After four days of deliberations, the jury announced they were hopelessly deadlocked. It turned out 10 of the jurors wanted to convict Betty of murder, but 2 held out for manslaughter. The holdouts apparently believed Betty lacked the malice aforethought (premeditation and intent) required for murder, possibly buying the argument that her mental state was akin to a battered spouse acting under extreme provocation. The jury foreman explained that the sticking point was indeed over "malice" and whether Betty had planned to kill or just snapped. Consequently, in November 1990 Judge Thomas Whelan declared a mistrial. Betty, who had been nearly catatonic with anxiety during the wait, smiled briefly upon hearing the word "hung jury". It was a small, if temporary, victory for her: at least two people had seen her actions as something less than murder. Still, the prosecution immediately announced they would retry the case. The tragedy and drama would have an encore.

The second trial took place in the fall of 1991, with essentially the same evidence and dueling narratives. The media coverage had only intensified by this time as Betty's case was now a fixture on tabloid TV and even Court TV aired the trial live, making it one of the earliest cases to get gavel-to-gavel cable TV coverage.

This time, the jury was less conflicted. On December 11, 1991, Betty Broderick was found guilty on two counts of second-degree murder. The lesser degree (second- instead of first-degree) suggested the jury did acknowledge some lack of pre-planning or extreme emotional disturbance, but ultimately, they held her responsible for intentionally killing Dan and Linda without justification. Betty showed little visible reaction as the verdict was read, but friends say she was stunned and devastated. Judge Whelan sentenced her to the maximum: 32 years to life in prison (15 years-to-life for each murder count, served consecutively, plus two years for the firearm use). At age 44, Betty faced the very real possibility that she would die in prison.

Public opinion remained split after the conviction. Some felt justice had been served and that no amount of marital discord could excuse sneaking in and shooting two people in their sleep. Others continued to view Betty with uneasy sympathy, as a woman who had been emotionally abused and tossed aside, only to break under the pressure. The case's notoriety even then was significant: within a year, two television movies were produced based on the Broderick saga (both starring Meredith Baxter as Betty). The trials themselves were a media spectacle, and Betty's story became emblematic of the archetype "woman scorned" gone too far. But beyond the headlines and sensationalism, the Broderick children were left to grapple with the awful fallout.

Dan and Betty's four children lost both of their parents in the blink of an eye; one to murder, the other to prison. For all the public discussion about Betty and Dan, their kids had to carry the trauma most intimately. During the trials, two of the Broderick children were called to testify, giving the world a glimpse of the family's internal suffering. Betty's eldest, 20-year-old Kim Broderick, took the stand and painfully recounted how the years-long war between her parents had affected their mother's behavior. It was Kim who described incidents like her mother burning her father's clothes in the yard in 1983, an event seared into her memory as a teenager. Kim also testified to her mother's erratic and cruel conduct during the divorce. In one incident, Betty was supposed to come visit Kim at her college apartment, but abruptly changed her mind, spewing venom instead. "All of a sudden, she said, 'I just remembered, I hate your guts. You betrayed me. You make me sick,'" Kim recalled in court, her voice cracking. One can only imagine how hearing those words from her mother affected young Kim. By the time of the murders, Kim's relationship with Betty was extremely strained. Betty seemed to perceive her eldest daughter's loyalty to Dan (Kim had been living with her father) as a betrayal and it seemed that this rift never fully healed.

Lee Broderick, the second-oldest at 18, also testified in her mother's criminal trial. Lee tearfully recounted the early morning phone call on November 5, 1989, when her mother confessed, "I shot Dad". Lee had been somewhat closer to Betty than Kim was, and that horrific call was a burden she'd carry forever. Lee also dropped a revelation in her testimony that hinted at issues with her father: she said that her dad had written her out of his will not long before his death. Apparently, Dan had decided that due to Lee's problems with school and some drug experimentation, he would leave her nothing; dividing his estate only among Kim, Danny, and Rhett. (This was confirmed by Dan's will, which the Los Angeles Times reported did indeed disinherit Lee.) It was a striking insight into the family's troubles: even before the murders, Lee felt a sense of rejection from her father, while Kim felt rejected by her mother. The two younger boys, Daniel IV (known as Danny) and Rhett, were only 13 and 10 when they lost their dad and mom. They did not testify at their mother's trial (too young, and likely spared), but their perspective emerged later in interviews.

In the immediate aftermath of Betty's arrest, the Broderick children's lives were upended yet again. With their father deceased and their mother jailed, the kids were shuttled around relatives. Ultimately, the two boys went to live in Colorado with an uncle's ex-wife, Kathy Broderick, who kindly took them in. Their sisters were already legal adults by then (Kim was 19 and Lee 18), but the family unit was shattered. Rhett later told Oprah Winfrey that the years following were chaotic. He moved between relatives and even ended up in a group home for troubled teens at one point. "I constantly felt like I was under the microscope," Rhett said of that period, "like everything I did they were trying to blame on my parents' situation." Both he and Danny struggled with behavioral issues in their adolescence, which is not surprising given the trauma and instability they endured.

Despite everything, all four children

maintained some relationship with their mother during her incarceration. In a 1998 interview from prison, Betty described how her children still visited her for her birthday and Mother's Day each year (though she asked them not to come on Christmas or major holidays, not wanting those memories tainted for them). She tried to remain a part of their lives through phone calls, letters, and visits. By 2010, the Broderick offspring were adults in their 30s with their own lives, yet the question of their mother's fate still loomed over them. That year, at Betty's first parole hearing, the children were divided about whether she should be released. Lee, who by then had reconciled with Betty, told the parole board she had a bedroom ready for her mother at her home. She felt Betty had paid enough price and "should be able to live her later life outside prison walls." Similarly, Rhett (who had spoken on Oprah years earlier, saying "she's not a danger to society; the only two people she was a danger to are dead") supported release. However, Kim and Danny vehemently opposed their mother's freedom. Danny said in 2010, "In my heart, I know my mother is a good person, but along the way she got lost. Releasing a lost person into society could be a dangerous mistake." He and Kim both felt that Betty was still stuck in the same destructive mindset and lacked true remorse for her actions. This family schism over Betty's future persisted into subsequent years.

As of today, the Broderick children have largely stayed out of the spotlight, striving to live normal lives. Sources indicate that they remain close to one another, bonded by the shared nightmare they endured. They also maintain varying degrees of contact with Betty. In a memoir Betty self-published in 2015, she wrote that she was, at that time, regularly speaking with and even seeing her children and grandchildren during prison visits. Rhett, on an Oprah follow-up special in 2005, remarked of his mother, "She's a nice lady. Everyone here would like her… if they spoke with her on any topic other than my dad." This poignant quote suggests that the children see more to their mother than the one act that defines her in the public's eyes. Still, the hurt and loss are everlasting. They lost their father, and in a very real sense, their mother on that November morning in 1989. No outcome could give them back what was taken. The Broderick children's story is perhaps the most tragic legacy of all: they are the survivors left to find healing and make peace with a past that could easily define their whole lives if they let it.

Betty Broderick has now spent over three decades behind bars. She was incarcerated in 1991 and remains in custody at the California Institution for Women in Chino, California. By most accounts, Betty has been a model prisoner when it comes to following prison rules. Jack Earley noted she had no disciplinary write-ups in prison. She kept busy by tutoring other inmates and even earned a reputation as a motherly figure to some. However, when it comes to rehabilitation of mindset, authorities have found Betty notably unrepentant. At her parole hearings, prosecutors and parole board members described a woman who still tends to justify or minimize her crimes. Deputy D.A. Richard Sachs, who observed Betty's parole hearings, said "She was unrepentant, unremorseful, and callous" in those proceedings. Indeed, during one hearing, Betty reportedly banged her fist on the table and referred to Dan as an "SOB", then in the next breath proclaimed to Dan's friends in the room, "I'm sorry you lost your drinking buddy." Such comments struck the board as flippant and deflecting blame; exactly the attitude that landed her in prison in the first place.

When questioned by the parole board, Betty has consistently framed herself as the victim. She acknowledges that killing Dan and Linda was wrong, but often in the same breath she insists she was driven to it by their actions. In one letter she sent to a reporter from prison, Betty claimed she had been "gang raped by the crooked courts", reiterating her belief that the legal system effectively conspired with Dan to abuse her. She wrote that Dan had "threatened" and "intimidated" her for years with his power. These statements mirror the very sentiments she expressed decades ago. To the parole examiners, this indicated that Betty Broderick has not experienced the kind of insight or remorse they require for release. As one board member put it, Betty remains "stuck in the same place" mentally as she was on the day she committed the murders.

Consequently, Betty's bids for parole have been denied time and again. In 2010, her first eligible year, the board refused her release, citing that she still showed no genuine remorse. She was denied again in 2011 and most recently in 2017, when she again failed to persuade officials that she took full responsibility for her actions. At that 2017 hearing, Betty's own words likely sealed the decision: when asked if she felt remorse, she responded, "I have remorse for the fact that my family was hurt, [but] I have no remorse for my actions… I regret my husband had no character." (In an earlier interview, she had famously said, "I have regrets, not remorse".) Such statements are red flags for parole boards, essentially demonstrating that the inmate still rationalizes the crime. It is therefore unsurprising that after 2017, the board issued Betty the longest denial possible and she will not be eligible for parole again until January 2032. At that point, Betty will be 84 years old. Unless something changes dramatically in her outlook, she may very well serve out her life in prison.

Day to day, Betty's life in custody is by now routine. Over the years she has given occasional interviews to the media, often by phone. In 1992, she was interviewed by Oprah Winfrey via phone on The Oprah Winfrey Show, vehemently asserting her side of the story to a national audience. She also cooperated with writers for books and articles about the case throughout the '90s. Later on, Betty decided to tell her own story in full: in 2015 she published a memoir titled "Telling On Myself", which reiterates her version of events and the grievances she holds toward Dan and the legal system. In it, she does express sorrow that her actions devastated her children's lives, but she continues to maintain that Dan's abuse, as she views it, was the precipitating cause. Prison officials have noted that Betty enjoys a certain infamy; she receives letters from supporters who see her as a folk hero of spurned wives, as well as letters of scorn from those who consider her a monster. Through it all, Betty's stance has largely remained: she wishes things hadn't ended the way they did, but she stops short of full remorse. As she bluntly wrote, "I didn't do the legal bullying. I wasn't the one who had the affair. I won't accept the blame for what happened."

GONE GIRL

Sherri Papini

Sherri Papini (born Sherri Louise Graeff in 1982) grew up in Shasta County, California. As a teenager and young adult, Sherri developed a troubling reputation for manipulation and dishonesty. In October 2000, when Sherri was 18, police reports show she stirred chaos within her own family: one report noted Sherri's sister accused her of trying to break into the sister's home, and an hour later Sherri was caught vandalizing her parents' house. A few years later, in 2003, Sherri's mother sought help from the sheriff's office, reporting that Sherri was harming herself and then blaming the injuries on her parents. Even those close to Sherri in her youth recalled her habit of bending the truth. An ex-boyfriend who dated her in the early 2000s described Sherri as an "attention-hungry person who told stories to try to get people's attention," noting that she fabricated tales of being the victim of abuse – first alleging family abuse, then later falsely accusing that same boyfriend after they broke up. A youth program supervisor who knew

Sherri as a teen said she "was good at creating different realities for people so that they would see what she wanted them to see, which got her really good attention." From a young age, Sherri Papini was honing the deceptive skills that she would use on a far larger stage years later.

Sherri's early adulthood continued in this pattern of calculated storytelling. In 2006, at age 24, she entered a marriage of convenience with an Army platoon sergeant named David Dreyfus. According to a later investigation, Sherri married him primarily to get health insurance coverage reportedly due to complications from her regular egg donations. The two never truly lived as a couple. Sherri traveled abroad to visit him during a deployment, but upon his return she abruptly asked him for a divorce, claiming she had found someone new. Sherri also told this first husband that her family had abused her while she was growing up; another dramatic lie. After the divorce in 2008, friends of Dreyfus told him that Sherri had long had a "history of lying," reinforcing what many in her hometown already knew about her character. By the time Sherri moved back to Shasta County in northern California, she had left a trail of deceit in her wake but she was ready to start fresh and rebuild her image in Redding.

Back in her hometown, Sherri rekindled a romance with her childhood sweetheart, Keith Papini. The two had first met as pre-teens; "It all started with a first kiss in middle school," Sherri wrote in a blog for their 2009 wedding. After years apart, fate brought them together again when Sherri returned to Redding. Keith was smitten with the girl who had been his first kiss in seventh grade. "You never forget your very first kiss," Keith said, recalling their innocent young romance and marveling at how "God had a plan" to bring them back together as adults. The couple married in 2009, and by all outward appearances, their love story seemed like a fairytale turned real.

By 2016, Sherri Papini was a 34-year-old mother of two, and she embraced the role of homemaker in Redding, California. She and Keith settled in the Mountain Gate area just outside town, where they were raising a toddler daughter, Violet, and a preschool-age son, Tyler. Keith worked hard as an audio-video specialist at Best Buy to provide for the family. Sherri was often described as a "super mom" by those who knew her, always doting on her children and involved in their activities. "My wife is a very involved mother… she is always doing stuff," Keith told a reporter, emphasizing that Sherri's life revolved around their kids and home. She loved traditions and went all-out for holidays. On November 1, 2016, the day after Halloween, Sherri had already begun pulling out boxes of Christmas decorations to transform their home for the season. That was the kind of person Sherri was in Keith's eyes: energetic, organized, and devoted to family. They seemed to be a happy, ordinary family. The Papinis were the picture of suburban contentment on the surface.

Yet, unbeknownst to those around her, Sherri's old patterns of deceit hadn't gone away. In secret, she maintained contact with men from her past. Keith had no inkling that in the months leading up to late 2016, Sherri had been exchanging flirtatious messages with at least one old flame and concocting elaborate personal dramas. To everyone who saw the Papinis around town, they appeared to be a loving young couple with two beautiful children and a bright future ahead. No one could have predicted the bizarre, twisted turn their lives were about to take.

Wednesday, November 2, 2016 started like any other day in the Papini household but by nightfall, it would become a day etched in true crime history. That morning, around 6:50 a.m., Keith Papini left the house to head to work, giving Sherri a hug and kiss goodbye as she tended to their two-year-old daughter. Sherri had a routine of jogging in the mornings after Keith left, once their son was at preschool or daycare. Sometime around 10:37 a.m., Sherri sent Keith a brief text message asking if he would be home for lunch for a romantic rendezvous. Keith didn't see the message right away as he was busy at work and typically kept his personal phone in the breakroom. When he eventually checked his phone around 1:30 p.m., he replied that he would be working late and not home for lunch. He had no way of knowing that by that time, Sherri was likely already gone.

Based on later accounts, investigators believe Sherri set out for her customary jog in the late morning, sometime around 11:00 a.m., shortly after sending that unanswered text. She loved running on the rural roads near her Redding neighborhood; an area around Sunrise Drive and Old Oregon Trail, surrounded by wooded trails and distant neighbors. Normally, nothing bad ever happened on those peaceful runs. But that day, Sherri Papini vanished without a trace. She never picked up her kids from daycare that afternoon, which was completely out of character. By early evening, as the autumn sun dipped low, a chain of events unfolded that threw her family and community into panic.

Keith Papini arrived home from work around 5:00 p.m., expecting to be greeted by the laughter of his children and the warmth of his wife. Instead, he opened the door to a silent house. No giggling kids, no Sherri bustling in the kitchen. Just an eerie quiet. Keith's stomach dropped. He quickly checked each room, calling out for Sherri and the kids. "I looked in different rooms and couldn't find anyone... I thought, 'Maybe they're outside,'" he later recalled of those first anxious moments. Stepping outside, he saw Sherri's car in the driveway, a sign she hadn't gone out to run errands. Confusion turned to dread as he realized the children were also missing. Keith's first thought was that perhaps Sherri had taken the kids on a walk to get the mail at the end of their rural driveway. But a check of the mailbox yielded nothing, and the kids were nowhere in sight.

Growing frantic, Keith phoned his mother to see if she'd heard from Sherri, but she had not. He then called the daycare center. "What time did Sherri pick up the kids today?" he asked. The answer made his blood run cold: "The kids are here," the daycare staffer replied. Violet and Tyler had never been collected that day. At that moment, Keith knew something was terribly wrong. He raced to his car with one goal in mind: find Sherri. Using the "Find My iPhone" app on his phone, Keith pinged Sherri's iPhone and saw that it was located somewhere near their mailbox, down the road about a mile or so from their house. Heart pounding, he drove the short distance to the intersection of Sunrise Drive and Old Oregon Trail, the area indicated on the map. There, on the ground, he made a discovery that confirmed his worst fears.

Lying in the dirt by the roadside were Sherri's cell phone and earbuds, as if casually dropped. The earbuds were tangled with strands of long blonde hair – Sherri's hair – ripped out and caught in the cords. It looked like a sign of a struggle. Keith's heart pounded as he picked up the phone. Oddly, the phone was placed neatly on the ground, screen facing up, as though someone had almost positioned it to be found. Keith later said it seemed too deliberately placed, describing it as "weird". In that chilling moment, with the sky growing dark, Keith's worst nightmare was unfolding. "Something is wrong, so wrong," he remembered thinking, realizing Sherri would never abandon her phone like this or leave the kids without any word. He immediately dialed 9-1-1.

At 5:51 p.m. on November 2, 2016, a distressed Keith Papini reported his wife missing to the Shasta County Sheriff's Office. In the recorded 911 call, his voice shook with panic. "I found her phone," Keith told the dispatcher. "It's got, like, hair ripped out of it, like, in the headphones, so I'm totally freaking out." Deputies arrived quickly and began combing the area by the roadside where the phone was discovered. They noted the phone and hair as evidence and carefully collected Sherri's earbuds lying about two feet off the road. The search for Sherri Papini had begun in earnest, and it would soon grow into a frantic nationwide effort to find the missing mother of two.

That night, law enforcement officers and volunteers fanned out across Shasta County with flashlights and bloodhounds, urgently searching for any sign of Sherri. Within hours, authorities organized search teams and put out a bulletin about the missing jogger. Sherri's disappearance was treated with high priority and the news of her disappearance spread quickly. A young mother vanishing in broad daylight under suspicious circumstances gripped headlines across the country. The community rallied to support the Papini family. Friends, neighbors, and even strangers showed up to help. More than 100 volunteers joined the search in the following days, scouring wooded trails, ditches, and backroads for any trace of Sherri. People who had never met Sherri found themselves emotionally invested, gripped by the fear that something terrible had befallen this beloved wife and mother.

Keith Papini, desperate to find his spouse, barely slept as days passed with no news. "People would see me and start crying and give me hugs… total strangers," he said of the outpouring of community empathy during the search. The Papini family set up a "Help Find Sherri Papini" Facebook page to coordinate updates, and a GoFundMe campaign raised over $40,000 to assist in search efforts. Keith and Sherri's relatives offered a $50,000 reward for any information leading to her return. Redding, a quiet Northern California city, found itself swarming with news cameras and reporters as Sherri's story began making headlines across the country.

Early on, Shasta County Sheriff Tom Bosenko cautioned that they had "no real viable leads" yet. Investigators could not immediately determine if Sherri's disappearance was voluntary or involuntary. Had she been abducted, or could she have walked away on her own? Those who knew Sherri fiercely rejected any notion that she left on purpose. "She would never just leave us," Keith insisted, utterly convinced his wife had been taken against her will. In media interviews, a teary-eyed Keith pleaded for her safe return: "Just bring her home. Please bring her back. The sooner the better," he implored whomever might have her. The Papini family's anguish was on full display, and it moved people nationwide.

As days turned into weeks, fear and speculation gripped the community. The absence of solid clues was agonizing. Rumors swirled on social media. Some speculated about possible suspects or motives; wild theories proliferated in Facebook groups and on talk radio. In whispers, a few skeptics questioned the bizarre circumstances...a cell phone carefully placed on the ground, a seemingly random disappearance in a safe neighborhood? But most people focused on hoping for Sherri's safe return. Women in Shasta County, especially those who enjoyed jogging alone, felt a chill of anxiety. "When that kidnapping story went down, there were many sleepless nights," said one local woman, recalling how she started carrying pepper spray on her solo runs during those weeks. The notion that an unknown kidnapper (or kidnappers) might be roaming the area put everyone on edge. Neighbors locked their doors a little earlier and kept their children closer, waiting for any news about what had happened to Sherri Papini.

Behind the scenes, law enforcement pursued every tip. They even quietly looked into Sherri's past for clues. Detectives interviewed people who knew Sherri, including two men listed in her phone contacts under women's names; signs that Sherri might have been hiding these relationships. One of these contacts, a man in Michigan (dubbed "Man 1" by investigators), admitted he and Sherri had been in touch and even discussed meeting up when he visited California in late October 2016. That meeting never happened, and he went home without seeing her, but it hinted at secrets in Sherri's life unknown to her family. Another old boyfriend ("Man 2") characterized Sherri to investigators as a habitual liar hungry for attention. These interviews, however, were not made public at the time. The authorities kept such leads confidential, so as not to jeopardize the search or cast aspersions without proof. To the public, the case still looked like an unsolved abduction.

For 22 agonizing days, Sherri's loved ones lived in limbo. Keith struggled with how to tell their young children why mommy was gone. Candlelight vigils were held, prayers offered, and yet each day ended with the question: Where is Sherri? The answer would come in the most dramatic fashion possible on Thanksgiving, a miracle, and more questions than answers.

November 24, 2016 was Thanksgiving

Day. In the pre-dawn hours, at approximately 4:30 a.m., the California Highway Patrol responded to a report that would send shockwaves through the community. Several 911 calls came in about a woman seen on the side of Interstate 5 in Yolo County, near Woodland, about 150 miles south of Redding. A truck driver had spotted a disheveled figure stumbling near the road and pulled over, alarmed. The woman was waving something which turned out to be a piece of fabric, possibly the restraints that bound her. A CHP officer arrived and found a petite blonde woman in distress, chained and badly injured, trying to flag down help. Incredibly, it was Sherri Papini. She was alive.

Officers quickly secured Sherri, who was terrified and emaciated. A chain was wrapped around her waist, tethering her left arm close to her, and her wrists and ankles bore ligature marks as if she had been tied up for a long period. She was wearing sweatpants and a thin shirt, the same clothes she had gone missing in, now dirty and tattered. The responding officers noted that Sherri had lost a considerable amount of weight. She was down to just 87 pounds, gaunt and starved. Her once long, flowing blonde hair had been chopped off to shoulder length in a jagged cut. Dark bruises, yellowing and fresh, mottled her face and body, and the bridge of her nose was broken. Sherri's skin showed burns and rash-like marks. Most chilling of all, there was a raw brand burned into the flesh of her right shoulder, a clear sign of deliberate torture. Sherri was shivering, exhausted, and in pain, but she was alive.

Paramedics rushed Sherri to Woodland

Hospital, and word was relayed almost immediately to Shasta County authorities and to Keith. It hardly seemed believable. After three weeks of fearing the worst, Sherri Papini had been found. Keith raced to the hospital to be by her side. Investigators warned him before he went in: "Brace yourself," they told the anxious husband, preparing him for her battered condition. Nothing could have prepared Keith for the sight of his wife in that hospital bed. "My Sherri suffered tremendously," he said, describing the moment he saw her covered in bruises from head to toe. "The mental prison I was in over the past three weeks was shattered when my questions of my wife's reality became known," Keith later recounted of that emotional reunion. He wept with both relief and horror as he gently held his wife's hand, careful not to hurt her. "I was filled with so much relief and revulsion at once," Keith said. "I was so happy to see her, but the condition she was in… it was indescribable".

News of Sherri's miraculous return spread on Thanksgiving Day like wildfire. In an era of grim headlines, this appeared to be a rare piece of good news: a missing mother had been found alive against all odds. Sherri was dubbed a "super mom" survivor by media outlets, and people across the country rejoiced for the Papini family. But as law enforcement and Sherri's relatives celebrated her safe return, they also urgently needed answers. Who had taken Sherri Papini? And why had they released her alive after 22 days of what appeared to be intense cruelty?

Still weak but determined to help catch her captors, Sherri began talking to Shasta

County sheriff's detectives from her hospital bed that very day. What she told them sounded like the plot of a Hollywood thriller. Sherri Papini claimed that on November 2, while she was out jogging, she had been abducted at gunpoint by two women. Specifically, she described her kidnappers as two Hispanic women who spoke Spanish and mostly kept their faces hidden. She said a dark-colored SUV had pulled up alongside her on the road that morning, and two Latina women had confronted her with a handgun. In an instant, they forced her into the vehicle and kidnapped her, speeding away as Sherri's phone and earbuds fell to the ground. Sherri recounted how she cried and pleaded for her life, thinking of her children, as the women restrained her.

According to Sherri's initial statements, her captors transported her to an unknown location where they held her against her will. She recalled being in a room – possibly a basement or a secluded house – where she was confined in a small closet much of the time. The two women spoke both English and Spanish, Sherri said, and they played "really annoying Mexican music" loudly as an apparent attempt to mask any noise or perhaps torment her with sound. During her 22-day captivity, Sherri said she was repeatedly abused physically. The women, she claimed, beat her, burned her skin, and even branded her shoulder with a heated tool as a form of punishment. (Shasta County Sheriff Tom Bosenko later confirmed that the brand was a disturbing message, but authorities withheld specifics, calling it "a message, not a symbol".) Sherri's beautiful long hair had been cruelly cut off. She was deprived of food, causing her dramatic weight loss. Sherri recounted one instance where she tried to escape her room, managing to get her wrists out of zip-ties and prying at the boarded-up window, but the captors caught her in the act. Enraged, they allegedly knocked her unconscious and decided to mark her permanently for her defiance, burning the brand into her skin. After that, Sherri said, they kept her chained whenever possible, tethering a cable around her waist that allowed limited movement so she could reach a bed but not the doors or windows.

Throughout this ordeal, Sherri told investigators, the two women spoke cryptically about some sort of human trafficking plan. She overheard them arguing and mentioning a buyer and at one point she caught a "sliver" of a conversation suggesting they were going to sell her to a law enforcement officer as part of a bizarre trade. She feared that any day might be her last. Then, as suddenly as it began, it ended. Sherri described how on Thanksgiving morning, her captors drove her out to a rural area in the pre-dawn darkness. They shoved her out of the vehicle off a road and left her there, still bound and blinding her with a pillowcase over her head. She heard the sound of a gunshot as they drove away, perhaps a warning not to move, and once she freed herself from some zip ties, she managed to partially pull off the bag over her head. Seeing vehicle lights receding into the distance, Sherri frantically ran to the road until finally a truck driver saw her silhouette and stopped. She was saved.

Sherri Papini's account was hair-raising and the details astonishing. Law enforcement treated her as a victim of a serious crime; a kidnapping case with two dangerous suspects on the loose. Sheriff Bosenko told the public that the suspects were "armed [and] considered dangerous", warning that these women had a firearm and had shown willingness to harm their victim. The authorities released a vague description: one woman was younger, about 20-30 years old with curly dark hair, thin eyebrows, and the other was older, around 40-50, with long straight black hair that had wisps of gray and thick eyebrows. Both were around average height (5'5" to 5'7") with medium builds. They were possibly driving a dark SUV. This was the extent of what Sherri could provide, since she said the women often kept their faces covered with masks. The FBI was called in and a nationwide bulletin went out. Sketch artists worked with Sherri over the next months to create composite drawings of the suspects, which would eventually be made public to aid the manhunt.

In those initial days after Sherri's return, sympathy for her overflowed. The media hailed her survival story; Sherri became something of a briefly celebrated figure as the mom who endured a nightmare and returned home alive. Keith Papini, once under a cloud of suspicion in some corners, was now vindicated and lauded for his devotion. He stood by Sherri unwaveringly, angrily dismissing any earlier skeptics. "The question isn't, 'Is she lying?'" one family statement read, "The question is, 'Who did this to her?'" The Papinis expressed gratitude for the support and focused on healing. Sherri's recovery from her physical injuries would take time, and the psychological trauma was presumed to be immense. Nonetheless, from her hospital bed, Sherri had given investigators vital leads. Now it was up to law enforcement to catch the monsters who had allegedly abducted her.

Yet, even as Sherri recovered at home in late 2016, quietly avoiding media appearances, doubts were quietly brewing beneath the surface. Some veteran detectives and FBI agents couldn't help but feel that parts of her story rang false or contradictory. Why would kidnappers release their victim unharmed (albeit injured) after weeks, without ransom or clear motive? Why target Sherri in the first place? Certain details like the strange decision to brand her only to set her free puzzled experts. And although Sherri was adamant in her story, concrete evidence to corroborate it was scant. The sketches drawn from her memory and the vague descriptions yielded no immediate suspects. As 2017 arrived, the case of Sherri Papini remained unsolved, and a troubling question loomed: Was Sherri telling the whole truth?

Publicly, the investigation into Sherri Papini's kidnapping stretched on into 2017 with few new clues. Almost a year passed without an arrest. In October 2017, the FBI released composite sketches of the two female suspects based on Sherri's descriptions, hoping to jolt loose new leads. The sketches showed two women with markedly different ages and features. One was younger with wild curly hair, the other older with straight hair and thick eyebrows. A $10,000 reward was offered for information leading to the kidnappers. Yet, even with the images broadcast on national TV, no credible tips surfaced. It seemed the mysterious Hispanic women had vanished into thin air, if they ever existed at all.

Behind closed doors, investigators were uncovering inconvenient facts that challenged Sherri's version of events. Forensic analysis of Sherri's clothing from the day she was found revealed a clue that she had never mentioned: male DNA on her sweatpants and underwear that did not belong to her husband Keith, nor to any unknown female. If Sherri had only encountered two women during her disappearance, how could a man's DNA be present on her clothes? The DNA was submitted to criminal databases, but initially there was no direct match. That's when the FBI turned to genealogical methods to search for familial DNA links. By mid-2020, technology had advanced, and the mysterious male DNA from Sherri's clothing was traced to a family member of a certain James Reyes who happened to be Sherri's ex-boyfriend.

This was the breakthrough investigators needed. It turned out Sherri had remained in sporadic contact with James Reyes, an old flame from years before. The revelation was stunning yet oddly logical. Could Sherri have run off to an ex-boyfriend's home? In August 2020, a surveillance team quietly collected an item from Reyes' trash, an empty iced tea bottle, to obtain his DNA. The DNA from the bottle was a match to the unknown male DNA on Sherri's clothes. Confronted with this evidence, James Reyes confessed what really happened during those 22 days in November 2016.

The real story was nothing like Sherri's fantastical kidnapping yarn. Reyes told investigators that Sherri had orchestrated her own disappearance. She had reached out to him for help, claiming she needed to escape her home life. In messages prior to November 2016, Sherri alleged that Keith was "abusing" her. She said she was scared for her safety and needed to get away. (Notably, there was no evidence whatsoever that Keith Papini ever harmed Sherri; by all accounts he was loving, loyal and gentle and Sherri's claims of abuse were just another lie.) James Reyes, feeling sympathetic to his distressed ex-girlfriend, agreed to help hide her. They devised a plan: Reyes would drive up from his home in Costa Mesa, Orange County (Southern California), to Shasta County (Northern California) and pick up Sherri on the day she planned to go jogging.

On November 2, 2016, the day Sherri disappeared, Reyes followed through. He rented a car (a rental SUV or perhaps a smaller vehicle; one report mentions a rented "sports car") and drove nearly 600 miles north to Redding. According to a federal affidavit, Sherri and Reyes communicated to coordinate the pickup. Sherri went out for her "run" as planned late that morning, and at a pre-arranged spot along her route, Reyes was waiting. Sherri willingly got into his car, after perhaps staging the drop of her phone and hair to make it look like a kidnapping struggle. In fact, investigators later found that Sherri had carefully placed her iPhone and earbud headphones on the ground herself; something Keith had sensed was odd from the start. Once Sherri was in the vehicle, they began the long drive back to Costa Mesa. The absurdity was stark: while an Amber Alert-style search effort launched up north, Sherri Papini was reportedly dozing in the backseat of Reyes' car as he transported her to safety in his apartment.

Reyes sheltered Sherri in his Costa Mesa apartment for the next three weeks. During that time, she never left the apartment once. Not to go outside, not to get medical care for self-inflicted injuries, nothing. While an entire community frantically scoured the woods for her, Sherri was essentially hiding out and watching TV. But this was no vacation for Sherri; she was on a mission to make her fabricated abduction look as convincing as possible. Reyes told investigators that Sherri did harm to herself: she starved herself to lose weight, hit herself to cause bruises, and even had him assist in creating some of her injuries. For example, the "brand" on Sherri's shoulder was actually inflicted at Sherri's request. Reyes admitted that he helped her by branding her skin with a wood-burning tool from a hobby supply store, an injury meant to bolster her kidnapping story. Sherri also cut her own hair short during her stay. The chain that was found around her waist? Sherri had asked Reyes to procure chains so she could appear to have been restrained. It was a hoax of unimaginable proportions: Sherri Papini was crafting a tableau of torment for the authorities and her family to find, thereby cementing her status as a crime victim.

Eventually, Sherri began to feel guilty or perhaps just homesick. By Thanksgiving 2016, she told Reyes she wanted to go back home to Redding. According to Reyes, Sherri was determined to return in a dramatic fashion consistent with the fake story she had devised.

In the early hours of November 24, Reyes drove Sherri north. They decided on a location near I-5 in Yolo County to drop her off, aiming for a time when someone would likely stop to help. Sherri bound her wrists and ankles loosely with zip ties (or had Reyes bind her) and remained in the passenger seat until they reached the spot. Following Sherri's instructions, Reyes pulled over and let her out, leaving her by the side of the road in the cold darkness, still in restraints so it would look like she had been dumped there by captors. Sherri even had him fire a gunshot into the air as they left as a final theatrical touch to scare her into staying put until help arrived. Reyes then drove off. Moments later, alone and suddenly truly helpless, Sherri did exactly what she had planned: she flagged down the first passing vehicle, which happened to be the truck driver who then called 911. Her hoax was successful, at least for the time being.

For law enforcement, Reyes' confession in 2020 was the final puzzle piece. The elaborate kidnapping tale that Sherri Papini told was a lie from start to finish. She had squandered resources, stoked fear in her community, and even vilified an entire demographic by blaming "two Hispanic women" for a crime that never happened. Investigators confronted Sherri with this evidence in August 2020. In a recorded interview, FBI agents and a detective laid out the DNA results and the ex-boyfriend's statements. They pointedly warned Sherri that it was a crime to lie to federal agents. But Sherri stuck to her story, incredibly doubling down on her lies. Even when told about the DNA linking to Reyes, she denied it, insisting she had been kidnapped as she described. The agents gave her every opportunity, even telling her that lying again would be a federal offense. Sherri simply wouldn't budge. She maintained her fictional story to the agent's faces, trying to weave around the evidence with new lies. This steadfast lying in 2020 sealed Sherri's fate. The investigators left that interview knowing they had the truth, even if Sherri wouldn't admit it. They began preparing to bring the hammer of justice down on Sherri Papini.

On March 3, 2022, more than five years after Sherri Papini's disappearance and dramatic return, the FBI decided it had enough evidence to make an arrest. Sherri was at home in Redding, where she had been living a relatively quiet life with her family, when agents showed up. In a scene dripping with irony, the woman who once had the nation's sympathy was perp-walked in handcuffs and charged as a criminal. Federal prosecutors charged Papini, now 39, with making false statements to federal officers and mail fraud related to the fraudulent financial benefits she had collected as a result of her fabricated kidnapping. According to the Department of Justice, from 2017 to 2021 Papini had bilked the California Victim Compensation Board and even the Social Security Administration out of over $30,000; money she claimed for therapy and recovery from her "abduction" and for disability payments due to PTSD. Now the truth was out, and Sherri was the one accused of wrongdoing. The arrest made headlines worldwide: "California Mom's Kidnapping Was a Hoax," blared news outlets, as the bizarre saga finally came to light.

Her family's reaction was initially one of disbelief and defensiveness. On the day of Sherri's arrest, the Papini family issued a statement saying they were "appalled" by how it was handled alleging that Sherri had been ambushed in front of her children when agents took her into custody. They suggested Sherri would have cooperated if asked, and expressed anger that the kids (now around 8 and 10 years old) witnessed their mother being arrested. This statement indicated that at least some of Sherri's relatives still believed (or pretended to believe) in her innocence at that point. But one key person was no longer in Sherri's corner: Keith Papini.

The revelations of Sherri's deceit devastated Keith. He had stood by her for years, vehemently denying naysayers, only to learn that the entire ordeal was a lie and that Sherri had betrayed him in the worst possible way. The indictment detailed how Sherri had been with her ex-boyfriend instead of being tortured, and Keith was reportedly blindsided by this truth. Within days of her arrest, as Sherri's duplicity became undeniable, Keith filed for divorce. On April 20, 2022, just two days after Sherri formally admitted the hoax in court, Keith Papini petitioned for dissolution of the marriage and for sole custody of their children. In his court filings, he described how he and the children had been "traumatized by [Sherri's] disappearance and her hoax kidnapping", emphasizing that Sherri's actions had shattered their family. After years of publicly supporting his wife, Keith now felt he "does not believe Sherri is in a position to make decisions on behalf of the children given her notoriety… and the dishonesty reflected in the charges brought against her" (as stated in his filing). It was a tragic but perhaps inevitable turn – the fairytale love story had ended in betrayal and heartbreak.

As Sherri's lies became public, outrage erupted from many quarters. Residents of Shasta County, who had lived in fear and poured their hearts out for Sherri in 2016, felt anger and resentment. "It was like a kick in the teeth to a community that didn't deserve to be treated like that," said one local woman who had helped search for Sherri, "She stabbed our community in the back with every step she took.". The Latino community in the area and beyond was particularly incensed by the hoax's racial component. "Ever since 2016, many of our Latino/Hispanic residents were forced to feel like the criminals in a twisted scheme that never, ever happened," wrote one Shasta County resident, recalling how Latino neighbors avoided driving together or walking in groups for fear of fitting Sherri's false description. Latino advocacy voices pointed out that Sherri Papini had played into racist stereotypes by casting Latina women as her villains, which in the charged political climate of late 2016 (right after a divisive election) only sowed more division and fear. "All this falsification in her story, it's just nasty and disturbing," said Araceli Gutierrez, a Latina business owner in Northern California, adding that Papini's lie "fed into racist tropes" and gave people reason to indulge hateful rhetoric. The backlash against Papini was intense. She had not only betrayed her family and supporters, but also wasted an estimated hundreds of thousands of taxpayer dollars in the massive law enforcement search and investigation. Shasta County Sheriff Michael Johnson (who succeeded Tom Bosenko) didn't mince words: "It is a case of calculated deception driven by her narcissistic behavior," he said, lamenting how Papini's lies had squandered resources and distracted from real victims.

Initially, she was hit with a 35-count indictment (34 counts of mail fraud for each reimbursement check and one count of lying to the FBI). Under the weight of evidence, Sherri's defense negotiated a plea deal. In April 2022, Sherri Papini agreed to plead guilty to two charges: one count of mail fraud and one count of making false statements to a federal officer. As part of the plea, she signed a detailed admission of the facts, finally conceding that the kidnapping was all a hoax. In a statement released through her attorney, William Portanova, Sherri broke her public silence to express contrition. "I am deeply ashamed of myself for my behavior and so sorry for the pain I've caused my family, my friends, all the good people who needlessly suffered because of my story," Papini said in April 2022, as she acknowledged the truth of her actions. "I will work the rest of my life to make amends," she added, in an attempt to begin repairing the damage. It was a stunning turnabout for someone who had stubbornly clung to her lies for years. The plea deal spared Sherri a trial that would have undoubtedly drawn even more intense media coverage but it did not spare her from punishment.

After pleading guilty, Sherri Papini awaited her sentencing. The saga that began in

2016 with her headline-grabbing "abduction" now reached its final chapter in a Sacramento federal courtroom on September 19, 2022. Papini's case had become notorious, and public interest in the outcome was high. Federal prosecutors, taking into account her cooperation in pleading guilty (and perhaps her personal circumstances as a mother of two), recommended a relatively lenient sentence of 8 months behind bars (split as 1 month in custody and 7 months supervised/home detention). The defense argued for even less time. They hoped Sherri might avoid prison altogether, citing her mental health and the humiliation she'd already suffered. Sherri's lawyer portrayed her as a deeply troubled woman, saying she was essentially "in pursuit of a nonsensical fantasy" when she carried out the hoax. Mental health evaluations had failed to pin a specific diagnosis on Sherri's behavior; even experts were baffled by what drove her, according to Portanova. He alluded to "a fierce storm… going on for a long time inside her head" to explain (but not excuse) her actions.

In the courtroom, Sherri Papini sobbed as she faced Judge William B. Shubb. She delivered a short statement taking responsibility: "I'm so sorry to the many people who have suffered because of me," she said, voice shaking. Turning toward the judge, she stated, "I am guilty, your honor. I am guilty of lying. I am guilty of dishonor… What is done cannot be undone. It cannot be erased.". It was perhaps the most honest declaration Sherri had ever made. But the prosecution was not convinced that Sherri's tears equated to genuine remorse. Assistant U.S. Attorney Veronica

Alegría argued forcefully that Sherri's courtroom apology was just more "manipulation." "At this point she would say and do anything to mitigate her punishment," Alegría told the judge, emphasizing that real harm had been caused by Papini's lies. The prosecutor enumerated those harms: "There was a community that lived in fear... Miss Papini took money from real victims," Alegría said, highlighting how actual victims might now hesitate to come forward or might be doubted by authorities "because of this hoax." She implored the judge not to let Papini off lightly.

Judge Shubb had plenty to say as well. He acknowledged that Papini's case was "unique, to say the least," and that there was little precedent for someone quite like her – a suburban mom who fabricated a violent kidnapping. But the judge was clearly disturbed by how long and persistently Sherri lied. "Miss Papini is a manipulator," Judge Shubb said bluntly from the bench, denouncing her deceit. He noted that Papini only admitted the truth when faced with overwhelming evidence years later. "It's not as if Miss Papini has seen the error of her ways... If she had not been caught, she'd still be living the lie," he declared sharply. Those words sealed Sherri's fate. In a decision that surprised some observers, Judge Shubb disregarded the prosecutors' mild 8-month suggestion and imposed a far stiffer punishment.

Sherri Papini was sentenced to 18 months in federal prison, to be followed by 36 months (3 years) of supervised release. This sentence was more than double what the government had asked for, making it a clear message of condemnation. The judge also ordered Papini to pay $309,902 in restitution to cover the costs of her fraud. That hefty sum included reimbursements to the California Victim Compensation Board (which had paid for her therapy and medical bills), the Social Security Administration (which had given her disability benefits after she claimed to be too traumatized to work), and the law enforcement agencies that expended resources on her case. "She has been ordered to pay every last dime back," the U.S. Attorney's Office said pointedly. Judge Shubb made it clear he believed a strong sentence was warranted to reflect the seriousness of the offense. "The court did what it thought was right, and frankly it's difficult to argue with the justice of the sentence," Sherri's own attorney conceded outside the courthouse, calling it "a fair sentence, even though it's longer than we wished.". The judge, he noted, wanted to "underline the wrongness" of Sherri's actions and "tattoo it further on her soul."

Sherri, flanked by her attorneys and a few family supporters, left the court in tears that day. She did not speak to reporters as cameras flashed. It was a somber end to a saga that began with such high drama. Papini's fall from grace was complete. In that moment she was not a victim or a survivor, but a convicted felon headed to prison.

In the wake of Sherri Papini's sentencing, the Papini case left a trail of broken trust and hard lessons. Sherri reported to federal prison on November 8, 2022 to begin serving her sentence. She spent her incarceration in a federal facility in Victorville, California, far from her Redding home. Her time behind bars was uneventful; Sherri kept a low profile, perhaps reflecting on the chain of lies that led her there. In August 2023, after roughly 11 months in custody, Sherri was transferred to community confinement (a halfway house) and then released early for good behavior – having served the majority of her 18-month term. In total, she served about 13 months in custody. Upon release, Papini, now 41 years old, was placed on supervised release, which will continue for three years until 2026. As of 2025, Sherri Papini is a free woman, though bound by the conditions of her supervised release and forever shadowed by her deceit.

Keith Papini and Sherri's children have moved on with their lives, apart from Sherri. In the immediate aftermath of the scandal, Keith was granted custody of the kids. He filed to have Sherri barred from any decision-making over the children, citing the notoriety and instability her actions caused. The divorce was finalized, and Keith has since sought to shield the children from the media spotlight and the painful truth of what their mother did. By many accounts, Sherri did not contest these arrangements strongly. She understood that her actions had forfeited her role as a wife and, at least temporarily, as an active parent.

Public interest in Sherri Papini eventually waned, but not before her name became synonymous with fraudulent victimhood. The media, which once heralded her brave survival story, now often uses her case as a cautionary tale. Opinion columns and TV commentators have dissected the Papini hoax's impact on society. In criminal justice circles, the case is cited as an example of why thorough investigation is crucial even when someone appears to be an innocent victim as things are not always as they seem. Law enforcement agencies in California quietly instituted policies to seek reimbursement in hoax cases, inspired in part by the costly Papini investigation. And genuine victims of violent crimes have expressed concern that such hoaxes make it harder for their stories to be believed. As prosecutor Alegría warned, "Victims of crimes may not believe they will be believed by law enforcement because of this hoax.". Advocates have had to reinforce the message that Sherri Papini's case was an anomaly, an outlier act of deception, and that real victims should still come forward.

In Shasta County, some positive change emerged from the community's sense of betrayal. Residents channeled their anger into unity, holding forums on rebuilding trust and even launching local campaigns to support real victims of crime and combat misinformation. There was also a local reckoning with the racial aspect of Papini's lie. In 2018, the county publicly declared it had "no room for racism," an effort partly driven by reflection on how Papini's story unjustly cast suspicion on people of color. One part-Latino resident summed up the community's feelings in an email to the Los Angeles Times, saying, "They [Latinos] were sent into shock during a time of already growing and rampant anti-immigrant... hatred. The Papini story just made it worse". Knowing now that it was all a lie was a relief, but it also left simmering resentment. As years pass, the name "Sherri Papini" still evokes a wince in Shasta County with a mixture of embarrassment for having been duped and anger at the damage done.

For Sherri herself, life after prison is undoubtedly very different from the life she once had. She returned to society as a convicted felon infamous for an elaborate con. She reportedly lived for a time with a relative (Keith's sister) after her arrest, and it's likely she continues to reside with family support since her release. Sherri is financially liable for that $309,000 restitution, a debt that will likely burden her for decades. (Judge Shubb remarked during sentencing that Sherri is unlikely to ever fully repay it "unless she wins the lottery.") There is little public information about her day-to-day life as of 2025, as she has understandably avoided interviews or public appearances. She's effectively a pariah in her old hometown; one can imagine it would be hard for her to walk the streets of Redding without drawing glares or comments.

The Papini case has earned a place in the annals of true crime lore, often compared to other notorious cases of false victimhood and hoaxes. Many have likened Sherri to Susan Smith, the South Carolina mother who in 1994 drowned her children and then falsely claimed a Black man had carjacked her, exploiting racist tropes to bolster her lie. Others mention Charles Stuart, who in 1989 blamed an unknown Black assailant for killing his wife, when in fact Stuart himself was the murderer. While Sherri Papini did not physically harm anyone (beyond herself), her willingness to accuse imaginary Latina women struck a similar chord of outrage.

It demonstrated how easily false narratives can tap into society's prejudices. As one commentator wrote, "Papini gave a face to the 'Latina kidnapper' that was never real, and that's one of the many reasons people won't soon forget her story."

In the end, Sherri Papini's story is one of a deeply deceptive manipulation that had very real consequences. She manipulated her family, her community, and the nation, all while the truth – mundane and bizarre in its own way – was that she longed for attention or escape at any cost. The emotional depth of the damage she caused is still felt by those closest to her. Keith Papini, in a victim impact statement, said he lost the woman he loved and the trust he once had: "The nation sought to help my wife; they gave me back a shattered shell of the woman I married," he lamented, describing how he and the children had to heal from not only her "kidnapping" but from the deception itself. The community, too, had to heal from being lied to on such a grand scale.

As of 2025, Sherri Papini lives quietly out of the public eye, likely attempting to rebuild some semblance of a life. She will be on federal supervised release until 2026, checking in with a probation officer and adhering to whatever restrictions are in place. Any misstep could send her back to prison. Those who followed the case doubt Sherri will ever return to the spotlight and many believe that is for the best. The consensus is that Papini's name will primarily serve as a warning: a reminder that even a "perfect" suburban mom can weave a wicked web of lies. In a twist of fate, Sherri Papini did become famous as she apparently desired but famous for all the wrong reasons, and at a price she will continue to pay for the rest of her days.

WOMB RAIDER

Taylor Parker

Taylor Parker was born December 8, 1992, and grew up in the tiny town of Simms in northeast Texas. By all accounts, Taylor's childhood and teen years were marked by compulsive lying and attention-seeking. Former classmates and acquaintances later recalled that Taylor would fabricate just about anything. Illnesses, relationships, pregnancies, all lies made up seemingly for sympathy or drama. She lied about having serious diseases like multiple sclerosis and cancer to elicit sympathy from others. She invented boyfriends and detailed romantic escapades that never happened. At one point, she even pretended to be pregnant as a teenager by stealing an actual pregnant woman's photo from social media, cropping out the woman's face, and claiming the swollen belly in the picture was her own. It was deception at a brazen level, even for a high-schooler.

Ironically, at around 18 years old, Taylor did become truly pregnant by a real boyfriend.

In 2010 she gave birth to a baby girl, whom she named Emerson. For a time, reality caught up with Taylor's lies as she was now a young single mother responsible for a daughter. But motherhood did not curtail Taylor's habit of falsehoods. Lying was like a second language to her, a reflex she would continue to use to manipulate those around her and try to shape her life into the drama she craved.

In 2011, 19-year-old Taylor met a man named Tommy Wacasey. Their romance moved quickly; within a few months of dating they married. Baby Emerson wasn't even a year old at the time, and soon Taylor was pregnant again, this time, with Tommy's child. The young couple welcomed a son in 2013. On the surface, it seemed Taylor was settling into family life. In 2014, after the birth of their son, Taylor underwent a tubal ligation (having her "tubes tied"), telling doctors she did not want any more children. She also traveled to Tijuana, Mexico, with an aunt that year to undergo gastric bypass surgery for weight loss. According to Tommy, Taylor later claimed that during that surgery doctors discovered a dangerous ovarian cyst and performed a partial hysterectomy, removing her uterus. This claim, like so many others from Taylor, was never proven and a physician would later testify that he did perform the tubal ligation on Taylor, but there was no reliable evidence she'd actually had a hysterectomy. It may well have been yet another lie to gain sympathy or attention. Even Tommy grew skeptical: Was Taylor telling the truth about anything at all?

As Tommy would later put it, "Looking back now, if I had known then what I know

now, it would have never happened. It's like our whole marriage was a lie. You would confront her about it, and it would turn into another lie." By the end of their marriage, Tommy realized he was dealing with a pathological liar. He filed for divorce, which was finalized in 2015. Tommy also sought custody of their son, and a judge agreed, granting Tommy full custody and ordering Taylor to pay child support of $225 a month. Taylor never paid a single dime. With the collapse of this marriage, Taylor lost the stable family she had briefly had, and her life descended further into fabrication to fill the void.

Not long after divorcing Tommy, Taylor met another man, Hunter Parker. They married quickly, and Taylor, now in her mid-20s, took Hunter's last name, becoming Taylor Parker. But this marriage was even shorter-lived than the first. Hunter deeply wanted children, and Taylor told him, as well as close friends at the time, that she couldn't have kids because her uterus had been "eaten up with cancer" and had to be removed. It's unclear if Hunter ever learned the truth that Taylor still had a uterus at least until 2014 and had chosen permanent sterilization. But he certainly knew they wouldn't be having children together. Taylor played the part of a tragically infertile young wife: she even approached two of her friends, McKenzie and Abby, asking if either would be willing to be a surrogate mother and carry a baby for Taylor and Hunter in exchange for $100,000. This astronomical offer raised eyebrows. Taylor had never been wealthy (holding down only modest jobs, if any), so where would she get $100k to pay a surrogate? Still, desperate to appease her new husband's wish for a baby, Taylor floated the idea among her friends.

What happened next was telling: McKenzie became pregnant on her own (not as a surrogate, just by coincidence) and announced she was expecting a baby girl. Taylor, despite having no stake in this pregnancy, acted overjoyed and heavily invested in McKenzie's condition as if living vicariously through her friend. Abby, the other friend, also ended up pregnant around that time, but with a boy. Taylor showed little interest in Abby's pregnancy. Observers later noted that Taylor's enthusiasm was oddly selective: she only seemed excited when her friend was having a girl, not a boy. Perhaps in Taylor's fantasy world, she imagined somehow acquiring a baby girl for herself. In any case, by April 2019, Hunter Parker had grown frustrated and suspicious of his wife. The lack of children, Taylor's strange behavior with her friends, and likely her incessant lying caused the marriage to crumble. Hunter and Taylor divorced, and Taylor's friendships with McKenzie and Abby soured as well. Both friends cut ties, likely sensing that something about Taylor was not right.

By mid-2019, Taylor Parker was twice-divorced, unemployed, and living in a spiral of lies. But she was also determined to cling to the life she wanted; a life of love, family, and wealth, even if it meant manufacturing every detail in her own imagination. Just weeks after her split from Hunter, Taylor latched onto a new romantic prospect: Wade Griffin, a hardworking "good ole country boy" from Texas. They met at a rodeo, where Wade, a tall and strapping man in his early 20s, was in his element. He worked for a roofing company and did side jobs like welding, hog trapping, and managing livestock. In Taylor's eyes, Wade represented stability and salt-of-the-earth goodness.

Taylor turned on the charm and reeled Wade in quickly. She cooked him home-made meals, helped take care of his house and farm animals, and even offered to organize his finances. She played the role of the devoted girlfriend so perfectly that Wade's friends later recalled she seemed "too good to be true." And indeed, she was. In the midst of doting on Wade, Taylor dropped hints that she came from serious money. She casually boasted about her family's wealth from oil and gas investments. According to Taylor, her family owned extensive lands rich with oil, and her grandmother had set up a special account to deposit the lucrative royalties. Taylor claimed she would soon have access to this fortune, implying that Wade's financial worries could all disappear if he just stuck with her.

Wade, being a humble, hard-working man, didn't pry too much into Taylor's stories of wealth. He figured her finances were her own business. But Taylor made sure he understood just how fabulously rich her family was. She told Wade they owned hundreds of acres of land that needed upkeep, and even offered to pay him $50,000 to clear brush and maintain the family property. For a young man like Wade, who had grown up ranching, this sounded like a dream side-job earning good money to work on a beautiful ranch. Wade accepted the gig. He even hired a friend, Juan, to help with the labor, happy to share the opportunity (Juan, a father of four, was grateful for the work).

In the beginning, Taylor made the lie convincing. She actually handed Wade an initial check to pay Juan for the first round of work, proving that the money was real, or so it seemed. But shortly after, Taylor abruptly pulled the plug on the project. She claimed her mother had found out about them spending money from the account and was furious; as a result, her mother supposedly froze the funds. Taylor apologized and explained that if Wade wanted to keep Juan working, he'd have to pay him out of his own pocket for now with Taylor promising to reimburse him later when she smoothed things over with her mom. Wade, trusting his girlfriend, continued paying Juan himself, believing he'd get paid back once Taylor's "family situation" was sorted.

This incident introduced a new dramatic element in Taylor's saga: the villainous mother. Taylor began telling Wade (and anyone else who would listen) that she and her mother, Shona, had a terrible relationship. According to Taylor, Shona resented her and would go to extreme lengths to sabotage her happiness. Taylor wove an outrageous tale: her mother not only harassed and threatened her regularly, but had even hired someone, a mysterious figure named Mandy Boyd, to send Taylor menacing emails and text messages. She claimed Shona despised her so much that at one point she put a hit out on her own daughter's life. In Taylor's telling, her mother was entangled with some kind of underground mafia and was involved in a violent shootout. This supposed shootout, Taylor said, was hushed up by the authorities to avoid scandal. The tale reached a crescendo when Taylor informed Wade that her evil mother Shona had finally met a dramatic end: after being taken into custody (for unspecified crimes), Shona had hung herself in jail.

It was a jaw-dropping story: a mother turned mortal enemy, a faked suicide, and a secret fortune held hostage. Wade had no way to know how much of this was true (in reality, almost none of it was). But Taylor told it with convincing emotion, and Wade, a trusting soul, accepted what his girlfriend said. In Taylor's mind, killing off her own mother in the narrative served a purpose: if Shona was out of the way (even if only fictionally), then Taylor could now claim full access to the family fortune. She presented herself as a wealthy heiress, finally free to live her life and oh, wouldn't it be wonderful if she and Wade moved in together now?

Sure enough, with the supposed inheritance imminent and Taylor playing the part of a wounded woman in need of love (now also grieving her mother's "death"), she persuaded Wade to let her move into his home. She even talked about buying land for the two of them and for her daughter, Emerson, to live on and build a family. By late summer 2019, Taylor Parker had firmly embedded herself in Wade Griffin's life, home, and finances. But she still wasn't satisfied. Wade's love and the fiction of wealth weren't enough. Taylor knew the surest way to bond herself to this man was the one thing that had blown up her previous marriage: a baby.

In August 2019, Taylor told Wade the "happy news": she was pregnant. Not only that, she claimed a doctor had already confirmed they were expecting twins. Wade was stunned and overjoyed. He had no idea that Taylor was medically incapable of conceiving (due to her tubal ligation, and certainly if her hysterectomy story were true, she'd have no womb at all). Taylor, however, had laid the groundwork for this deception. She had lied to so many people about her health that few knew the real facts. Wade did not know Taylor's reproductive history, and after only a few months of dating, he had little reason to doubt her claim of pregnancy. Twins on the way, a wealthy future, a doting girlfriend...it all seemed almost too good to be true for Wade.

But Taylor Parker was an expert at creating elaborate illusions. As soon as she announced the pregnancy, she began orchestrating ways to support her lie. Behind the scenes, Taylor searched online and ordered items from a website that catered to exactly this kind of deception: fakeababy.com. Incredibly, this site sold phony pregnancy bellies and even realistic ultrasound sonogram prints customized with the buyer's name, a chosen date and clinic, and the gender of the baby. (One can only shudder that such a market exists, but Taylor eagerly took advantage of it.) If Taylor was going to convince everyone she was carrying twins, she needed all the props including a false belly that would grow over time and ultrasound images to show off. And she got them.

Before long, Taylor was flashing a sonogram picture of twin babies and talking about doctors' visits. Wade's family, however, remained skeptical. Wade's mother, Connie, and his sister, as well as some close friends, sensed that Wade wasn't truly in love with Taylor. It seemed he was more caught up in her schemes than in a genuine romance. They suspected Taylor might be lying about the pregnancy just to keep Wade around. And they had good reason to be wary: by late 2019, Wade was finding himself entangled in one bizarre financial promise after another because of Taylor's grand stories.

For instance, Taylor was determined to win over Wade's family to prove she was the real deal. In early 2020, she did something dramatic: she gifted Connie (Wade's mom) her dream car, a brand-new Nissan Altima. Connie was astonished. The car she'd always wanted, appearing out of thin air courtesy of her son's girlfriend? Taylor insisted that, thanks to her inheritance, money was no object. Around the same time, Taylor encouraged Wade to elevate his own lifestyle in anticipation of their coming wealth. She pushed him to buy a new $29,000 all-terrain vehicle (ATV) and a heavy-duty pickup truck worth over $90,000, and to invest in about 20 head of cattle for $21,000. All of these, Taylor promised, would be paid off soon because her millions were just around the corner. Eager to build a life with Taylor and dazzled by the prospect of wealth, Wade went along with these purchases, financing them on credit. Each new expenditure sank him deeper into debt, but Taylor assured him repeatedly that once her inheritance came in, she'd wipe the slate clean.

The extravagant gift-giving didn't last

long. Just a few weeks after giving Connie the new Altima, Taylor asked to borrow it back under a flimsy pretext. She told Connie there was a factory recall and she needed to take the car to the dealership for repairs. Reluctantly, Connie handed the car over. But something told her to double-check Taylor's story. She called the dealership and learned the truth: there was no recall at all. The car was slated for repossession. Taylor had never paid for it in the first place. The Altima had been nothing more than a prop in Taylor's ongoing charade, and now the dealership was reclaiming it. Connie realized, with a sinking feeling, that Taylor had conned them.

Wade, too, was beginning to feel the pressure. By early 2020, with loan payments mounting for the ATV, the truck, and the cattle, Wade confided to Taylor that he was in over his head. He hadn't seen a penny of the promised inheritance money and was watching his bank account bleed dry. "We are not financially able to keep everything we've bought," he told her in frustration. "None of the money was coming through, and I'm losing faith it ever will." Taylor knew she had to keep Wade believing in the fantasy just a little longer. To ease his doubts, she produced yet another lie: Wade began receiving text messages from someone claiming to be Taylor's Aunt "Katie Jo." In these messages, Aunt Katie Jo affirmed that the family estate was being settled and that extra acres of land would be set aside for Taylor and Wade to raise cattle on. It was exactly what Wade needed to hear to refresh his hope that his patience (and mounting debt) would pay off. Of course, Taylor herself was almost certainly impersonating this aunt, sending texts from a fake number. Every person involved in Taylor's grand stories, from her mother, to her family lawyer, to this aunt, was ultimately just Taylor in disguise.

Amid all these wild financial schemes, Taylor continued to advance the narrative of her pregnancy. In February 2020, she claimed that she had lost one of the twins due to a tragic accident. She told Wade that her father, Mark, had texted her about a farming accident. A piece of equipment called a bush hog had broken, and as Taylor helped a family friend with the repairs, a winch line snapped and struck her in the stomach. The impact, Taylor implied, caused one of the babies to miscarry. It's unclear if she said she lost both twins or just one, but soon after, Taylor announced that she was pregnant again. By this time, it was early 2020 and she set a new due date: September 22, 2020. Whether this represented a continuation of the twin pregnancy now reduced to one baby, or a completely "new" pregnancy after an alleged miscarriage, she left vague. What mattered was the timeline. Everyone was now expecting Taylor to deliver a baby in late September.

The year 2020 dawned with Taylor juggling multiple high-stakes lies. She was faking an entire pregnancy, complete with social media posts and even a gender reveal party, and simultaneously trying to keep her collapsing financial fictions alive. In March 2020, as the COVID-19 pandemic cast a pall over normal life, Taylor pressed forward with her personal drama. She organized a lavish gender reveal event to announce the sex of her (imaginary) baby. In true country flair, she brought out a baby calf adorned with a big pink bow to reveal she was expecting a girl. Family and friends gathered as Taylor and Wade happily declared they would soon welcome a daughter, whom they planned to name Clancy Gaile (a name Wade loved and had chosen). A photo of Taylor smiling beside the little cow with its pink bow went up on her Instagram. In attendance were Wade's mother Connie, his boss Roger, Roger's wife Angela, Taylor's father Mark, and even Taylor's young daughter Emerson. For those few hours, under the spring sun, everyone played along with the joyful charade.

Indeed, Wade's mother and others were growing increasingly suspicious. The more Taylor tried to substantiate her lies, the more mistakes she made. One weekend, during a visitation with her son (the boy from her first marriage), Taylor told the little boy that he was going to be a big brother and mommy was having another baby. When the boy went home, he innocently repeated this to his father, Tommy Wacasey. Tommy was alarmed: he knew Taylor couldn't be pregnant. He had been married to her through her supposed hysterectomy and the tubal ligation; he knew having another child was physiologically impossible for her. Tommy realized that if Taylor was claiming to be pregnant, she must be deeply entangled in some deceit, and whoever her current partner was could be in danger of getting hurt or defrauded. Wanting to warn Taylor's new boyfriend without getting personally entangled, Tommy sent an anonymous text message to Wade. The message essentially said: Taylor can't get pregnant. It's a lie and she's a compulsive liar about many things.

When Wade showed Taylor the anonymous warning text, Taylor didn't miss a beat. She immediately blamed it on the usual suspect, her "crazy" mother or someone on her mother's side of the family trying to ruin her life. Taylor insisted that certain people just wanted to "make her look bad" and sabotage her happiness, weaving it into her ongoing narrative of being persecuted by her family. Wade apparently chose to accept Taylor's explanation, or at least he did not sever the relationship. After all, by this point he had invested so much emotionally and financially into Taylor's promises that walking away was hard. He was in love with the idea of the life they were building: the ranches, the baby on the way, the happy family.

However, as spring turned to summer 2020, the cracks in Taylor's story were widening. One of Wade's friends, Angela, who was the wife of Wade's boss, had been politely skeptical of Taylor from early on. Angela had heard all about the dramatic "mom" saga and the inheritance, and she had attended the gender reveal. Being a shrewd woman, Angela kept an eye on Taylor's claims. On April 9, 2020, Angela received an email from Taylor, asking her for a favor: Taylor needed Angela to print out an attached "pregnancy verification letter" from a clinic. The letter, purportedly from a medical professional, confirmed Taylor's pregnancy and listed her due date as September 22, 2020. Taylor perhaps thought that providing official-looking documentation would silence the doubters. But Angela looked closely at the letter and immediately spotted something fishy. The name of the nurse who "signed" the letter was exactly the same as the patient's name on the form. In other words, Taylor had likely forged a letter and clumsily put her own name in both the patient and provider fields. Confronted with this odd discrepancy, Taylor became upset and defensive. She claimed that the clinic must have a mole, planted by her nefarious mother, who intentionally falsified the letter to make her look bad. It was an absurd excuse, but consistent with Taylor's pattern of blaming every inconsistency on her phantom enemy, "Mom."

Angela wasn't buying it. She politely but firmly told Taylor that to put everyone's mind at ease, they should go to the clinic together, immediately, and get an actual pregnancy test done. Perhaps cornered and panicking, Taylor agreed. The two women drove to a Health Express clinic in Mount Pleasant, Texas that day. Due to COVID-19 restrictions, extra people weren't allowed to accompany patients into exam rooms, so Angela waited in the lobby while Taylor went in alone to give a urine sample. Angela watched Taylor walk in carrying only her small wallet. After some time, Taylor emerged from the back, holding a piece of paper with lab results. Stapled to it was a letter that looked very similar to the one she had emailed Angela earlier. This letter indicated a positive pregnancy test and confirmed the due date of September 22nd. Taylor beamed, showing Angela: see, I'm really pregnant!

But Angela noticed something strange: the paper was not folded. Taylor hadn't brought a purse in that could conceal a full-size document, and she went in empty-handed. So how did she come out with a printed letter in hand? It was as if the letter had materialized out of thin air. Angela would later puzzle over this. Did Taylor somehow plant a pre-written letter in the restroom or convince a nurse to print it? During Taylor's eventual trial, evidence showed that the urine test she took at the clinic proved she was not pregnant. Yet somehow, she had walked out with paperwork saying the opposite. To this day, even investigators aren't entirely sure how Taylor pulled off that little magic trick. Such was Taylor Parker's devotion to deceit, she was willing to brazenly falsify medical results right under a friend's nose.

Despite her clever maneuvering, Taylor's credibility was deteriorating fast among Wade's circle. By the summer of 2020, word had quietly spread among some folks in town and former acquaintances that Taylor Parker's pregnancy was likely a sham. On July 2, 2020, Taylor made a social media post asking for prayers for herself and baby Clancy, saying she had a lot of doctor's appointments and scans that day likely in an attempt to garner sympathy and reinforce her narrative. But the post drew skeptics. Some people who knew Taylor's history left pointed comments, essentially trying to call her bluff by asking probing questions about her pregnancy.

Additionally, Taylor's own former coworkers were catching on. It turned out Taylor had once worked at an OB/GYN clinic in 2014. In the ultrasound image she had shared online, the doctor's name listed was "Dr. Mason" – a physician at that very clinic. Employees there recognized the scenario and thought Taylor's supposed pregnancy was bizarre. Alarmed, they actually contacted the local hospital in early fall 2020 with a warning: there's a woman in the community faking a pregnancy; we're worried she might try to steal a baby from the hospital. One hospital official later testified, "There was no indication that a crime was going to be committed. We just wanted to make sure our babies were going to be safe in our hospital." In other words, Taylor's reputation for lying was so known in certain circles that people instinctively feared she could do something extreme like abduct a newborn. They weren't wrong to worry but they severely underestimated what Taylor was capable of.

Through all this, Wade remained publicly supportive of Taylor. Astonishingly, at the end of August 2020, roughly eight months into the "pregnancy", Taylor and Wade posed for a professional maternity photoshoot. In the photos posted online, Taylor is dressed in flowing maternity attire, cradling a very convincing baby bump, with Wade by her side, his hand on her belly. They look like a happy couple eagerly awaiting their child. It is chilling in hindsight to see those images and know that Taylor's swollen abdomen was a prosthetic; beneath it was nothing but the void of her lies.

By September 2020, Taylor Parker was trapped in the lie of her fake pregnancy and time was running out. Her due date of September 22nd arrived with no baby to show. She needed a plan, and she needed it fast. Every lie she had told was converging into a terrible predicament: how could she produce a real baby to present to Wade, to her family, to everyone she had deceived? The only way to keep from being exposed (and to hold onto the life she so desperately wanted) was to obtain a baby by any means necessary.

Taylor's initial thought might have been to stage a kidnapping at a hospital. Many who later studied the case noted parallels to another infamous crime: in 2004, a woman named Lisa Montgomery had faked a pregnancy and then murdered a pregnant woman to cut out and steal her baby. Taylor may or may not have known of that case, but the similarities are eerie. Hospital staff had been warned about Taylor, making a snatch-and-run in a maternity ward far more difficult. Taylor likely realized that her best chance was to target a pregnant woman directly, someone near full-term whose baby she could take and pass off as her own. Disturbingly, a perfect target was already within Taylor's inner circle: Reagan Hancock.

Reagan Hancock was a 21-year-old woman from New Boston, Texas, the same small town where Taylor often stayed with Wade. Taylor and Reagan were not complete strangers. In fact, earlier in 2019, Reagan had hired Taylor (who did photography as a side hobby) to take her engagement photos. Reagan was a friendly, trusting young woman; she was newly married to her high-school sweetheart, Homer Hancock, and they were excited to start a family. Taylor even photographed Reagan and Homer's wedding in spring 2019. After that, the two women stayed in touch on social media, though they weren't extremely close.

By mid-2020, Reagan was pregnant with her second child, a baby girl. (She and Homer already had a 3-year-old daughter, Kynlee.) When Taylor learned that Reagan was expecting and due around late October 2020, she saw an opportunity. Taylor reached out to Reagan under the friendly guise of two pregnant moms bonding. Reagan, being kind-hearted, responded positively. Throughout the summer, as Taylor carried on her own fake pregnancy, she would chat with Reagan about baby preparations. Perhaps Reagan felt sorry for Taylor, who claimed to have so much family drama; maybe she believed they were genuine friends.

Taylor's elaborate planning kicked into high gear in late September. She knew she had to get rid of Wade on the day she would carry out her plan; whatever that plan ultimately was. Around her supposed due date, Taylor contacted a hog farmer in Oklahoma (about four hours away) using the name "Taylor Griffin", essentially using Wade's last name as an alias. She inquired about buying a large number of pigs, but the farmer became suspicious when she seemed ignorant of basic farming logistics and regulations. He suspected a scam and refused the sale. Taylor, undeterred, kept pressing. She messaged the farmer again on September 27, claiming she had sorted out transport for the hogs. The farmer still rebuffed her. It appears that Taylor's goal was never really to buy livestock. Rather, it was to create a scenario to send Wade on a wild goose chase far from home.

Whether or not she secured an actual seller, Taylor decided to stage the hog sale regardless. On the morning of October 9, 2020, a date by which she was overdue and growing desperate, Taylor told Wade that he needed to go meet the seller to finalize the purchase of some hogs. She provided an address out in the country, seemingly coordinating via text messages with the "seller." Wade, trusting this was legit, set off early that morning, towing a trailer for the animals. Taylor had meticulously faked a whole text conversation on her phone to show Wade, making it appear she'd arranged this deal. In truth, every single person in those messages was Taylor talking to herself – the farmer, the aunt, the mom, were all fabricated characters to support her lies.

Wade arrived at the designated rural location around 7:30 AM, but found nothing but an empty farm. The bewildered property owner came out, confused as to why a stranger was there with a trailer. Wade showed him the text messages he had, supposedly from the owner, confirming the sale. The man shook his head. He had never texted with Wade or anyone about selling hogs. Only then did it dawn on Wade that he had been deceived. He immediately tried calling Taylor... but by that time, Taylor was already executing the final, gruesome phase of her plan.

With Wade safely out of town, Taylor Parker drove to Reagan Hancock's home in New Boston on the morning of October 9, 2020. She knew that Reagan's husband, Homer, would be at work and that 3-year-old Kynlee would likely be at home with her mom. We know from later evidence that Taylor actually visited Reagan the night before as well when she dropped by on October 8th with a little gift for the baby and a Starbucks drink for the expectant mom. Reagan was touched by the kindness; she even thanked Taylor in a Facebook post that evening, not knowing it was part of her friend's twisted pre-meditation. Taylor's friendly visit likely served two purposes: it put Reagan at ease, and it allowed Taylor to scope out Reagan's house and routine one last time.

That fateful morning, some time after 8:00 AM, Taylor entered the Hancock home. It's not clear if she knocked and Reagan willingly let her in, or if Taylor found another way inside. But based on later reconstruction, what happened next was pure horror. Taylor attacked Reagan with sudden, brutal violence. A later autopsy and blood spatter analysis indicated that Reagan fought desperately for her life and for her unborn child. The struggle moved through four to five different areas of the house from a bedroom, into a hallway, the kitchen, and the living room. Reagan, five months shy of her 22nd birthday and heavily pregnant, tried everything to fend off her attacker. She sustained extensive defensive wounds on her arms and hands, meaning she raised them to block blows. But Taylor was relentless.

At some point, Taylor managed to bludgeon Reagan with a blunt object. Later evidence suggested she grabbed a claw hammer and used both the metal head and the claw end to smash Reagan's skull. Reagan suffered at least five skull fractures and a broken nose, likely from hammer strikes. Taylor also grabbed a large mason jar filled with sand, heartbreakingly, it was a decoration from Reagan's own baby gender reveal party, and used it as a weapon, bashing Reagan with the jar until it shattered, mixing pink and blue sand with blood on the floor. Amidst this beating,

Taylor repeatedly stabbed Reagan with a knife. Investigators would count over 100 stab wounds across Reagan's body, an absolutely frenzied onslaught.

Finally, Taylor overpowered the gravely wounded Reagan and forced her onto the living room floor. Reagan was alive but incapacitated and her nightmare had only worsened. Taylor's ultimate goal was now at hand. She retrieved a medical scalpel from her purse (she had come prepared with surgical tools) and began to cut open Reagan's abdomen. The initial knife she had used wasn't efficient enough for the crude cesarean she intended, so the scalpel was necessary. In a grotesque procedure, Taylor sliced Reagan from hip to hip across the lower belly. She cut deep, opening the uterus itself, and carefully extracted Reagan's unborn baby girl, along with the placenta. Remarkably, through this unimaginable torture, Reagan remained alive, perhaps barely, but alive as her child was stolen from her womb.

In a final act of callous cruelty, as Taylor lifted the premature infant from her mother's body, she brought the baby's face close to Reagan's and taunted, "Say goodbye to Mommy." It was a chilling, tragic mockery. Taylor forcing a newborn to "say bye" to the dying mother who could only watch in helpless horror. Immediately after, Reagan succumbed to her injuries. Whether from blood loss, shock, or further wounds (her throat had been cut as well, and the medical examiner could not rule out strangulation), Reagan's fight for life ended as her child was taken from her.

Just when you thought it couldn't get any worse, this entire savage attack occurred while little Kynlee, Reagan's 3-year-old, was also in the house. Miraculously, Kynlee did not wake up during the commotion or if she did, she mercifully did not come out of her room. The toddler was found unharmed physically, still in her bed later that morning. One can only imagine what would have happened if the child had wandered out during the assault. But Taylor had one objective and once she had accomplished that, she left Kynlee alone and turned her focus to covering her tracks.

At approximately 9:14 AM, Taylor Parker fled the murder scene, carrying Reagan's infant daughter who was weakly clinging to life. Before she left, Taylor grabbed Reagan's cellphone, shoving it into her own pocket or purse. She knew that Homer, Reagan's husband, would likely start calling or texting when he couldn't reach his wife and Taylor intended to intercept those messages to buy herself time. As she drove away from Reagan's home, Taylor indeed used Reagan's phone to send out text messages. In fact, around 8:30 AM (possibly while Reagan was still fighting for life), Homer had received some odd texts from his wife's number. They were likely sent by Taylor, pretending to be Reagan, perhaps saying she was busy or everything was fine. These phony messages ceased after 8:30, probably because by that time Taylor was racing away and focused on staging her own "birth" scenario.

Back at the gruesome crime scene, a neighbor noticed something amiss around 9:30 AM. The Hancocks' dog was loose and wandering outside, and Reagan wasn't answering the door. The neighbor contacted

Homer at work to let him know their puppy was out. This immediately alarmed Homer; it was unlike Reagan to ignore calls or let the dog roam free. He called Reagan repeatedly with no answer. Growing worried, Homer called Reagan's mother, Jessica Brookes, and asked if she could go by the house to check on Reagan and Kynlee. Homer himself left work and began rushing home.

Jessica Brookes arrived at her daughter's home shortly after 10:00 AM. She could never have been prepared for the sight that awaited her. Upon entering, Jessica found the living room drenched in blood. There was blood on the floors, the furniture, the walls – and there, in the midst of it, lay her daughter Reagan, lifeless and mutilated. The horror was overwhelming. Jessica immediately dialed 911, and in the recorded call, her screams conveyed the anguish of a mother encountering the worst thing imaginable. "Help me! My daughter's been murdered!" she cries. "There's blood everywhere! Oh, my babies! Oh my God!" In the background, Jessica can be heard frantically calling out for Kynlee and wailing in despair as she realizes Reagan's unborn baby is gone, cut out of her. She then desperately asked her husband about Kynlee, and is relieved to find her granddaughter alive, though soaked in her mother's blood. Police arrived within minutes, and soon after, a distraught Homer pulled up to a scene swarming with flashing lights and officers.

Meanwhile, not long after 9:30 AM, about 13 miles away over the state line in Oklahoma, State Trooper Tonyli Boyd was on patrol when he noticed a car speeding and driving erratically near the town of Idabel, Oklahoma. He initiated a traffic stop. To his astonishment, the driver, Taylor Parker, immediately cried out that she had just given birth and that her newborn baby was not breathing. Taylor was covered in blood from head to toe; on her hands, face, legs, everywhere. She was cradling a tiny infant in her lap, still connected to what looked like an umbilical cord trailing into Taylor's pants. A passing motorist even stopped to help upon seeing the commotion, and together with the trooper they tried to render aid.

Trooper Boyd observed several red flags. The blood on Taylor appeared dry and coagulated, not fresh as one would expect from an abrupt roadside delivery. There was an umbilical cord, yes, but bizarrely it was not attached to the baby's abdomen in the normal way and instead, it seemed to be coming from inside Taylor's pants. While Taylor was caked in blood, the newborn girl was relatively clean, and the driver's seat of the car had almost no blood on it. If Taylor had really just given birth in the driver's seat, the scene should have been far messier. Taylor, however, stuck to her story. She insisted she had gone into labor unexpectedly and that her doctor was in a town across the border (likely part of her earlier ruse). She pleaded to be taken to a hospital in Oklahoma rather than back to Texas.

The trooper called for an ambulance and had Taylor and the baby transported to McCurtain Memorial Hospital in Idabel, the closest hospital, which happened to be in Oklahoma. Upon arrival, Taylor continued to simulate the role of an exhausted new mother.

She hunched and shuffled as she walked, as if weakened from the labor of childbirth. But any hopes she had of fooling medical professionals were quickly dashed. The ER staff, alarmed for the infant's condition, began treating the baby and examining Taylor. What they found was damning: an external physical exam revealed that Taylor did not have a uterus at all (whether due to a past surgery or because it had been removed that very morning from Reagan's body, it was clear she hadn't carried a child to term). An internal exam showed no signs of a recent birth. There was no tearing, no bleeding, not even a cervix (Taylor's partial hysterectomy claim might have been true after all). A blood test confirmed there were zero pregnancy hormones in Taylor's system. In short, Taylor Parker had not given birth that day, or any recent day.

Confronted with this evidence, Taylor clung to her lie. She grew agitated and continued to insist she had delivered the baby. But the pieces were falling into place rapidly now. The newborn infant was in distress. She was very premature, later determined to be about 34 weeks gestation (roughly six weeks early) but she was alive for now. The hospital staff worked to stabilize the baby girl, whom Taylor claimed as her own. However, due to the violent way she had been brought into the world and likely oxygen deprivation, the baby had suffered severe brain damage. Despite doctors' efforts, the infant's condition deteriorated. At 1:22 PM on October 9, 2020, the baby was pronounced dead. By that time, law enforcement had been alerted that a woman matching Taylor's description had been found with a newborn, and that back in Texas there was a murdered young mother with a missing baby. It didn't take long for authorities in Oklahoma and Texas to connect the dots.

Hospital staff, horrified by the unfolding truth, informed the Oklahoma State Bureau of Investigation (OSBI) and local police that this woman did not give birth to this baby. The DNA tests later would conclusively show the infant was Reagan Hancock's daughter, not Taylor's. As this confirmation came in, Texas authorities notified Oklahoma that a capital murder had been discovered in New Boston, and the baby belonging to the victim was unaccounted for until now. By early afternoon, Taylor Parker was placed under arrest at the hospital.

Wade Griffin arrived at the Idabel hospital that afternoon as well, having learned that Taylor was there with the baby. Completely unaware of what had truly happened, he thought Taylor had gone into labor that morning and delivered their child while he was away. Imagine his shock when he was met not with congratulations but with law enforcement who promptly handcuffed him in the hallway. Initially, Wade thought this must be about that strange hog sale; maybe he'd inadvertently trespassed or broken a law. But investigators quickly explained that Taylor was accused of a heinous crime: kidnapping and murder. Wade was dumbfounded. He told officers that he was on his way to meet Taylor at the hospital for an induction of labor. He truly had no idea what was unfolding. It became immediately clear to police that Wade had been duped like everyone else; he was not involved in the crime, just another one of Taylor's victims. They released him once his innocence was established. Wade was left stunned and heartbroken, grappling with the revelation that the woman he loved had never been pregnant at all, and that the baby he thought was his had been violently stolen from another family.

In custody, facing an avalanche of evidence, Taylor Parker initially stuck to absurd denials. During early interrogations, her story was "all over the place," investigators later said. At first, Taylor concocted a heroic rescue narrative: she claimed she had visited Reagan and somehow they got into a fight, which led to Reagan falling and suffering a grievous head injury in the garage. In this invented scenario, Taylor said Reagan, in her injured state, begged Taylor to save her baby; to cut it out of her to save its life. Taylor insisted she performed an emergency C-section only at Reagan's pleas, and that Reagan tragically died in the process. When asked why Reagan had severe neck wounds, Taylor unbelievably suggested that after she delivered the baby and set the scalpel down, Reagan might have grabbed it and slashed her own throat. This wild story didn't align with the physical evidence at all, certainly not with 100+ stab wounds, hammer blows, and a staged fake birth. Investigators pressed further, calling out the inconsistencies. Taylor then tried shifting blame: perhaps someone else was involved, or it wasn't how it looked. But these attempts failed. Finally, faced with no way out, Taylor confessed the core truth: she admitted she had never been pregnant and that she killed Reagan Hancock to steal her unborn baby and claim the child as her own. In that moment, all of Taylor's lies, piled high over years, came crashing down under the weight of reality.

Texas authorities charged Taylor Parker with capital murder (for killing Reagan in the commission of another felony), kidnapping, and murder for the death of baby Braxlynn (Reagan's family had already lovingly named the lost child). The gravity of the crime, often termed "fetal abduction" in legal parlance, sent shockwaves through the region. Taylor's bond was set at $5 million, ensuring she would remain behind bars through the long pre-trial process. Reagan's devastated family and the community mourned the young mother and baby whose lives were savagely taken. Little Kynlee had lost her mother and baby sister in one morning and would be raised by her father and grandparents, carrying that trauma forever.

It took nearly two years for the case to go to trial, delayed in part by the COVID pandemic and the sheer volume of evidence to be gathered. Finally, in September 2022, Taylor Parker's capital murder trial commenced in Bowie County, Texas. It would last about six weeks, becoming one of the most chilling and closely watched trials in Texas that year. The prosecution laid out the full, astonishing timeline of Taylor's deceit and brutality. Witness after witness testified to her pattern of lying and manipulation.

Her first husband, Tommy Wacasey, recounted how convincingly Taylor could lie, and how he eventually realized their entire marriage had been built on her falsifications. Her former friends described the fake illnesses and pregnancies. Wade Griffin took the stand to share his story. He shared how Taylor tricked him with phantom inheritances and a nonexistent pregnancy, how he had genuinely believed he was about to be a father that day, only to learn the horrifying truth. Evidence from Taylor's digital devices showed the extent of her planning: internet searches for fake pregnancy bellies, research on performing C-sections, and the many fake personas (like "Shelly Linx" and "Katie Jo") she used in emails and texts to prop up her lies. The forged documents for land purchases and the bizarre email purportedly from her "dead" mother were presented, showing the jury just how far Taylor would go to weave deception.

Crucially, a fellow inmate from jail testified that Taylor had confided in her, admitting details of the crime that only the killer would know. This inmate relayed the chilling moment Taylor described holding the newborn up to Reagan's face and saying, "Tell mama bye." The medical examiner and a crime scene reconstruction expert provided the graphic details of Reagan's injuries, confirming the brutality of the attack and debunking any notion that this was an altruistic "rescue surgery." They found, for instance, the tip of that small scalpel blade still embedded in Reagan's neck during the autopsy, indicating the ferocity of the stabbing. The prosecution painted Taylor as a calculating, remorseless liar who murdered out of selfishness and greed.

Taylor's defense attorneys had an almost impossible task. The evidence of guilt was overwhelming, so their focus shifted to the penalty phase, trying to save Taylor from a death sentence. They portrayed Taylor as a deeply "flawed and unwell" individual. They brought up mental health counselors who had seen Taylor in the past. One counselor testified that Taylor had come to her claiming trauma from medical issues like multiple sclerosis and even a stroke – all illnesses that prosecutors demonstrated Taylor never actually had. The counselor admitted she was shocked to learn what Taylor had done, saying she never saw any signs that Parker was violent or lying during therapy. Another jail counselor testified that Taylor seemed to thrive in the structured environment of prison, manipulating other inmates and even guards to her advantage, and notably never once expressing remorse for her actions. This hinted at a personality profoundly bent on control and devoid of empathy.

By early October 2022, the jury had heard it all. They deliberated on the guilt phase for only about 90 minutes, an astonishingly short time for a capital murder case, before returning a unanimous verdict: Guilty on all counts. Taylor Parker was convicted of capital murder for Reagan's death (which in Texas encompassed the baby's death as an aggravating factor), as well as the lesser charges related to the baby. The trial then moved to the sentencing phase, where the same jury would decide whether Taylor should face the death penalty or life in prison without parole.

Prosecutors argued that the heinousness of the crime, combined with Taylor's manipulative, deceitful nature, warranted the death penalty. They emphasized how much planning and cold calculation went into every step. This was not a crime of passion or opportunity, but a premeditated slaughter of a young mother for personal gain. Taylor's defense pleaded for her life, citing her mental health issues, alleged past abuse, and the fact that she had family (two children from her first marriage) who might still want to know their mother was alive. The jury weighed these factors for several days.

On November 9, 2022, the jury delivered its decision. They chose the ultimate punishment. Taylor Parker was sentenced to death by lethal injection. As the judge formally pronounced the sentence, he ordered, "You can remove her and take her to death row," keen to swiftly enforce the jury's verdict. Taylor, at 29 years old, became one of only a handful of women on Texas's death row.

During the sentencing hearing, Reagan's family had the opportunity to deliver victim impact statements, addressing the woman who had so monstrously harmed them. Reagan's mother, Jessica, spoke through tears and fury directly to Taylor. In a voice shaking with emotion, she said: "My baby was alive, still fighting for her baby, when you tore her open and ripped her baby from her stomach. All of this in front of her little girl. You're an evil piece of flesh. A demon. You watched her die. You did not care about Braxlynn, either, spending so much time making sure you would not get caught. We all know you think this is about you. But Reagan was one of the very few people on this Earth that cared about you. So, every time you think to yourself, 'Oh, poor me, nobody cares about me,' know that's the truth." Jessica went on to vow that while she would not let Taylor consume her thoughts, she would make sure the world never forgets the evil that was done to her daughter and granddaughter. "I will continue to remind people – the world – how evil you are for the rest of your life, however short that may be," she said coldly. "But only if I hear mention of your name. Otherwise, I will not speak of you. Only of my beautiful baby girl, Reagan, and grandbaby, Braxlynn, who were a light God will continue to use in this dark world. You took their breath, but you did not get their beauty and light that will shine for years to come."

Tellingly, none of Taylor's own family members showed up at her sentencing hearing to support or speak on her behalf. Not her mother (who, despite the lies, was very much alive), not her father, not any sibling or relative. Taylor had burned every bridge; she stood utterly alone, facing the consequences of her actions.

Taylor Parker now sits on Texas's death row, awaiting the lengthy appeals process that accompanies any capital case. She will likely spend years in prison as her case is reviewed by higher courts, but the odds of overturning such a rock-solid verdict are slim. In prison, by some accounts, Taylor continues to manipulate those around her; a testament to the ingrained pathology that drove her for much of her life. She is a woman who lied and schemed habitually, with no evident remorse. Psychologists who have studied the case suggest Taylor Parker exhibits traits of a pathological liar and a narcissistic, manipulative personality. Even in incarceration, she has tried to bend reality to her will, though her world now is reduced to concrete walls and steel bars.

The story of Taylor Parker is a cautionary tale of how a desperate desire for acceptance and love can spiral into delusion and violence. Taylor was so intent on creating a life she could be proud of complete with a loving partner, financial status, and a baby that she didn't care who she hurt, manipulated, or even killed along the way to make her lies a reality. Each lie she told was like a stepping stone leading her further into darkness, until finally there were no more lies that could save her, only horrific action.

For the community of New Boston and the families involved, the scars will never fully heal. The Hancock family had to bury a beloved daughter and the infant grandbaby who never got to take a first breath in the world. Kynlee will grow up cherished by her father and grandparents, but without the mother and baby sister who were stolen from her. Wade Griffin had to face bankruptcy and the wreckage of a life built with someone who never truly existed; he, too, was a victim, left with emotional trauma and financial ruin. Taylor's own two children were also victims of her deceit. They have had to learn that their mother committed an atrocity, and they will live with that legacy and absence.

In the end, Taylor Parker's story serves as a grim reminder of the depths of human deceit and the horrifying extreme of fetal abduction; a crime so rare and appalling that it captures headlines and haunts the public consciousness. Taylor's lies caught up with her in the most tragic way possible. Now, as she sits on death row, she has all the time in the world to contemplate the carnage she caused. But if the testimonies are true, Taylor Parker feels little genuine remorse. Her story, however, will not be remembered for the fantasy life she tried to create. It will be remembered for the real lives she destroyed and for the truth, finally revealed, that put an end to her deadly deceit.

THE LULULEMON MURDER

Brittany Norwood

Shortly before opening time on Saturday, March 12, 2011, store manager Rachel Oertli arrived at the Lululemon Athletica in Bethesda, Maryland and immediately sensed something was wrong. The front door, which should have been locked overnight, was ajar. Inside, the upscale yoga apparel boutique was a wreck. Merchandise was scattered, hangers and mannequins knocked over, and every cash register lay open and emptied. As Rachel cautiously stepped in, the lights were blazing and she could hear a faint, distressing moan from the back of the store. Fearing intruders might still be inside, she backed out and rushed to find help.

Outside, a line had already formed next door at the Apple Store for a new product launch. Rachel spotted a young man in line, 27-year-old Ryan Haugh, and urgently asked if he would accompany her inside, explaining that something terrible had happened. Ryan agreed without hesitation. Together they re-entered the

Lululemon store, Rachel holding back while Ryan moved further into the dim interior, following a trail of bloody shoe prints leading toward the employees' area.

Nearing the back hallway, Ryan was met with a scene of unfathomable violence. On the floor lay the lifeless body of a woman face-down in a huge pool of blood. A length of rope was cinched tightly around her neck. Her face was so savagely beaten that Ryan could not even recognize her features, only her long dark hair and clothing suggested the victim was female. Shocked, he turned to call out to Rachel that someone was dead but then he heard a soft whimpering nearby.

Following the sound into a bathroom, Ryan discovered a second woman collapsed on the tile floor, alive but in agony. She was bound hand and foot with plastic zip-ties and covered in blood. Her yoga pants were blood-soaked and curiously slit open at the crotch, as if cut by a blade. Cuts and gashes crisscrossed her arms and abdomen, and a bleeding laceration split her forehead. Though injured, this woman was breathing and semi-conscious, moaning in pain. Ryan shouted for Rachel to call 911 and tell them an ambulance was needed immediately.

Only then did Rachel realize with horror that the two victims were her own employees – 30-year-old Jayna Murray and 28-year-old Brittany Norwood, who had closed the store together the night before. Minutes later, at 8:00am, Montgomery County police and paramedics arrived to a crime scene as perplexing as it was gruesome.

First responders found Jayna Murray face-down in a pool of blood, no pulse, clearly deceased. Brittany Norwood, the apparent survivor, was drifting in and out of consciousness, still bound by zip-ties around her wrists and ankles. Medics gently placed Brittany on a stretcher; she appeared battered but her wounds, though bloody, were not immediately life-threatening. She had a deep cut on her forehead and numerous shallow cuts and bruises. In chilling contrast, Jayna's injuries were obviously catastrophic. A clerk covering the body noted a metal merchandise bar lying nearby streaked with blood, and other makeshift weapons strewn about including a wrench, a hammer, a knife, even a jagged rock – all apparently used in a vicious attack. The sheer volume of blood spatter on walls and floor told investigators that whoever assaulted Jayna did so with unstoppable rage. Bloody shoeprints tracked through the store, appearing to come from two different pairs of shoes: one set was relatively small, possibly a woman's, but the other set was notably larger; size 14 men's sneakers, investigators estimated, from the dimensions of the prints. These larger prints wandered through the blood and then mysteriously stopped at a sink in the back with no trail leading out of the store. On the surface, it looked like two assailants, one possibly female, one male, had rampaged through the store during a robbery gone terribly wrong.

Police quickly secured the scene as a possible double-victim crime. Jayna's body was removed for autopsy, and Brittany Norwood was rushed to Suburban Hospital for treatment of her injuries. As detectives began collecting evidence, they noted more odd details. The store's safe had been opened and emptied of its bank deposits, and the cash drawers were indeed cleaned out, consistent with robbery. But aside from the money, nothing obvious seemed to be missing; pricey leggings and merchandise were still in the store (albeit scattered). Could the robbers really have inflicted such extreme violence over just the contents of a safe?

Meanwhile at the hospital, doctors examined Brittany Norwood. She had numerous cuts on her arms, chest, and legs, but most were relatively superficial, more like scratches than deep stab wounds. Only two wounds required stitches: the gash on her forehead and a cut on her right hand. She was badly bruised and understandably shaken. Notably, a sexual assault exam found no physical evidence of rape. Brittany's undergarments were intact, though her yoga pants had a long slit in the crotch area, suggestive of a staged sexual assault rather than a real one.

As detectives cautiously interviewed Brittany in her hospital bed, her account of the night before began to shine a light on the nightmare that had unfolded.

Through tears and obvious trauma, Brittany Norwood told investigators that the previous evening, Friday, March 11, 2011, she and Jayna Murray had closed the Lululemon store together around 9:45 pm. They left the shop at the same time. Jayna headed to her car, and Brittany began walking to the nearby Metro station for her commute home. But a few minutes later, Brittany realized she had left her wallet (containing her Metro transit card) back at the store. It was nearly 10:00 pm and she didn't have the store keys or Jayna's phone number. Desperate not to be stranded, Brittany said she phoned another co-worker and eventually reached Rachel, the store manager, who provided Jayna's cell number. Brittany called, and Jayna, being a helpful colleague and friend, offered to meet her back at the store to let her in and retrieve the forgotten wallet.

According to Brittany, Jayna soon returned and parked right out front. The two young women went back inside the closed store around 10:05 pm, a timestamp later confirmed by the store's alarm records. They found Brittany's wallet, chatted briefly, and were preparing to leave again when, as Brittany described it, ambush struck.

Brittany recounted in harrowing detail how two strange men suddenly slipped in through the unlocked front door behind them. She described the attackers as two men dressed entirely in black, wearing gloves and ski masks. One was taller than the other, and one carried a backpack. Before the women could react, the men pounced. One grabbed Jayna and the other grabbed Brittany. Brittany claimed she saw Jayna get smashed over the head with something, dropping her to the floor unconscious, while Brittany herself was dragged by her hair to the back bathroom by the second assailant.

In the darkness, Brittany said, she mostly heard the horror unfolding: the sickening thuds and Jayna's high-pitched screams echoing from the next room as Jayna was beaten mercilessly. Brittany told police her own attacker began taunting and torturing her. He produced a utility knife or razor, she said, and slashed at her clothing and stomach. She recalled him hurling racist and misogynistic slurs at her and though she admitted she never clearly saw his face or skin, she "felt" he was a white male from his voice and the insults he used. In a chilling allegation, Brittany said this man then sexually assaulted her: first raping her, and then violating her with a wooden clothes hanger from the store's racks. She was sobbing as she told detectives how utterly helpless and terrified she felt, hearing Jayna pleading for her life outside the bathroom door. "Talk to me. Don't do this… What's going on?" followed by Jayna's screams for help and cries of "God help me… please help me!"

After what felt like an eternity, the store fell eerily quiet. Brittany said the two attackers then regrouped, breathing hard from exertion. They allegedly dumped Jayna's limp body in the hallway and, in a final act of cruelty, threw Brittany on top of her friend's bloodied corpse, telling Brittany that they were sparing her life only because she was "more fun to fuck". With that obscene remark, the intruders reportedly used zip-ties to hogtie Brittany's wrists and ankles, then left her on the bathroom floor, bleeding but alive. Brittany remembered the men rifling through the cash registers and safe on their way out. Then they were gone, disappearing into the night and leaving the store in silence.

Brittany wept as she expressed guilt to detectives: if only she hadn't forgotten her wallet, Jayna would still be alive. The police were sympathetic. This was an unimaginably traumatic ordeal for the young woman. For the moment, they treated Brittany as a victim and primary witness. Montgomery County detectives immediately launched a manhunt for two unknown male perpetrators, driven by Brittany's detailed description of the savage "robbery." The Bethesda community, upon hearing news of the attack, was gripped by fear that violent predators were on the loose.

As Brittany recovered in the hospital that weekend, investigators worked around the clock to corroborate her story and catch the supposed killers. Initially, there were a few leads. Surveillance cameras at the Apple Store next door had captured two men dressed in black walking by on Bethesda Avenue around the relevant time on Friday night. One taller, one shorter, one carrying a backpack. The footage didn't show their faces, but it fit Brittany's description closely enough that police released the images to the public, hoping for tips. The local news flashed headlines about a shocking attack at the high-end yoga shop, urging anyone with information about the two mystery men to come forward. For a brief moment, it seemed the case might break quickly.

That hope faded when detectives actually tracked down the men from the video within days. They turned out to be two restaurant workers walking home from their shift, still in their black server uniforms, and they had solid alibis. They were not involved. Another early angle involved a local homeless man who frequented the area; police questioned him as a person of interest, but he was soon cleared of any connection. With those leads dead-ended, investigators were left with the evidence inside the store itself. But some of it was not lining up neatly with Brittany Norwood's account.

Crime scene technicians had noted the unusual bloody shoe prints at the scene. One set was small and likely came from one of the women's own shoes. The other set, however, was from a pair of men's size 14 sneakers, suggesting an unidentified male intruder. But in scouring the store, technicians actually found that very pair of size-14 shoes tucked away in a Lululemon stockroom. They were Reebok cross-trainers kept in the store for customers to wear while trying on hemmed pants. The soles perfectly matched the bloody footprints. This was a major red flag: why would outside attackers take the time to don a pair of the store's spare shoes during the assault, then leave them behind? Detectives began to wonder if the crime scene had been deliberately staged. A forensic specialist examining the pattern of the prints had another keen observation. The smaller shoe prints (presumed to be Jayna's or Brittany's) always underlay the larger prints. Not once did a big shoe print overlap a small one. It looked as if the person leaving those large sneaker prints had walked through the blood after the smaller prints were already there. In other words, one person could have made both sets of tracks, at different times.

Other evidence strained the credibility of Brittany's story. The binding on Brittany's wrists raised eyebrows: the ends of the plastic zip-ties had human teeth marks on them, as if bitten and pulled tight by the person wearing them. It appeared Brittany might have actually bound herself. And while Brittany's leggings had been cut open, her medical exam showed no signs of sexual assault. Even Brittany's own injuries were telling: they were relatively minor and concentrated in places she could reach on her own body (like the scratches on her abdomen). She had no defensive wounds on her arms or hands except a single cut on one hand; unusual if two men had attacked her with weapons. In stark contrast, Jayna Murray's injuries were utterly devastating. When the medical examiner's report came in, detectives were stunned. Jayna had sustained at least 331 separate wounds including cuts, stabs, and blunt-force traumas from head to toe. In one horrific tally, over 100 of those wounds were identified as defensive injuries to her hands and arms, meaning Jayna had fought desperately for her life. Her skull had been fractured repeatedly with one blow so savage it essentially severed her spinal cord, which was likely the final, fatal strike. Dr. Mary Ripple, the deputy chief medical examiner, later testified that Jayna was alive through nearly the entire attack, bleeding and conscious as hundreds of wounds were inflicted. "She had a pulse, she had blood pressure, she was bleeding into the wounds. She was alive," Dr. Ripple emphasized on the stand. Such prolonged torture was hardly consistent with a quick-hit robbery by panicked thieves. It spoke to a sustained, personal rage.

Detectives were now looking at the supposed victim Brittany Norwood in a very different light. The more they analyzed, the more the puzzle pieces pointed inward. For one, Brittany's timeline had a glaring hole: Jayna's missing car. Brittany had told police that Jayna parked directly out front when returning to the store that night. But when officers looked for

Jayna's vehicle after the crime, it was nowhere on Bethesda Avenue. Brittany herself expressed surprise that Jayna's car was gone suggesting maybe the assailants had stolen it as a getaway car. In fact, an observant patrol officer recalled seeing an unattended car with out-of-state plates left in a nearby parking lot around midnight on March 11, just a couple hours after the presumed time of the attack. Sure enough, police found Jayna's silver Pontiac Coupe in that lot, three blocks from the Lululemon store. Inside Jayna's car they found traces of blood on the steering wheel and interior. Further testing determined the blood to be a mix of Jayna's and Brittany's blood. Even more damning, investigators found a Lululemon-branded cap in the car with a bloodstain on the inside forehead band. The blood matched Brittany Norwood's head wound. This indicated that Brittany had been inside Jayna's car after the bloodshed. When confronted with this evidence, Brittany suddenly "remembered" a new detail: she now claimed that the masked men had forced her at knifepoint to move Jayna's car for them, threatening to kill her if she didn't return within 10 minutes. In this newly minted story, Brittany said she even walked past a police officer while moving the car but was too afraid to say a word. The detectives couldn't believe what they were hearing. Brittany's story was literally changing by the day, growing more convoluted and implausible.

Then came the revelations about Brittany's motive. As suspicion mounted, police quietly dug into Brittany Norwood's background and character. Co-workers and friends painted a picture of a charming, athletic woman and also a compulsive thief and liar. Former roommates and teammates recounted how Brittany had a habit of things going missing around her: jewelry, cash, personal items swiped from purses and gym bags. At a previous Lululemon store where she worked, Brittany had been let go for suspected theft. In fact, at the Bethesda branch, she'd only been employed for about six weeks, and already managers had raised concerns. Employees quietly suspected Brittany of stealing merchandise and money from lockers, and the team had implemented bag checks at closing time to curb the losses. The night of March 11, that very policy may have set tragedy in motion. As they closed up, Jayna believed she spotted a pair of expensive yoga pants in Brittany's bag that hadn't been paid for. When Jayna asked to inspect the bag, Brittany allegedly protested that another employee had already checked her, dropping a co-worker's name. Jayna double-checked with that employee and found the claim was a lie. No one had verified Brittany's bag. Jayna reported her suspicions to the store manager by phone after leaving that night. The manager told Jayna they would deal with it the next morning. Brittany likely realized that Jayna had caught her and informed management. She was about to be exposed and fired.

Within minutes, Brittany made the fateful call asking Jayna to return to the store, luring her kind-hearted colleague into a deadly trap. Investigators theorized that once Jayna was back inside, Brittany confronted her in a fury, perhaps begging her not to tell, perhaps enraged that Jayna hadn't let the matter slide. A violent argument erupted. Brittany snapped and attacked Jayna with whatever objects she could grab. The evidence showed at least five to eight different weapons were used in the assault, including a wrench, a hammer, a metal merchandise peg, a box cutter, a knife, and a length of rope used as a garrote. At some point Jayna tried to flee toward the employee entrance, leaving a trail of blood behind her, but Brittany overtook her before she could escape the back door. For an agonizing 15 to 20 minutes or more, Brittany mercilessly beat, stabbed, and slashed Jayna, who remained alive and conscious, fighting back with her bare hands until the very end. "Think about how long this took. Jayna is alive through almost all of this," prosecutor John McCarthy later told the court, highlighting that Jayna suffered dozens of wounds even after trying to crawl away. "This was not slow. This was not painless. This woman struggled to survive."

When Jayna finally lay dead, Brittany faced the aftermath of what she had done. In a whirlwind of panic and calculation, she staged the crime scene to support a fictional tale of masked intruders. She dragged Jayna's body to the back hallway and tied a rope around her neck to suggest strangulation by attackers. She changed shoes, putting on the men's size 14 Reeboks and tracking footprints through Jayna's blood to mislead investigators. She deliberately overturned merchandise and left the cash registers gaping, then even opened the safe and removed cash bags to simulate a robbery. Brittany then took Jayna's keys, drove Jayna's car a few blocks away to get it out of sight, and returned to the store on foot. In the final touch, she used a razor blade or knife on herself: cutting her forehead and slicing shallowly at her limbs to create the appearance of injuries, and cutting open her own pants to fabricate the sexual assault. She tightly zip-tied her wrists and ankles (using her teeth to pull the ties closed), smeared herself with Jayna's blood, then lay down in the bathroom and waited. Brittany Norwood spent the rest of that long, dark night on the floor, feigning unconsciousness until morning light when her manager would discover the carnage and cast Brittany once more in the role of "victim."

By the time police had assembled this narrative from the evidence, their initial sympathy for Brittany had evaporated. One week after the murder, on March 18, 2011, detectives invited Brittany to the station under the pretense of clarifying her statement. Brittany arrived, perhaps sensing suspicion, and grew defensive as investigators methodically laid out the mountain of contradictions in her story. Finally, they confronted her directly: We know you did this, Brittany. The 28-year-old shook her head and simply asked, "Can I go home now?". It was the same flat denial she'd maintained even when her own brother and sister, brought into the interrogation room, begged her to tell the truth. Brittany refused to confess. But the evidence spoke loudly enough. She was placed under arrest and charged with first-degree murder for the slaying of Jayna Murray, the co-worker she had so cunningly tried to frame as a fellow victim.

The Bethesda community was stunned. For a week, everyone had feared that crazed killers were on the loose. Jayna's family had even felt a degree of sympathy for Brittany Norwood, the young woman who survived the "attack". They even thought to send her flowers while she was in the hospital. Now the truth was out: there never were any masked men. The brutal murderer had been among them at the candlelight vigil. The sense of betrayal was palpable. "The woman portrayed as the brave survivor… never existed," one journalist noted. Brittany Norwood had fooled them all.

Brittany's trial began in late October 2011 at Montgomery County Circuit Court, drawing intense media attention. Prosecutors presented a chillingly comprehensive case, using forensic experts, surveillance timestamps, and witness testimony to methodically dismantle Brittany's lies. They even brought in the Apple Store employees who shamefully admitted they had heard the assault through the wall that night but wrote off the screams and thuds as "just drama". Judge Robert Greenberg would later rebuke those Apple staff for their "callous indifference" in failing to call police. The centerpiece of the state's case was the sheer barbarity of Jayna's injuries and the elaborate cover-up. Jurors saw graphic photos of the blood-soaked scene and the array of improvised weapons used. Montgomery County State's Attorney John McCarthy argued that the duration and savagery of the attack proved premeditation: Brittany had ample time to reconsider as she rained blows on Jayna, but instead she chose to escalate the violence and then carefully stage a false crime scene.

In a notable strategy, Brittany Norwood's own defense team conceded that she was the killer, hoping honesty might win some measure of leniency. Defense attorney Douglas Wood admitted in his opening statement that "Jayna was killed by Brittany", but argued it happened in a sudden eruption of anger rather than a planned murder. "There was no premeditation. Brittany lost it. She lost control," Wood told the jury, describing the incident as a "horrific fight" that got out of hand. The defense urged a second-degree murder conviction, implying that Jayna's death was the result of momentary rage after a workplace argument about theft. They portrayed Brittany as a woman who snapped under pressure, not a cold-blooded monster.

But this argument faced an uphill battle against the forensic evidence. Prosecutors countered that nothing about the scene suggested a mere momentary lapse. This was a prolonged, calculated slaughter. In closing arguments, Prosecutor McCarthy enumerated Brittany's deliberate lies and actions: "Could you begin to even count the number of times she lied? It's almost impossible," he said of her intricate web of deceit. He reminded jurors that Brittany had "10 hours to make this scene look the way she wanted" after the murder; hardly the behavior of someone who "lost control" only momentarily. The evidence of staging and the ferocity of the attack, McCarthy argued, pointed to intent every step of the way. The jury saw through Brittany Norwood's final deception just as clearly as the detectives had.

On November 2, 2011, after only about an hour of deliberation, the jury returned a verdict of guilty of first-degree murder. It was a swift, decisive end to the question of Brittany's culpability. Juror Donny Knepper later told reporters that the evidence was "overwhelming" and left no doubts. In Maryland, first-degree murder carries a maximum of life in prison, and the state did not seek the death penalty in this case. The only remaining question was whether Brittany Norwood would ever have a chance of parole.

At the January 2012 sentencing hearing, Brittany Norwood faced Jayna Murray's family and a packed courtroom. She spoke publicly for the first time about the crime, offering an apology. "I know what I say today won't take the pain away… I am truly sorry," Brittany said haltingly, turning toward the Murrays. She begged the judge to give her "some hope" of eventually regaining freedom, asking for the possibility of parole after decades in prison. Jayna's family, however, remained unmoved. They had heard enough of Brittany Norwood's lies.

Judge Robert A. Greenberg delivered a scathing rebuke as he pronounced sentence. Looking Brittany straight in the eye, Judge Greenberg methodically recounted the brutality of her actions and the cold-blooded cover-up that followed. "On several different levels this case exemplified the worst of human behavior," he declared, condemning both Brittany's savagery and the neighboring Apple Store employees who heard the attack and "didn't do a blessed thing" to help. The judge even illustrated the length of the assault by pounding his fist on the bench 330 times. It took him eight minutes, driving home how long Jayna's suffering must have lasted. "After every blow, you had a chance to think about what you were doing," he admonished Brittany, emphasizing that each stab and strike was a conscious choice to continue. As for her elaborate deceit: "You are one hell of a liar, ma'am," Judge Greenberg said with contempt. In his view, a person capable of such manipulative brutality stood "very little chance of being rehabilitated".

In the end, the judge rejected any notion of mercy. He sentenced Brittany Norwood to life in prison without the possibility of parole. "You will live," Judge Greenberg told her. "You will see another sunrise, another sunset... There'll be Christmases, there'll be telephone calls, there'll be visits. The only visits Jayna Murray will have are those to her grave." With that, Brittany Norwood, at 29 years old, was led away to begin a lifetime behind bars. (Multiple appeals filed on her behalf were later denied, and her conviction stands.)

For the family and friends of Jayna Murray, the outcome provided some measure of justice, but little solace. Jayna had been a vibrant, accomplished young woman on the cusp of a new chapter in life. Raised in Texas (after being born in Kansas), she was the beloved only daughter of Phyllis and David Murray. She had a contagious smile, excelled in athletics and academics, and embraced adventure; even bungee jumping over a waterfall to celebrate her 30th birthday. At the time of her death, Jayna was nearing completion of dual graduate degrees and had a serious boyfriend, Fraser, who had quietly begun shopping for an engagement ring with plans to propose. All of those hopes were annihilated in one night of senseless violence. Jayna's mother later described the grief as "a pain that ripped through our bodies… like a lightning strike". In a letter to the court, Phyllis Murray wrote of her daughter's killer: "This individual must be removed from society forever." And so she was.

On June 24, 2011, three months after the murder, the Lululemon store in Bethesda reopened its doors, transformed by renovation and bearing a beautiful tribute to Jayna. Above the entrance, a colorful stained-glass mosaic with the word "Love" was installed in her honor. The memorial was later gifted to the Murray family, but while it graced the shop it reminded every visitor of the compassionate soul lost from their community. To this day, those who knew and loved Jayna Murray celebrate her life and spirit. Friends recall her passion for dance and travel, her warmth and generosity. Strangers, too, have come to leave flowers and notes, paying respects at the site of the tragedy. The story of the Lululemon murder remains one of the most shocking crimes the Washington, D.C. area has ever seen and a cautionary tale of deception and lethal greed behind a polished façade. In the end, Brittany Norwood now lives out her days in prison as one of the very wicked women she once tried so hard to pretend she wasn't. And Jayna Troxel Murray's memory lives on as more than a victim of a wicked act but as a cherished daughter, sister, and friend whose vibrant legacy will not be forgotten.

STAGE FIVE CLINGER

Shayna Hubers

Shayna Michelle Hubers was born on April 8, 1991, and grew up in Lexington, Kentucky. By all accounts, she was a bright and driven young woman. In high school, Shayna was an honor student and was known to be highly intelligent. In fact, one psychologist later noted she had a "superior" IQ. Her friends and family saw her as hardworking and personable. Shayna's mother, Sharon, was a school teacher and her father, Michael, was a carpenter. They raised her in a strict, religious household, instilling traditional values and a strong work ethic. As a child and teenager, Shayna excelled academically and participated in school activities. However, behind her achievements, there were signs of emotional turbulence that few knew about.

In her late teens, Shayna reportedly experienced trauma that would later be cited in her defense. She was allegedly sexually assaulted during high school, though she never reported it at the time. Whether or not this event occurred as described, it suggests that Shayna carried unseen emotional scars into adulthood. Despite any private struggles, she pushed forward with her education. After high school, Shayna attended the University of Kentucky in Lexington, where she majored in psychology and graduated cum laude. By age 21, she was pursuing a master's degree in school counseling, striving for a career where she could help guide young students. Those around her saw a motivated, successful student with a bright future.

Beneath the surface, though, Shayna could be very emotionally intense. Friends would later describe her as extremely talkative, social, and even *clingy* in relationships. She had a deep fear of abandonment and craved love and validation. When Shayna fell for someone, she tended to fall hard. These traits didn't fully reveal themselves until she began her tumultuous relationship with a young attorney named Ryan Poston – a relationship that would ignite Shayna's most unstable impulses and ultimately turn deadly. Before delving into that volatile romance, it's important to understand who Ryan was and how his path crossed with Shayna's. Ryan Carter Poston was born on December 30, 1982, roughly nine years before Shayna, and was raised in Northern Kentucky. He came from an accomplished and affluent family. Ryan's mother, Lisa Carter, was warm and supportive, and his father, Jay Poston, was a successful businessman and a Fortune 500 advertising executive. After his parents separated, Ryan also grew close to his step-father, Peter Carter, and he became a protective big brother to his three younger half-sisters, Alison, Katherine, and Elizabeth.

Those who knew Ryan describe him as brilliant, kind-hearted, and a bit "nerdy" in the best way. He had a quick smile and a sharp mind. As a teenager, Ryan even attended prestigious international high schools due to his family's travels. He studied at the International School in Manila, Philippines, and later in Geneva, Switzerland. So, he developed a worldly perspective at a young age. For college, Ryan returned stateside and attended Indiana University, where he triple-majored in history, geography, and political science. His passion for learning was evident; he was the type of person who could debate politics one minute and crack a self-deprecating joke the next.

After college, Ryan pursued a career in law, driven by a strong sense of justice and a desire to help others. He earned his Juris Doctor at Northern Kentucky University's law school. By his late twenties, he was practicing as an attorney in Cincinnati, Ohio, just across the river from his Kentucky hometown. He worked in the same office building as a mentor and friend, attorney Ken Hawley, who shared Ryan's love of chess. In fact, Ryan was an avid chess player; his competitive matches with Ken would stretch over days, the board pieces left in place between sessions. This thoughtful, strategic hobby was a reflection of Ryan's personality: patient, intelligent, and calm.

Friends would later say that in over a decade of knowing him, they never saw a dark or violent side to Ryan. He was polite, gentle, and *"super nerdy, super sweet,"* as one longtime friend put it. He had a charming but unassuming demeanor. Tall and exceptionally handsome, with a winning smile, Ryan had no trouble meeting women, but he was ultimately looking for a genuine connection. By 2011, at age 28, he had a promising career and a stable life. What he didn't have was the right partner to share it with.

In the spring of 2011, fate – or rather, Facebook – brought Shayna Hubers and Ryan Poston together. Ryan was 28 and Shayna just 20 when their paths first crossed online. Ryan's cousin (by marriage) Carissa Carlisle was actually friends with Shayna, and through that connection, Ryan stumbled upon Shayna's Facebook profile. Her profile photo caught his eye. Shayna was young, pretty, and full of energy in pictures from a recent spring break trip. On a whim, Ryan sent Shayna a friend request and introduced himself. She accepted, and they began chatting casually through social media.

Before long, Ryan and Shayna decided to meet in person. Their first face-to-face meeting took place in Lexington, Kentucky (where Shayna was in school) sometime in April 2011. According to later accounts, this initial meet-up was brief. They "talked some" and then went their separate ways that day. Yet, there was enough chemistry that they met again shortly afterward. The second time they got together, Ryan ended up spending the night with Shayna, marking the unofficial start of their romance.

At the beginning, the attraction between the two was strong. Ryan was taken by Shayna's intelligence and vivacious personality. She was not only beautiful but also one of the top students in her class, and they could engage in lively conversations. Shayna, for her part, was smitten with Ryan. Here was an older, handsome, and successful lawyer showing interest in her. He was charming, attentive, and came from the kind of successful family that impressed Shayna. On the surface, they *"looked good together,"* as one account later put it. In photos from that period, they indeed appeared to be a picture-perfect couple: Ryan with his confident smile and suit jackets, Shayna with her bright eyes and polished look.

However, even in those early days, there were hints that this relationship might be less than ideal. Despite their affectionate moments, Ryan was not as "all-in" as Shayna was. He enjoyed Shayna's company but also valued his independence. He was nearly 30, established in his career, while she was barely out of her teens and still in college. To put it simply, they were at different stages in life and small red flags began to emerge. Shayna could be intense and clingy, wanting to spend every moment with Ryan, whereas Ryan sometimes pulled back. Nevertheless, through mid-2011, things were mostly happy. They texted frequently and saw each other when they could, given the 80-mile distance between Lexington and Ryan's home in Highland Heights, KY. Friends observed that Shayna sent *far more* texts to Ryan than he sent to her, which hinted at who was more invested, but in those first months it didn't seem like a serious issue.

As 2011 turned into 2012, Ryan and Shayna's relationship became a rollercoaster of passionate highs and explosive lows. They were on-again, off-again multiple times in the roughly 18 months they dated. Friends and family recall the relationship as *"tumultuous"*. One week they'd be inseparable; the next, Ryan would be trying to break things off, only to reconcile with Shayna after she pleaded with him to stay. This cycle would repeat over and over.

Looking back, there were numerous red flags. One major incident occurred in April 2012, about a year into their courtship. Shayna had heard that Ryan had been saying unkind things about her to others, calling her names behind her back. She confronted Ryan about these "degrading" comments, and the fight escalated dramatically. According to Shayna (who later testified about this event), Ryan lost his temper and became physically violent: he allegedly picked her up and threw her out the door of his condo, then slammed the door against her body as she tried to re-enter to grab her belongings. Shayna claimed she was bruised and shaken by this altercation. If true, this was a shocking escalation. But importantly, this account comes from Shayna herself. At the time, no police report was filed, and Ryan's friends never saw evidence of injuries. This incident does, however, align with a pattern in Shayna's later stories: she would portray Ryan as abusive, while Ryan's circle would insist they never knew him to be violent. The truth of that April 2012 fight remains contested, but it set the stage for an even more toxic dynamic going forward.

After that blow-out in April, Ryan and Shayna broke up for a while. In fact, there was a stretch between April and July 2012 where they were apart. Ryan seemed intent on freeing himself from the drama. During that break, he tried to move on but Shayna wasn't going to let go so easily. In July 2012, the couple reconciled yet again. But when they got back together this time, Ryan tried to lay down some *ground rules*, reflecting his frustrations from the past year. According to Shayna's later testimony, Ryan placed "conditions" on her if they were to continue dating :

- She needed to talk less around him. He told her to cut her talking by about 25% because her constant chatter annoyed him.
- He insisted she find a hobby to keep herself occupied whenever she stayed at his condo, rather than focusing all her attention on him.
- Disturbingly, Shayna claimed Ryan pressured her to participate in threesomes or sexual encounters with other women, essentially demanding she engage in sexual acts involving additional partners.

If these assertions are true, it paints Ryan as controlling and insensitive. Indeed, Shayna told friends that Ryan would criticize her frequently. In public, he sometimes made fun of her eating habits or her appearance, which was humiliating for her. He also told her she needed to lose weight and even suggested she get cosmetic enhancements like a breast augmentation or a facelift. By Shayna's account, Ryan was very focused on looks and would comment on her body in ways that hurt her self-esteem. She was so desperate to please him that she underwent an unusual procedure known as a "G-shot" (an injection intended to enhance a woman's sexual experience) after Ryan expressed frustration that she could not orgasm with him. Shayna hoped this would make him happier in their sex life. These details, shared later by the defense, reveal how far Shayna was willing to go to try to satisfy Ryan. But again, these accounts are all from Shayna, and Shayna alone.

From Ryan's perspective, as related to his friends, he felt smothered by Shayna. He found her behavior increasingly erratic. She would show up unannounced at his condo in Highland Heights after driving 80 miles, sometimes letting herself in with a spare key she had, even when he wasn't home. If Ryan ignored her texts, Shayna would bombard him with dozens more. His coworkers observed that Shayna would call his office receptionist if he didn't answer his cell, just to track him down. "It was relentless," said Lori Zimmerman, who worked in the same building. Shayna simply could not tolerate being out of contact with Ryan. Attorney Ken Hawley, Ryan's friend and mentor, recalled that Shayna might send Ryan *50 to 100 text messages in a day* when she was upset. She would essentially wear him down. Eventually, "he would say, 'OK, Shayna,'" giving in to see her because it was easier than continuing to resist. Ryan's loved ones saw this as a toxic dynamic: he was too compassionate (or perhaps too conflict-averse) to firmly cut ties with Shayna, and she exploited that to keep pulling him back.

Carissa Carlisle (the mutual friend who introduced them) had a front-row seat to the drama as well. Carissa later testified that Ryan "repeatedly tried to end the relationship" but struggled to do so because he hated to hurt Shayna's feelings. Each time he'd attempt a breakup, Shayna would blow up his phone with apologies, declarations of love, or even anger. She would also physically appear wherever Ryan was, refusing to let the breakup stand. According to Carissa, Shayna's post-breakup behavior was, as she phrased it, *"restraining order level crazy"*. That is to say, Shayna's obsessive persistence after each breakup was extreme enough that most people would consider getting a restraining order. In fact, about two weeks before his death, Ryan walked into his office looking upset and confided to a receptionist, *"How do you break up with someone that doesn't want to break up with you?"* He even asked her how one would go about filing for a restraining order, indicating he was seriously contemplating it.

Shayna's jealousy was another volatile element in the relationship. She distrusted Ryan and would snoop to catch him talking to other women. In one incident, while staying at her friend Carissa's apartment, Shayna *stole Carissa's phone* because she suspected Carissa might be communicating with Ryan behind her back. "Please, Shayna, don't take my phone," Carissa begged when she realized what happened. But Shayna had already slipped out with it. Using Carissa's phone, Shayna managed to read private conversations between Carissa and Ryan. In those messages, Ryan confided to Carissa that things with Shayna *"weren't supposed to happen"* and that *"he never meant to hurt her"*, implying he regretted getting so entangled with Shayna. Learning this likely infuriated Shayna and only intensified her fear of losing him.

Shayna also went to creative lengths to

keep tabs on Ryan. She made fake accounts and phone numbers to contact him. In May 2012, she bragged to Ryan in a text that she had obtained an out-of-state phone number so she could reach him even when he was avoiding her; she admitted she did it because she knew he wouldn't answer if he realized it was her. Another time, on October 1, 2012, just days before the fateful night, Shayna used a friend's cell phone to pose as a potential client seeking Ryan's legal services, just to get him to respond. Once he replied, thinking it was a client, she revealed it was actually her and sent him insulting messages, venting her hurt and anger. These were not the actions of a stable, trusting girlfriend; they were the acts of someone *obsessed* and afraid of being cast aside.

Perhaps the most disturbing red flags were Shayna's own statements about Ryan in the days leading up to his death. On October 1, 2012, that same day she tricked him with a fake text, Shayna also texted a friend about going to a shooting range with Ryan that evening. In that message she wrote, *"When I go to the shooting range with [Ryan] tonight, I want to turn around, shoot and kill him and play like it's an accident."* She half-jokingly (or not jokingly at all) fantasized about murdering him during target practice. In another text to a friend, she admitted *"a part of me wanted to turn around and shoot him"* at the range. Other messages from that period showed her swinging between love and hate, saying things like *"my love has turned to hate"* and *"I hate him."*. She even messaged a friend who was a dentist and, referring to Ryan's vanity about his appearance, wrote, *"[Ryan's] been begging me to ask you if you could do his veneers, but please 'F' them up and make him ugly so he'll never get another girl. I hate him.*". These communications reveal a chilling shift as Shayna was oscillating between desperate love and violent hatred.

There were even reports that just hours before the incident on October 12, Shayna made a frightening remark. While shopping at the mall that day, she allegedly told a store employee that she was going to kill her boyfriend. A sales clerk named Tara Filliater later testified that Shayna matter-of-factly said she was going to *"kill her boyfriend"* soon. This comment was apparently overheard and remembered once news of what Shayna did broke. In hindsight, it was a dire warning sign of what was to come.

For Ryan's part, as these red flags accumulated, he knew he was in a toxic situation and wanted out. He told a close friend shortly before October that he intended to break up with Shayna *face-to-face* soon, since all his prior attempts by text or "hints" hadn't worked. That friend believed Ryan was likely going to cut ties for good *the day he died*. Indeed, another colleague noticed that on Ryan's last day alive, he came into work looking unusually upbeat and relieved. He told her he had a date that night with another woman and smiled at the prospect of a fresh start. When the coworker asked if he had ended the relationship with Shayna, Ryan said they had broken up and he planned to tell Shayna he had a date. It was a risky move, but Ryan was trying to reclaim his life.

That new woman was Audrey Bolte, 2012's Miss Ohio USA winner. Ryan had met Audrey on Facebook as well, and they arranged to meet for drinks on Friday, October 12, 2012. Audrey later said she was genuinely looking forward to getting to know Ryan on that first date. Ryan no doubt saw this as a hopeful opportunity. Audrey was beautiful, outgoing, and completely uninvolved in the chaos that had consumed his life with Shayna. Unfortunately, Shayna got wind of Ryan's plans. The prospect of losing Ryan to another woman was unthinkable for her. As prosecutor Michelle Snodgrass would later put it, *"losing him was not an option"* in Shayna's mind. The stage was set for a tragic confrontation.

Friday, October 12, 2012, began with tension already in the air. The night before, Ryan and Shayna had been together and it hadn't gone well. In fact, on Thursday night (October 11), they had one of their classic blow-up fights – possibly the worst one yet. They went to a dinner event with Ryan's parents, which perhaps gave Shayna hope that their relationship was on solid ground, but afterward an argument erupted. That night, Ryan reportedly *"lit into"* Shayna about the differences between their families, essentially belittling her background, saying cruel things about her mother, her education, "where she's from, her appearance". The class difference had always been a sore spot (Ryan's family was wealthy and prominent; Shayna's was middle-class and modest), and now he allegedly used it as ammunition in a drunken tirade. Yet, despite this nasty argument, the two ended up having sex later that night. It was an unhealthy pattern: conflict followed by intimacy, leaving Shayna feeling more confused than ever about where she stood.

In the early morning hours of October 12, after that volatile night, Shayna experienced something like a panic attack. She woke up with chest pains and a terrible sense of foreboding. Frightened, she did something very out of character. She called her mother in the middle of the night for help. This was unprecedented; Shayna normally wouldn't involve her mom in her relationship drama at that hour. Sensing her daughter's distress, Sharon Hubers drove over to Ryan's condo to pick Shayna up. Shayna left Ryan's condo (with Ryan still asleep or cooling off from the fight) and went back to her parents' home to rest. She spent most of Friday with her mother, who later said she had "an awful, foreboding feeling" about Shayna going back to see Ryan.

However, by the evening of October 12, Shayna did return to Ryan's condominium in Highland Heights. Accounts differ on whether Ryan invited her or whether she came on her own. Given that Ryan had a date scheduled for 9:30 PM with Audrey, it's likely Shayna insisted on coming over, possibly under the pretense of "talking things out" or picking up some belongings. What we do know is that Shayna was at Ryan's condo when he got home that evening after work. Ryan arrived at his apartment sometime after 8 PM, presumably intending to change clothes and head out to meet Audrey. Instead, he walked into another confrontation with Shayna.

According to Shayna's later statements, Ryan was in a "dark mood" as soon as he walked through the door that night. He was upset, likely because he truly wanted to break things off and get to his date, but Shayna's presence complicated everything. Shayna would later claim that Ryan snapped and began a final, vicious argument. He allegedly hurled a cascade of insults at her: calling her names, attacking her self-worth, saying she was crazy, mocking her family and her looks. "He was critical of everything there is to be critical of," defense attorney David Eldridge described it, channeling Shayna's version of events. Shayna said Ryan's eyes, normally a calm blue, appeared "completely black" with rage that night.

What happened next is a matter of dispute, with two starkly different narratives:

Shayna has maintained that Ryan became physically violent first. She says that as she tried to retreat into the bedroom to grab her things and leave, Ryan exploded in a fury. He allegedly grabbed her with both hands, lifted her up by her shoulders (or by her bra and pants, as she described), and literally threw her down in another room. She claims he was manhandling her, at one point falling on top of her with all his weight, yanking her hair and choking her. Shayna said she was genuinely terrified because she thought *"he was going to snap her neck"* as he dragged her around while she screamed. She described a chaotic fight: wrestling on the floor and then up on their feet again, with Ryan allegedly still attacking and shouting.

At some point during this melee, Shayna says they ended up near the dining table. She was on the floor, crying hysterically, and Ryan was looming over her, still enraged. Shayna attempted to stand up, but Ryan shoved her back down into the chair or floor. Then, according to Shayna, Ryan grabbed his 9mm handgun that was sitting on the dining table. He pointed the weapon directly at her and chillingly said that he could kill her and get away with it. In Shayna's telling, this was the breaking point. Ryan then put the gun down on the table momentarily as he perhaps repositioned himself or continued to yell. Shayna seized what she perceived as her one chance: she lunged for the gun on the table. Not sure if he was reaching to grab it again or possibly to grab her, Shayna picked up the firearm and opened fire.

She fired multiple shots at Ryan. The first hit caused Ryan to cry out in a way that sounded *"like an animal,"* according to Shayna. He fell to the floor. Shayna says he was still twitching and making noises, which "freaked her out". In a state of panic, she claims she then fired additional shots to "put him out of his misery." As she later bluntly told a 911 operator, *"He was twitching and I knew he was going to die anyway—and he was making funny noises—so I shot him a couple more times. He was twitching so bad, and I didn't want to watch him lay there and twitch."* In total, Shayna shot Ryan six times. She would even remark during interrogation that she *"gave him the nose job he wanted"* by shooting him in the face, since Ryan had supposedly been very vain about his nose.

After the gunfire stopped, Shayna says the condo fell silent with Ryan on the floor. She took a moment to collect herself. Instead of immediately dialing 911, the first person she called was her mother. Phone records later showed that Shayna placed not one but two calls to her mom in the moments after shooting Ryan. Only after speaking with her mother (who urged her, "It has to be self-defense," according to the defense's opening statement) did Shayna finally call 911. That 911 call came in at 8:53 PM, roughly 10-15 minutes after the shooting.

On the 911 call recording, Shayna's voice was frantic and breathy. She immediately declared that she had killed her boyfriend in self-defense. *"He beat me and tried to carry me out of the house,"* she told the dispatcher, *"and I came back in to get my things and he was right in front of me and he reached down and grabbed the gun and I grabbed it out of his hand and pulled the trigger."* In that moment, Shayna portrayed the situation as one where she wrestled the gun from Ryan's hand during a struggle and shot him. When asked how long ago this happened, she said, *"Not even that long – 10, 15 minutes ago."*. The dispatcher, sounding surprised, repeated *"10 or 15 minutes ago?"* and Shayna affirmed it. This admission that she waited so long to call for help struck responders as odd. As one police lieutenant later remarked, "Someone shooting someone and then waiting 15 minutes to call – that in itself was bizarre".

Despite Shayna's account of what happened, investigators would soon uncover a very different picture of what likely happened in that condo. Physical evidence and neighbor testimony contradicted key elements of Shayna's self-defense story. For starters, the two neighbors living directly below Ryan, an elderly couple named Vernon and Doris West, heard the gunshots and they distinctly remembered the pattern. They testified that they heard two shots, then a pause of several seconds (about 6 seconds), followed by four more shots. Vernon West even said he heard the sound of a body hitting the floor after the first two shots, before the final four were fired. Crucially, neither neighbor heard any shouting, screaming, or sounds of a struggle before the gunfire erupted. The apartment was otherwise quiet. This directly undercuts Shayna's claim of a prolonged loud fight leading up to the shooting. If Ryan had been throwing her into furniture and yelling, one would expect the downstairs neighbors to hear thumps or raised voices but they heard none of that.

Crime scene evidence further undermined Shayna's version. When police entered Ryan's condominium after 911 dispatch instructed Shayna to step outside with her hands visible, they found Ryan's body on the floor by the dining table. The scene was oddly calm: no furniture overturned, no broken items, no signs of a violent struggle. In fact, the living room was *orderly*, and dust on the furniture was undisturbed. Shayna had said Ryan threw her into the television, yet the TV was still in its place and coated with dust indicating it hadn't been hit or moved at all. She claimed he was reaching across the table for the gun, but items on the table hadn't even been knocked over. The only obvious disarray was whatever clutter Ryan normally had; his father later explained Ryan was a bit of a slob, so some mess was typical, but nothing suggested an altercation had occurred.

Moreover, when officers took Shayna into custody, they immediately checked her for injuries consistent with an assault. They found no visible wounds or bruises on her, except for a slight discoloration on one shin. There were no marks on her neck, no scratches, no signs that she had just been in a life-and-death brawl. If Ryan truly had slammed her against walls and yanked her hair, one would expect some physical evidence of it on her body. The absence of such evidence made police very skeptical of Shayna's self-defense claim from the start.

As detectives processed the scene, they noted Ryan's position. He had been shot six times and was found lying on his back near the table. He was unarmed; the handgun was on the floor. Later ballistic analysis and autopsy would reveal the trajectories of the bullets. As Highland Heights Police Chief Bill Birkenhauer described, Ryan was shot on pretty much every side of his body. His chest, back, arm, and face were all hit, almost as if Shayna had moved around while firing. In fact, prosecutor Kyle Burns would later assert that Shayna walked around the table to shoot Ryan again and again in locations that would ensure he died. The pattern of shots (two, then four after a pause) fits with Shayna shooting him, seeing him fall, and then circling the table to fire more rounds into his body to finish him off.

Back in the immediate aftermath, after officers secured the scene, Shayna was taken down to the Highland Heights police station for questioning. What unfolded in that interrogation room would soon become infamous.

On the night of October 12, 2012, just hours after Ryan's death, Shayna Hubers sat in a small police interrogation room, still wearing the clothes she had on during the shooting. The video recording of her three-hour interview with police would later shock everyone who watched it.

At first, Shayna appeared upset. She had been crying, and her eyes were red. Lt. David Fornash of the Highland Heights PD began by asking her basic questions. Shayna initially invoked her right to an attorney, saying she might want a lawyer present. The detectives halted any direct questioning at that point. However, in a rather unusual turn, Shayna soon began talking unprompted, waiving her earlier request. Once she started talking, it was as if a dam broke. Shayna talked, and talked, and talked. She seemingly could not stop herself from spewing out her version of events, along with many bizarre tangents.

During the interrogation, Shayna claimed repeatedly that she shot Ryan in self-defense because he was attacking her. She insisted that he had been *"throwing me around like a ragdoll"* in the moments before the shooting. She told the officers that Ryan was *"whacked on drugs,"* an assertion perhaps referencing the fact that Ryan did have a combination of prescription Xanax and Adderall in his system (to manage anxiety and ADHD). A toxicologist would later testify for the defense that such a mix could *potentially* cause aggression, but there was no evidence Ryan was out of control that night aside from Shayna's story. Shayna described Ryan as "evil" during the interrogation, at one point stating that he *"deserved it"* – a disturbing choice of words for someone claiming the killing was unintentional.

Crucially, as she recounted the shooting

to the detectives, Shayna began to incriminate herself further the more she spoke. She admitted that after the initial shots, Ryan was down but twitching, and she shot him again to put him out of his misery. *"He was twitching some more. I shot him a couple of more times just to make sure he was dead 'cause I didn't wanna watch him die,"* she explained matter-of-factly. The officers listening couldn't believe what they were hearing. This sounded less like self-defense and more like an execution. Chief Birkenhauer later noted, *"She didn't say that she was worried about him sufferin', she said that she couldn't stand to see that, is why she finished him off."*. As CBS correspondent Peter Van Sant astutely asked, if someone you love is wounded and twitching, wouldn't your instinct be to try to save them or call an ambulance, rather than shoot them again? *"Or call 911,"* the chief added pointedly.

Perhaps the most infamous moment came when Shayna nonchalantly quipped about Ryan's vanity. She told the officers that Ryan had always wanted a nose job and that by shooting him in the face, *"I gave him his nose job he wanted."*. This morbid joke stunned the police. Chief Birkenhauer's jaw "hit the floor" when he watched that clip as he thought, *"Did she really just say that?"*

And Shayna didn't stop there. When left alone in the interrogation room, she engaged in behavior so bizarre that it's hard to believe until you see the footage. Knowing she was alone (but being recorded), Shayna paced the room, occasionally dancing and twirling like a ballerina, even performing a little pirouette. She looked nothing like a woman traumatized by a life-or-death situation. At one point, she began singing "Amazing Grace" softly to herself. In another moment, she stood in front of the mirror and said aloud, *"I did it. Yes, I did it. I can't believe I did that,"* followed by *"I'm so good at acting."* The comment about acting especially struck investigators. Was she admitting that her sorrowful demeanor was all an act?

When Lt. Fornash eventually came back into the room to formally arrest her, he informed Shayna, *"I'm gonna have to charge you with murder."* Shayna, still oddly composed, simply asked, *"What degree?"* Lt. Fornash replied, *"Murder. There's no degree."* (In Kentucky, "murder" is a single charge; there's no first or second degree label at the charging stage). And with that, Shayna Hubers was booked for the murder of Ryan Poston.

Later, Prosecutor Snodgrass would reflect on that interrogation video, saying that while people react strangely to trauma, she'd never heard of someone dancing and literally snapping their fingers saying "I did it!" when in shock. To Snodgrass and the police, Shayna's behavior looked less like shock and more like an unremorseful performance by a person relieved that they'd finally done what they set out to do. The evidence gleaned from Shayna's own mouth that night would become a cornerstone of the prosecution's case against her.

With Shayna in custody, charged with murder, and held on a $5 million bond, attention turned to preparing for trial. The next two and a half years would see a slow path to justice, as both sides built their cases in what was shaping up to be one of Northern Kentucky's most dramatic murder trials in recent memory.

Shayna Hubers's first trial for the murder of Ryan Poston began on April 13, 2015, in Campbell County, Kentucky. By this time, Shayna had spent over two years in county jail awaiting trial, unable to afford the enormous bail set after her arrest. The case had attracted local media attention. A young, pretty graduate student charged with brutally killing a handsome young attorney made for salacious media coverage but Judge Fred Stine kept proceedings focused and professional.

Commonwealth's Attorney Michelle Snodgrass led the prosecution, joined by prosecutors Kyle Burns and others. From the outset, they painted a picture of Shayna Hubers as an obsessive, jealous girlfriend who refused to let Ryan go and who chose to eliminate him when he tried to leave her for good. In opening statements, Snodgrass and her team described Shayna as *"jealous, calculated, and manipulative"*. Kyle Burns told the jury, *"She wanted Ryan Poston... losing him was not an option."* The prosecutors emphasized that Ryan had not been abusing Shayna; rather, *"one thing Ryan was not was abusive"*, Burns said flatly. Instead, Ryan had often tried to appease Shayna and avoid conflict, effectively *placating* her to keep the peace.

The state's theory was simple: by October 2012, Ryan was determined to end the rocky relationship for good, and when Shayna realized he truly intended to break up and even worse, that he had a new date lined up, she became *"desperate"* and decided to kill him. They argued it was a conscious, intentional act, not a heat-of-the-moment defensive reaction.

Burns vividly recounted the events of the fatal night from their perspective: Ryan came home to get ready for his date with *"everything Shayna feared: tall, beautiful, and blonde"* (referring to Audrey). Shayna, unwilling to be cast aside, tried everything. *"She begged for food... she begged for sex"*, Burns said, attempting to distract or delay Ryan from leaving. She put on a guilt trip, cried, argued and when none of it worked, she "pulled the trigger". She shot Ryan, then walked around the table and kept shooting him as he lay wounded. *"She shot and killed Ryan Poston and played like it was self-defense,"* Burns told the jury pointedly.

To back up this narrative, the prosecution presented a wealth of evidence:

- **Text Messages**: They showed the jury numerous text messages that Shayna had sent in the weeks and days before the murder, demonstrating her obsession and increasing hostility. Notably, they introduced the October 1 text where Shayna said she wanted to *"turn around and shoot"* Ryan at the gun range and make it look like an accident. They also showed messages where Shayna's "love turned to hate" and she outright said *"I hate him."* These were damning because they suggested a motive (anger and premeditation) inconsistent with pure fear or self-defense.

- **Witnesses about the Relationship**: Multiple friends and family members testified that the couple's relationship was indeed volatile. Carissa Carlisle took the stand and shared how Ryan had been trying to gently extricate himself from

Shayna. She even read aloud some text exchanges with Ryan, in which Ryan expressed dread and anxiety about Shayna's reactions. Carissa confirmed that Ryan was *"trying to avoid conflict"* with Shayna as he planned to break things off.

- **Plans for a Date**: Ryan's stepfather, Peter Carter, testified that just the night before the murder, Ryan confided in him about the upcoming date with Audrey Bolte and explicitly said he was afraid to tell Shayna about it. This showed that Ryan anticipated Shayna might react badly implying he had reason to fear her volatility, not the other way around.

- **Audrey Bolte**: Audrey herself testified, confirming that Ryan had made a date with her for that night, October 12, and that he never showed up. Hearing from Audrey, a poised beauty queen, likely made the motive quite tangible for the jury: Shayna knew Ryan was about to slip out of her grasp and into the arms of another woman.

- **Ryan's coworkers**: Ken Hawley and Lori Zimmerman recounted how Shayna would harass Ryan at work when he tried to avoid her by calling the office incessantly and even showing up uninvited. They described Ryan as worn down and exhausted by her behavior. This bolstered the idea that Ryan was not a controlling abuser, but rather a man overwhelmed by an overly attached girlfriend.

- **Neighbors' Testimony**: The Wests (the

downstairs neighbors) provided their account of hearing two shots, then a pause, then four shots and no sounds of a fight beforehand. This strongly supported the prosecution's claim that Shayna's self-defense story was fabricated.

- **Physical Evidence**: Police investigators testified about the pristine condition of the apartment (no sign of struggle) and the lack of injuries on Shayna. Crime scene photos and diagrams showed where Ryan's body fell and bullet trajectories, consistent with him being shot, pausing, then shot more while on the ground. Chief Birkenhauer himself took the stand to explain how the dust on the TV and undisturbed table items contradicted Shayna's claims.

- **Shayna's Interrogation Video**: Perhaps the most powerful evidence was Shayna's own taped police interrogation. The jury saw segments where Shayna spoke at length that night. They heard her calmly explain how she shot Ryan extra times to end his twitching. They witnessed her chilling "nose job" comment on video, in Shayna's own voice: *"I gave him his nose job he wanted."* And they saw her dancing and singing alone in the interrogation room, displaying an eerie lack of remorse. It's hard to overstate how damaging that footage was to Shayna's credibility as a supposedly frightened victim. As Prosecutor Snodgrass argued to the jury, *"Someone in shock does not pirouette...*

Within hours of putting six bullets into Ryan Poston and watching him die, she danced and sang." The tape made it painfully clear that Shayna was not behaving like a traumatized woman acting in genuine self-defense.

- **Jailhouse Confessions**: The prosecution also had an unexpected ace in the hole: Shayna's former cellmate from jail. A woman named Cecily Miller, who was housed with Shayna after her arrest, testified about Shayna's chilling jailhouse admissions. Miller said that Shayna actually bragged about killing Ryan, laughing about shooting him in the face and giving him the nose job he always wanted. Miller further testified that Shayna discussed her legal strategy openly, saying she was going to plead insanity but thought better of it because she was "too smart," claiming she had *"the IQ of Einstein,"* so she'd go with a battered woman defense instead. In other words, Shayna allegedly admitted to this cellmate that her defense was a calculated tactic, not the truth. The image of Shayna laughing about the murder while behind bars and boasting of her intelligence was likely the final nail in the coffin for her defense.

Shayna's defense team in the first trial, led by public defenders, stuck to the story of self-defense. They argued that Ryan had been emotionally and physically abusive and that Shayna had reason to fear for her life that night. They tried to flip the script: depicting Ryan as controlling, with a bad temper fueled by stress and possibly substance use, and Shayna as a battered, terrified young woman who reacted in panic.

They pointed to the Xanax and Adderall in Ryan's system, suggesting that could make someone irritable or aggressive. They reminded jurors that Shayna had no history of violence, whereas Ryan allegedly had shown a darker side in private (citing the April 2012 door-slamming incident and any other anecdote they could). Shayna's attorneys weren't allowed to bring in everything they wanted, however. The judge had set some limits on evidence. For instance, any irrelevant inflammatory details or certain hearsay might have been excluded. In fact, after the trial, the defense complained that they were "not allowed to present evidence and witnesses that would have shown Hubers killed Poston in self-defense" though it's unclear what those were specifically, it suggests the judge barred some testimony perhaps about past incidents or Ryan's character that the defense wanted in.

One strategic decision the defense made was not putting Shayna on the stand in the first trial. Instead, they relied on the police interrogation tape to convey her version of events. This was risky because, while the tape did show Shayna claiming self-defense, it also showed all her bizarre and damaging behavior. The defense likely figured that Shayna's demeanor on the stand might not play well with the jury either, and cross-examination by the prosecution could trap her in lies or inconsistencies. So, they let the taped statements speak for her.

The defense did call some witnesses to support Shayna's claims of being a victim. For example, Shayna's mother Sharon Hubers testified. Sharon told the court that Ryan *"gave her the creeps."* She likely recounted how she had to pick Shayna up the morning of the shooting because Shayna was distraught, and possibly any signs she observed of Shayna being in an unhealthy relationship. The defense also presented an expert toxicologist who spoke about Ryan's medication (Xanax and Adderall), saying that combination could, in some users, lead to volatility or violent behavior. This was meant to bolster the idea that Ryan might indeed have snapped that night in a drug-fueled rage.

Additionally, a clinical psychologist or psychiatrist may have been brought in to discuss Shayna's mental state. If so, it wasn't heavily publicized, but the defense might have subtly introduced the idea that Shayna had some trauma (like the unreported sexual assault in high school) and possibly borderline personality disorder or PTSD making her reactions intense. However, this first trial defense was more straightforward: Shayna simply acted out of *fear* and *extreme emotional disturbance*, not malice. They requested that the jury, if they disbelieved full self-defense, at least consider a lesser charge like manslaughter under extreme emotional disturbance (a provision in Kentucky law that can reduce murder to voluntary manslaughter if the defendant was under a reasonable extreme emotional disturbance).

After two weeks of testimony, the case went to the jury. Deliberations in the first trial were relatively brief; only about five hours. On April 23, 2015, the jury returned with a verdict: Guilty of Murder. They flatly rejected Shayna's self-defense claim. The evidence of premeditation and lack of remorse had simply been overwhelming. Jurors did have the option to convict on lesser charges (the judge had instructed them on manslaughter degrees and reckless homicide as possible alternatives), but they chose the top charge of murder, indicating they found her actions intentional and not justified.

During the sentencing phase of the trial, the same jury recommended a sentence of 40 years in prison. In Kentucky, at that time, a life sentence was an option, but the jury opted for 40 years, possibly considering her age (she was 24 by then) and lack of criminal record. However, under Kentucky law, a person convicted of a violent offense must serve 85% of their sentence before parole eligibility. This meant Shayna would ordinarily have to serve 34 years (85% of 40) before parole, effectively keeping her behind bars until she was in her mid-50s.

Shayna's defense attorneys made a last effort to mitigate. They filed motions asking the judge to consider recognizing Shayna as a victim of domestic violence, which under Kentucky law could drastically reduce the time before parole eligibility (down to serving 20% of the sentence, if the judge found she had been an abuse victim). They argued that the evidence showed Shayna had been emotionally and physically battered by Ryan, citing whatever supportive testimony they could. But Judge Fred A. Stine, who presided over the trial, was not convinced. At the formal sentencing in August 2015, Judge Stine denied those motions and pointedly stated he did not believe Shayna was a victim of domestic violence. In fact, he remarked that Ryan's murder was *"as cold-blooded an act as I've been associated with in the criminal justice system."* This was a strong statement from a seasoned judge, underscoring how unnecessary and planned he viewed the killing. He went so far as to say he had considered giving her more than 40 years, but ultimately he honored the jury's recommendation.

Thus, in 2015, Shayna Hubers was formally sentenced to 40 years in prison, with parole eligibility after 20 years (because the jury's domestic-violence-victim request was denied, she'd still need to serve 85%, but her attorneys had hoped to reduce that). As she was led away in cuffs, it seemed like the final chapter of this tragic saga had been written. But Shayna Hubers's story was not over yet.

In an unexpected twist, Shayna's conviction was overturned the following year due to a legal technicality. In August 2016, it came to light that one of the jurors from her trial had a prior felony conviction on his record. In Kentucky (as in most states), convicted felons are not allowed to serve on juries. This juror had failed to disclose his old felony during jury selection (possibly he had rights restored and didn't realize it barred him, or he intentionally hid it). Regardless, when the defense discovered this, they moved for a new trial. Judge Stine, as much as he surely disliked vacating the verdict, had little choice but to grant it. On August 25, 2016, Shayna's 2015 conviction was formally thrown out. She would get a second trial.

For Ryan's family, it was a painful delay of justice; for Shayna, it was an unexpected second chance to avoid spending most of her life in prison. In preparation for the retrial, Shayna hired a prominent new attorney, David Eldridge, from out of state. The retrial was initially set for fall 2017, then postponed to January 2018 at Eldridge's request for more prep time, and ultimately it began in the summer of 2018, nearly six years after Ryan's death.

Shayna Hubers's second trial kicked off in Campbell County in August 2018. This time around, the defense adjusted its strategy. They still claimed that Shayna had acted out of fear, but they put less emphasis on proving an immediate physical self-defense scenario and more on portraying Shayna as a mentally troubled young woman acting under extreme emotional disturbance. Kentucky law recognizes "Extreme Emotional Disturbance" (EED) as a mitigating factor that can reduce a murder charge to first-degree manslaughter if the defendant acted under a sudden and intense disturbance of emotion with a reasonable explanation. Eldridge's goal was likely to get a manslaughter conviction instead of murder, which would carry a lighter sentence.

In his opening statement, attorney David Eldridge acknowledged that both Shayna and Ryan were *"deeply flawed people"* and that their relationship was dysfunctional. He did not attempt to paint Shayna as entirely innocent, but he urged jurors to understand the psychological context. Eldridge argued that Shayna suffered from Borderline Personality

Disorder (BPD), which made her emotions intense and her reactions extreme. He explained that people with BPD have unstable interpersonal relationships, fear abandonment, and can be emotionally immature or overreactive; a description that matched Shayna's behavior to a tee. The defense also brought up Shayna's past trauma, like the alleged sexual assault in her teens, to show she carried emotional damage into this relationship.

Most significantly, Eldridge shifted the narrative to verbal and psychological provocation. Even if the jury believed Shayna was not in immediate physical danger, perhaps they could be swayed that Ryan's cruel treatment pushed her into an emotional breaking point. Eldridge told the jury their focus would be on how Ryan *"berated her constantly"* and that on Oct. 12, Shayna was acting under extreme emotional distress rather than in cold blood. Essentially, "Yes, she pulled the trigger, but she was not in her right mind. Rather, they claimed, she was in a state of extreme turmoil caused by his abuse."

The defense furthermore presented lurid details to paint Ryan as a bad boyfriend. Shayna testified at length this time, giving her own account from the witness stand (a big change from the first trial where she didn't testify). She spoke about their sex life issues and how Ryan pressured her for threesomes, criticized her body, and belittled her for not being able to orgasm. She even mentioned she got that G-shot for him. This was intended to shock the jury: to show Ryan as sexually selfish and demeaning. Then, Shayna recounted every alleged incident of Ryan's aggression: the door incident in April

2012, a time he supposedly picked her up and threw her into a hallway, and the final night's attack where he supposedly grabbed and shook her. She described being called crazy, being told to shut up, being tossed around, all to support that she reasonably feared him. Eldridge highlighted that Shayna tried hard to be a good girlfriend by cooking and cleaning for Ryan, doting on him, and wanting a real relationship while Ryan treated her as a disposable object for sex. The implication was that Ryan psychologically tortured her by reeling her in and pushing her away.

A defense psychologist, Dr. J. Reid Meloy or a similar expert, testified that Shayna showed signs of PTSD from abusive episodes and definitely had Borderline Personality Disorder. The psychologist explained that Shayna's mental illnesses would greatly affect her perception and reactions. (Interestingly, the prosecution's own expert, Dr. Edward Wygant, examined Shayna and concurred on the BPD diagnosis, though he concluded she still knew right from wrong during the shooting. The defense also reminded jurors that Shayna had been an *"honor student"* and a fundamentally good person before all this, subtly suggesting that something must have unhinged her. Namely, Ryan's treatment of her.

During her testimony, Shayna did make some damning admissions under cross-examination. She conceded that she had exhibited "possessive and controlling" behaviors during her relationship with Ryan. She openly admitted that if Ryan tried to break up with her, she would indeed send countless texts, and even when he did not respond, she'd continue sending messages. She admitted going to Ryan's condominium uninvited and entering when he was not there because she had a key. She admitted to searching Ryan's phone because she did not trust him, accessing his Facebook to "block" other women, and contacting his neighbors to see if he was home when she was not in the area. Additionally, she acknowledged lying to Ryan about her dating other men (pretending she had other interests to make him jealous). She even faked a heart condition during one breakup to gain his empathy. These were all hallmarks of stalking behavior, which Shayna more or less copped to, likely in an attempt to "own" her flaws before the prosecution could use them to label her as crazy. She also admitted to deceptive ploys like the fake phone number and fake client text message. Perhaps her lawyers felt honesty about those misdeeds would make her overall testimony more credible. She wasn't painting herself as perfect, but as a woman driven to extremes by love and mental illness.

Shayna stuck to her claim that on the night of the shooting, she truly believed Ryan was about to kill her. She recounted through tears (genuine or not) that Ryan pointed the gun at her and said he could get away with murdering her. She described the final moments in line with what she had told police (minus the flippancies): he set the gun down, continued to rage, and when she saw him reaching, she grabbed it and fired in blind fear. One new detail she added in this trial was that at some point Ryan had locked himself in his bedroom to avoid a confrontation, and she was so anxious to talk to him that she picked the lock with a bobby pin to get in. (This tidbit actually made Shayna look more like the aggressor because if true, he was trying to get away from her and she wouldn't allow it.)

The prosecution in the second trial largely stuck to their original evidence, but they also had some new witnesses and angles, since more time had passed and more information had come out. Carissa Carlisle again spoke about the relationship. This time, Carissa also revealed how Shayna had stolen her phone to contact Ryan, as mentioned before, highlighting Shayna's invasiveness. Carissa told the jury that Shayna's feelings and reactions toward the relationship were extremely unstable, and that by the end, Ryan was trying hard to cut ties with her. The coworkers reiterated Ryan's fear of not being able to break up with Shayna and the restraining order question he'd asked. Multiple cellmates from the jail testified at the 2018 trial, not just Cecily Miller. In addition to Miller, two others, Donna Dooley and Holly Nivens, took the stand. These women had spent time behind bars with Shayna and recounted jaw-dropping conversations...

Donna Dooley testified that Shayna described the murder to her and even admitted that *before* shooting Ryan, she threw things around the condo to be loud and make it appear that Poston was abusing her. Shayna told Dooley she did this to fool the neighbors into thinking Ryan was attacking her, essentially a preemptive cover story. Shayna also allegedly told Dooley that she shot Ryan because he wanted her to leave so he could go on a date, essentially admitting the real motive was the impending date with Audrey. Dooley remembered the conversation clearly because Shayna "had no remorse at all" when talking about the killing.

Holly Nivens recounted that initially Shayna stuck to the abuse story with her too, claiming Ryan had attacked her. But over time, Shayna admitted to Nivens that actually she was the aggressor and that Ryan had not abused her on the night of the shooting. Shayna confided that Ryan locked himself in his bedroom apparently to avoid a fight, and Shayna was the one who picked the lock with a bobby pin to get in and confront him. Nivens testified that Shayna said on other occasions she would throw things around the condominium to convince neighbors that she and Ryan were fighting, and she would show neighbors self-inflicted bruises, pretending Ryan gave them to her. After some time, Shayna told Nivens bluntly that she shot Ryan because he was breaking up with her, and gave details about that night. Nivens also described Shayna's demeanor in jail: she would pretend to cry on the phone (with family or her attorney), but once off the call she'd smile and wink at her fellow inmates, as if her sorrow was just an act.

Cecily Miller again testified in the second trial, reinforcing what she said before: that Shayna often laughed when talking about Ryan's death and did not appear to have any genuine remorse. Shayna told Miller she *knew* Ryan was supposed to go on a date with Miss Ohio that night, and she killed him after he asked her to leave. Shayna also stated she intended to claim Ryan had "beaten and raped" her, even though it was untrue, as a strategy to defend herself. Like Dooley, Miller recalled that

Shayna showed no remorse for what she'd done.

The mall witness, Tara Filliater, told the jury about overhearing Shayna casually threaten to kill her boyfriend only hours before the shooting. This was new evidence that hadn't been presented in the first trial.

The prosecution also called rebuttal experts to counter the defense's psychological angle. Dr. Edward Wygant, a forensic psychologist for the state, agreed Shayna had Borderline Personality Disorder. But he concluded that in his opinion, Shayna's BPD and any other mental health issues did not impair her ability to form intent or understand her actions on October 12, 2012. He pointed out that Shayna was able to clearly recall how she felt during the shooting and immediately afterward, which indicated she was not in a dissociative state or blackout. She was aware of what she was doing. Essentially, mental illness or not, she made a choice to shoot Ryan multiple times.

In closing arguments, Prosecutor Snodgrass hammered home that Shayna's actions were those of a scorned lover, not a legitimately fearful abuse victim. She reminded jurors of Ryan's own words before his death; asking how to break up with someone who won't let you and of Shayna's texts about wanting to kill him, which spoke to motive. The testimony of the cellmates, Snodgrass argued, showed that Shayna's self-defense claim was a calculated lie and that her lack of remorse was telling. All the evidence, from the lack of injuries on Shayna to the neighbor who heard no fight, pointed to murder in cold blood.

After another dramatic trial, the second jury also did not buy the defense's story. On August 28, 2018, Shayna Hubers was once again found Guilty of Murder. The deliberation lasted around five hours, similar to the first trial, indicating the jury reached a consensus without great difficulty. The wealth of corroborating evidence, especially Shayna's own admissions to inmates, made it hard to see this as anything but murder.

This time, because Shayna was now a convicted murderer for the second time and had shown no real remorse, the jury went a step further in punishment. They recommended a sentence of life in prison. In Kentucky, a life sentence still allows for the possibility of parole after a minimum period. Due to the time Shayna had already served since 2012 (about 6 years in custody before and during the retrial), it was calculated that she would be eligible to seek parole after serving 17 more years, in the year 2032, when she would be about 41 years old. The judge imposed the life sentence as recommended on October 18, 2018.

As the courtroom cleared, Ryan Poston's family and friends perhaps felt a measure of relief that the justice system, however delayed, ultimately held Shayna accountable. Yet it was a somber victory. Nothing could bring back Ryan or fully heal the wound of his loss.

Throughout the trials, a portrait emerged of Shayna Hubers that was complex and deeply troubling. On one hand, she was a high-achieving young woman. She was intelligent, educated, and outwardly polite. On the other hand, she displayed behavior consistent with someone with serious emotional and psychological issues.

Both the defense and prosecution experts agreed that Shayna Hubers has Borderline Personality Disorder. BPD is characterized by unstable moods, intense interpersonal attachments, fear of abandonment, impulsivity, and often manipulative or self-destructive actions. Shayna's life with Ryan checked nearly every box for BPD: her frantic efforts to avoid being abandoned by him (constant texting, refusing to accept breakups, even faking a heart problem during one breakup to gain sympathy); her pattern of idealization turning to devaluation (professing love then saying "I hate him" and fantasizing about his death); her emotional instability (moments of extreme joy with him followed by despair or rage when he pulled away). People with BPD often have a distorted self-image and can oscillate between feeling like a victim and feeling justified in extreme actions. We see this in how Shayna at times painted herself as the devoted girlfriend just trying to please her man, and at other times embraced the role of a vengeful woman scorned who "gave him what he deserved."

Shayna also demonstrated narcissistic and histrionic traits. She had an extremely high opinion of her own intellect, telling her cellmate she had the "IQ of Einstein". She believed she could outsmart the system (initially musing about an insanity plea, then opting to claim abuse as a strategy). Her behavior in the interrogation room – dancing, singing, and theatrically crying only when an officer was about to leave – suggested an almost performative aspect to her personality, as if she were putting on a show. When she said *"I'm so good at acting,"* it was eerie because it rang true: Shayna was acting, both for the police and perhaps for herself. She knew how to turn on the waterworks or the fearful facade when needed, but when she thought no one was watching, her true affect was disturbingly nonchalant.

The lack of genuine remorse is a striking element of Shayna's profile. Multiple inmates independently observed that Shayna laughed about the killing and never appeared actually sorry that Ryan was gone. When she cried, it seemed to be for her own predicament rather than for Ryan's death. This emotional shallowness and self-centeredness lean toward psychopathic tendencies, although no expert labeled her a psychopath outright. It might be more that her intense focus on herself (a narcissistic streak) combined with the devaluation of Ryan (she described him as an *"evil person"* in messages) allowed her to justify or detach from the horror of what she did.

In court, Shayna's demeanor was noted at times to be oddly upbeat. During the 2018 trial, observers saw her smile or smirk occasionally when entering the courtroom, as if confident in how things were going. When discussing graphic or intimate matters on the stand, she sometimes lacked the embarrassment or discomfort one might expect. She did tear up when describing feeling afraid during the alleged fight, but some jurors reportedly found her tears insincere or inconsistent. Meanwhile, when witnesses testified against her (like the cellmates), Shayna often scribbled notes furiously or whispered to her attorney, appearing annoyed more than ashamed. This comportment likely did not endear her to the jury.

One particularly telling detail was what Shayna did during the retrial period: she got married in jail. In June 2018, while awaiting her second trial, Shayna married a fellow inmate named Unique Taylor, a transgender woman incarcerated for an unrelated matter. On January 14, 2019, just a few months after her conviction, Shayna filed for divorce, stating the brief jailhouse marriage was "irretrievably broken". This bizarre episode suggests that even facing life in prison, Shayna was seeking attention, connection, or control in any way she could. It was as if she couldn't stand being irrelevant or alone so she made a dramatic personal decision (with no practical benefit, given she was behind bars) that grabbed headlines. Some have interpreted this as further evidence of her impulsivity and need for validation, even in jail.

Ultimately, mental health experts concluded that while Shayna had personality disorders and perhaps past trauma, she was not legally insane or delusional. She knew right from wrong. Dr. Wygant's evaluation underscored that Shayna was able to recall her actions and feelings, meaning she was not in an unconscious haze when she shot Ryan. In other words, her psychological issues help explain *why* she might do something so extreme, but they don't excuse *that* she did it.

Shayna Hubers can be seen as a case study in the dangerous intersection of obsessive love and mental instability. She was a young woman who could excel in school and seem utterly normal to casual acquaintances, all while harboring deep emotional dysfunction that erupted in violence. The psychological profile that emerged (borderline personality, narcissistic tendencies, manipulative behavior, and lack of remorse) is one that, in hindsight, spelled disaster when combined with a tumultuous relationship and the stress of rejection.

MONSTER

Aileen Wuornos

Aileen Carol Wuornos has been called many names. *America's first female serial killer*, the *Damsel of Death*, even a "monster." But behind these lurid labels lies the true story of a woman shaped by a nightmarish childhood, tumultuous relationships, and a notorious killing spree. From her troubled early life in Michigan to the murderous highway encounters in Florida, and finally to her dramatic trial and execution, her life story is as tragic as it is infamous. In this chapter, we'll walk through Aileen Wuornos's journey from birth to death, sticking to the facts of her case while also noting how Hollywood and the media sometimes got it wrong.

Aileen Wuornos was born Aileen Carol Pittman on February 29, 1956, in Rochester, Michigan. Her start in life was anything but stable. Aileen's mother, Diane, was just 14 years old when she married Aileen's father, Leo Dale Pittman, who was 18. The young marriage fell apart quickly. Diane filed for divorce only two months before Aileen was born. Aileen never even met her father. And perhaps for the better: by 1967, Leo Pittman was in prison for sexually assaulting a child and was diagnosed with schizophrenia; he ended up hanging himself in prison in 1969.

When Aileen was almost four years old, her mother Diane abandoned her and her older brother Keith, leaving them with their maternal grandparents, Lauri and Britta Wuornos. The grandparents legally adopted Aileen and Keith in March 1960. Unfortunately, this new home was far from loving. Lauri and Britta were known to be alcoholics, and Aileen later recounted severe abuse at the hands of her grandfather. According to Aileen, her grandfather would beat her and even sexually assault her when she was a child, sometimes forcing her to strip off her clothes before these beatings. In one especially disturbing incident, he even made the young Aileen watch him drown a kitten for disobeying him. It's no surprise that Aileen developed an explosive temper and struggled to fit in with other kids. Her childhood was effectively a nightmare behind closed doors.

By the time she was about 11 years old, Aileen was acting out in alarming ways. She began engaging in sexual activities at school in exchange for cigarettes, food, or small change. Local boys cruelly nicknamed her "cigarette pig" for trading sexual favors for loose change and smokes. Aileen also admitted that during her childhood she had consensual sexual encounters with her own brother Keith. The abuse and dysfunction around her normalized unhealthy behavior at a young age. She ran away from home multiple times and spent time living in the woods or in abandoned cars near her home in Troy, Michigan. Neighborhood gossip hinted at even darker abuse. Some neighbors later said that Aileen's 14-year-old pregnancy (more on that in a moment) was caused by an older friend of her grandfather.

At age 14, Aileen became pregnant. She told her family that a family friend had raped her, resulting in the pregnancy. In January 1971, Aileen was sent to a home for unwed mothers in Detroit to have the baby. She gave birth to a baby boy on March 23, 1971, when she was just 15. The infant was immediately put up for adoption, and Aileen never had a chance to raise him. This traumatic chapter is often glossed over in the sensationalized versions of Aileen's story, but it had a profound effect on her. Just weeks after giving birth, Aileen dropped out of school for good. Around the same time, her grandmother Britta died of liver failure, and Aileen's grandfather Lauri finally threw the troubled 15-year-old out of his house entirely. Essentially homeless, Aileen began living in the woods near her old home and turned to prostitution to support herself as a teenager. By any measure, Aileen Wuornos's youth was traumatic and chaotic. Less than five years later, in 1976, Aileen's grandfather Lauri committed suicide as well (much like her father had), leaving yet another dark footnote in her family history. By that time, Aileen had already left Michigan behind. She hitchhiked across the country as a drifter, surviving in part through sex work and petty crime. It was a rough, itinerant life that set the stage for the violence to come.

In the mid-1970s, Aileen Wuornos was

living a transient lifestyle, making her way down to Florida and getting into frequent trouble. At just 18 years old, she had her first major run-in with the law. On May 27, 1974, in Jefferson County, Colorado, Aileen was arrested for drunk driving, disorderly conduct, and firing a .22-caliber pistol from a moving vehicle. When she failed to show up to court for those charges, a warrant was issued for her arrest; an early sign of her tendency to flout authority. This was only the beginning of Aileen's rap sheet.

In 1976, at age 20, Wuornos hitchhiked from the Midwest down to sunny Florida, perhaps hoping for a fresh start. Instead, she found more trouble and an unlikely marriage. That year in Florida, Aileen met a wealthy 69-year-old man named Lewis Gratz Fell, who was the president of a local yacht club. Despite their five-decade age difference, the two had a whirlwind romance. In a bizarre turn of events, Aileen and Lewis quickly married, and their nuptials even made it into the local society pages of the newspaper. For a moment, it must have seemed like Aileen had stumbled into a Cinderella story but it didn't take long for this marriage to collapse in spectacular fashion.

Within weeks, Aileen's fiery temper erupted. She frequently got into bar fights in the local saloons. In one incident, she even assaulted someone with Lewis's own cane! Her elderly husband took out a restraining order against her after only a few weeks of marriage, describing Aileen as having a "violent and ungovernable temper". Aileen countered by claiming that he had attacked her, but either way the relationship was doomed. She left

Florida and headed back to Michigan in mid-1976, angry and empty-handed. On July 14, 1976, just two months after the wedding, Aileen was arrested in Mancelona, Michigan for assault and disturbing the peace after she threw a cue ball at a bartender's head during yet another bar altercation. Only a few days after that incident, Aileen's brother Keith (whom she had been close to, perhaps too close) died of esophageal cancer on July 17, 1976. Keith's death did bring one silver lining for Aileen: she received a $10,000 payout from his life insurance.

Aileen and Lewis officially annulled their short-lived marriage on July 21, 1976. It had lasted only about nine weeks. The $10,000 inheritance from her brother didn't last long either. By August 1976, Wuornos had blown through the money on luxuries and a new car, which she then wrecked in an accident shortly after buying it. She also had to pay a $105 fine for drunk driving that year. The rapid collapse of her marriage and squandered inheritance left Aileen back where she started – drifting and broke.

The late 1970s and 1980s saw Aileen Wuornos bouncing around Florida and the South, accumulating *arrests* like souvenirs. She attempted suicide at least six times during her youth (between ages 14 and 22), revealing her deep despair even as she kept up a tough front. Her criminal record grew longer each year. In May 1981, Aileen was arrested in Edgewater, Florida for armed robbery after she had held up a convenience store at gunpoint, stealing a grand total of $35 and a couple of packs of cigarettes. For that crime, she ended up serving just over a year in prison (sentenced in 1982 and released in June 1983). By this point she was in her late 20s and well-known to police. Aileen had a pattern of committing bold, reckless crimes. (An anecdote often mentioned: during one robbery attempt, she was reportedly wearing a bikini under a jacket. It was an image that perhaps says a lot about her devil-may-care attitude and the Florida heat!)

After her release, Wuornos continued bouncing between odd jobs (mostly sex work) and unlawful antics. In 1984, she was arrested in Key West for trying to pass forged checks. By 1985, she was a suspect in the theft of a revolver and ammo in Pasco County. In January 1986, she was detained in Miami driving a stolen car, carrying a loaded gun, and using a fake ID with her aunt's name. Just a few months later, in June 1986, a man accused her of threatening him with a gun for money; police found a .22-caliber pistol under the passenger seat where Aileen had been sitting. In short, by her early 30s Aileen had a long rap sheet: offenses ranging from assault and armed robbery to theft, forgery, resisting arrest, and weapons charges. One police report even noted her attitude as "POOR". She was known to be belligerent and easily angered during arrests. Aileen was a volatile person, constantly in trouble with the law, and surviving by the skin of her teeth.

In 1986, Aileen Wuornos's life took a turn when she met the woman who would become her lover and later, her betrayer. At a Daytona Beach gay bar called Zodiac, 30-year-old Aileen struck up a conversation with a 24-year-old motel maid named Tyria Moore. Sparks flew. The two women quickly became inseparable, moving in together and beginning an intense romantic relationship that would last about four and a half years. Aileen, who often went by the nickname "Lee," was deeply in love with Tyria. *"It was love beyond imaginable. Earthly words cannot describe how I felt about Tyria,"* Aileen later said, looking back on their relationship. Even shortly before her execution, Aileen claimed she was still in love with Tyria. This love would drive many of her actions for better or worse.

The couple eked out a living on society's margins. Tyria held occasional low-wage jobs (housekeeper, maid, etc.), while Aileen earned most of their money the way she knew best: sex work along Florida's highways. They often drifted between cheap motels, trailer parks, and rented rooms around the Daytona area. By all accounts, Aileen was possessive and jealous with Tyria, not even liking it when Tyria went to work and met other people. The two of them also had run-ins with the law as a pair. For example, on July 4, 1987, police questioned Aileen and Tyria after they were accused of attacking a man with a beer bottle in a bar fight. Neither woman was charged in that specific incident, but it shows how Aileen's combative behavior persisted. Still, Tyria Moore stuck by Aileen's side through thick and thin during those years...at least until the bodies started piling up.

In an often-overlooked detail, Aileen's relationship with Tyria was actually her second serious relationship with a woman. Her first female relationship happened before Tyria, though little is publicly known about it. But Tyria Moore was the relationship that mattered most in Aileen's life. Aileen was desperate to keep Tyria's affection and support. As we'll see, that desperation would lead Aileen down a very dark path.

According to Aileen, it was during her time with Tyria that something in her finally snapped. By late 1989, with Aileen now in her mid-30s, she was still prostituting herself to strangers on the highway to keep money in their pockets. Years of abuse, rape, and hardship had filled her with rage. As documentary filmmaker Nick Broomfield later speculated, *"I think this anger developed inside her... and finally exploded into incredible violence. That was her way of surviving."* Aileen herself would later claim that by this point, she hated men and humanity in general. That she had "hate crawling through my system". Whatever the exact trigger, Aileen Wuornos was about to embark on a year-long killing spree that would make her one of the most infamous serial killers in American history.

From late 1989 through late 1990, the bodies of several middle-aged men were found dumped in central Florida. They had one thing in common: they died violent deaths on the side of the road. The perpetrator turned out to be Aileen Wuornos, who would later confess to murdering seven men in the span of about twelve months. All of her victims were men who encountered Aileen in the context of her prostitution along highways. She would be picked up or approach them at rest stops, offer sexual services, and then events turned deadly. Here is a rundown of the murders Aileen committed during her infamous spree:

- Richard Charles Mallory, 51 – Aileen's first known victim. Richard Mallory was an electronics store owner in Clearwater who, on November 30, 1989, picked up Aileen (likely for sex) and drove to a secluded area. According to Aileen, Mallory brutally beat and raped her in his car, and she shot him in self-defense. Mallory's body was found on December 13, 1989, in a wooded area; he'd been shot several times, with two bullets to his left lung being the cause of death. (Interestingly, it later came out that Mallory had a history of violence. He had a prior conviction for attempted rape but this fact wasn't known to Aileen at the time and was not admitted as evidence in her trial.) Mallory's car was discovered abandoned, which helped lead investigators to connect his case with later victims.

- David Andrew Spears, 43 – A construction worker from Winter Garden. He was reported missing in mid-May 1990. On June 1, 1990, his nude body was found along U.S. Route 19 in Citrus County. Spears had been shot six times with a .22 caliber pistol.

- Charles Edmund Carskaddon, 40 – A part-time rodeo worker. He was killed around May 31, 1990. His body was found on June 6, 1990 in Pasco County. Carskaddon had been shot nine times with a .22 weapon. His body was wrapped in an electric blanket and badly decomposed by the time it was discovered. Evidence later showed Aileen had been seen driving Carskaddon's car and had pawned a gun belonging to him.

- Peter Abraham Siems, 65 – A retired merchant seaman and Christian missionary. In June 1990, Siems set out from Jupiter, Florida, heading toward New Jersey, but he never reached his destination. In July 1990, his car, a Pontiac Sunbird, was found crashed in Orange Springs, Florida. Witnesses spotted two women later believed to be Aileen and Tyria walking away from the accident scene. A bloody palm print on the car's interior door handle was matched to Aileen Wuornos. Peter Siems's body has never been found, and Aileen would later say she left his corpse in a remote location but she couldn't recall exactly where. Because no body was recovered, Siems's case never went to trial, but authorities have little doubt he was one of Aileen's victims.

- Troy Eugene Burress, 50 – A sausage salesman from Ocala. Burress went missing on July 31, 1990. On August 4, 1990, his body was found in a wooded area along State Road 19 in Marion County. He had been shot twice. By this time, multiple murder cases were clearly being linked to the same female suspect. It was a highly unusual scenario that had the Florida media buzzing about a possible female serial killer roaming the highways.

- Charles Richard "Dick" Humphreys, 56 – A former Air Force major, police chief, and Florida state child-abuse investigator. On September 11, 1990, just after retiring, Humphreys was travelling when he crossed paths with Aileen. His body was found the next day, September 12, in Marion County. He was fully clothed (unlike some other victims) and had been shot seven times in the head and chest. Humphreys's car was later found in Suwannee County.

- Walter Gino Antonio, 62 – A truck driver, security guard, and reserve police officer. He was Aileen's final known victim. Antonio's partially disrobed body was found on November 19, 1990, near a remote logging road in Dixie County. He had been shot four times. Five days later, his car was found in Brevard County, abandoned.

Seven men in total lost their lives. Most of them were shot repeatedly with a small caliber handgun, their bodies dumped in secluded spots. Robbery was also a motive as Aileen often took their cash, credit cards, and valuables, and in several cases drove their cars for a while or pawned their belongings. In fact, throughout this period, Aileen would return home to Tyria with various "borrowed" cars and items from her victims, which she pawned off to keep them afloat financially. She used fake names and ID when pawning items, making the trail harder to follow. But with so many bodies showing up, the police were on the hunt for a suspect and they had a hunch it might be a woman.

Aileen initially claimed that each killing was in self-defense. That each man had either raped her or attempted to rape her during their encounter. It's true that in at least Richard Mallory's case, Aileen's account of being violently raped aligns with known facts about Mallory's predatory past. But as the killings went on, the self-defense story became harder to believe. Some victims, like Dick Humphreys, were found fully clothed and were upstanding men with no indication of violence or assault. Years later, Aileen admitted that for the later murders, robbery was the primary motive and she killed to eliminate witnesses. In one interview, she confessed that her claims of self-defense were a lie for all but Mallory, saying *"I wanted to confess to you that Richard Mallory did violently rape me... but these others did not. [They] only began to start to."* This chilling statement suggests that after Mallory, Aileen may have begun initiating the violence herself as soon as she sensed any threat or opportunity, fueled by a mix of anger and opportunism.

The idea of a female serial killer murdering strangers was sensational in 1990, so much so that the press inaccurately dubbed Aileen Wuornos *"America's first female serial killer,"* even though other women had killed multiple people before her. She also earned the grim nickname "Damsel of Death" in headlines. These monikers sold newspapers, but they oversimplified the reality of who Aileen was and what drove her. Unlike many serial killers, Aileen's crimes weren't driven by sexual sadism or meticulous planning; they were chaotic, born out of desperation, rage, and a lifetime of abuse. Still, seven men were dead, and by the end of 1990 the law was closing in on Aileen Wuornos.

By the fall of 1990, Florida authorities realized that the string of murdered men found near highways was likely the work of the same perpetrator and witnesses had spotted two women near some of the victim's abandoned vehicles. A task force was formed to track down the suspects in what newspapers were now calling the case of Florida's female serial killer. One major break came on July 4, 1990, when Aileen and Tyria crashed Peter Siems's car while driving it near Orange Springs. A witness, Rhonda Bailey, saw two women (matching Aileen and Tyria's descriptions) at the scene and later gave this info to police. Investigators found Aileen's palm print on the car and soon discovered that items belonging to various victims had been pawned under different aliases by the same woman. Crucially, one pawn shop thumbprint from a stolen item matched Aileen Wuornos's prints in the police database. By December 1990, authorities had a name: Aileen Carol Wuornos, a known 34-year-old street prostitute with a long criminal record. They also publicly released composite sketches of "two women" seen with victim Peter Siems's car, hoping for leads on their whereabouts.

Tyria Moore, sensing the heat, had actually left Florida a couple months earlier, in late 1990, and gone to Pennsylvania to stay with her family. That left Aileen on her own in Florida. On January 9, 1991, Aileen Wuornos was finally arrested at a biker bar in Port Orange (near Daytona) called The Last Resort. Ironically, this grungy establishment was indeed her "last resort" and she was captured there on an outstanding warrant (for a minor firearm charge under one of her aliases) as a ruse, while police built the murder case against her. She didn't realize it immediately, but the jig was up.

After Aileen's arrest, police quickly tracked down Tyria Moore in Pittston, Pennsylvania the next day. Faced with the possibility of being charged as an accomplice, Tyria agreed to cooperate with investigators in exchange for immunity. Detectives flew Tyria back to Florida and set her up in a motel, where over the course of three days in mid-January 1991, she made numerous recorded phone calls to Aileen at the jail, pleading with Aileen to help clear her name. Tyria played her part well. She cried, told Aileen she was scared of being implicated, and begged Aileen to confess to the killings so that Tyria wouldn't get in trouble. Aileen, who was fiercely protective of Tyria, took the bait.

On January 16, 1991, Aileen Wuornos confessed to the murders during one of these phone calls with Tyria. "I'm the one who did it," she told her, admitting to killing those men but insisting that she only did it to protect herself when the men tried to rape her. Once she realized Tyria had turned on her, Aileen didn't hold back in taking full responsibility. She later said she did it out of love because she couldn't bear the thought of Tyria being blamed. Indeed, Aileen told police that her motivation was that she was *"desperately in love"* with Tyria and didn't want her to get in trouble. In a twisted way, her confession was a final act of devotion.

With Aileen's taped confession and Tyria's testimony, the case against Wuornos was ironclad. In a curious side development, an evangelical born-again Christian couple named Arlene and Jerry Pralle saw Aileen's mugshot in the news and decided to reach out to her in jail in 1991. In an exceedingly *odd* and often overlooked twist, this couple actually legally adopted Aileen Wuornos in November 1991, while she was awaiting trial. Arlene Pralle, the woman who became Aileen's "adoptive mother," claimed she felt a spiritual calling to support Aileen, and Aileen welcomed the affection and religious guidance. The adoption had no real legal effect on the case but added to the media circus surrounding Wuornos. (Documentaries later suggested the Pralles may have been more interested in fame or profit than genuine charity, a point of controversy.) It was just one more strange chapter in an already bizarre story.

Aileen Wuornos's day in court arrived in early 1992, and it was as dramatic as expected. Her first trial was for the murder of Richard Mallory, the first victim. It began on January 14, 1992. Florida prosecutors faced a challenge: normally, you can't bring up a defendant's other crimes in a single murder trial. But this was no ordinary case. Using a provision known as the Williams Rule in Florida, the prosecution was allowed to introduce evidence from Aileen's other six murders to show a pattern of criminal behavior. This meant the jury heard about all the slain men, not just Mr. Mallory.

Aileen's former lover, Tyria Moore, took the stand as a star witness for the prosecution. Tyria's testimony was devastating. She recounted how Aileen had confessed some of the killings to her. In particular, Tyria testified that the day after Mallory was killed, Aileen told her that she had shot and killed a man that had tried to rape her. Tyria also told the court about items Aileen brought home from victims.

Her cooperation and inside knowledge helped secure Aileen's fate.

During the trial, Aileen's defense tried to argue that Mallory had been violent with her. They attempted to introduce evidence of Mallory's 1950s conviction for attempted rape and his time in a correctional facility for sex offenders. Indeed, records showed Mallory had been committed for treatment as a sex offender and was described as having "strong sociopathic trends" back in 1961. This could have supported Aileen's claim that she truly feared for her life with Mallory. However, the judge ruled this evidence inadmissible and refused to allow it in court. The jury never heard about Mallory's dark past. In the end, it may not have mattered much. Aileen's credibility was low, given the sheer number of people she had killed after Mallory.

On January 27, 1992, the jury found Aileen Wuornos guilty of first-degree murder in the Mallory case. The verdict was hardly a surprise. At the sentencing phase, Aileen's defense brought in psychiatrists who testified that she was mentally unstable, diagnosing her with borderline personality disorder and antisocial personality. The prosecution, however, emphasized the cruelty of the crimes. Aileen herself, when given a chance to speak, didn't do much to help her cause; she often vacillated between stating that she'd been raped and expressing anger. She even muttered, "may your wife and kids get raped" to the male prosecutors or police, showing the fury still inside her.

Four days after the guilty verdict, on January 31, 1992, Aileen Wuornos was sentenced to death by electrocution (later changed to lethal injection) for the murder of Richard Mallory. She was 35 years old, and now the second woman ever sent to Florida's death row in modern times.

After the Mallory trial, Aileen decided to cut to the chase on the other cases. On March 31, 1992, she pleaded "no contest" to three more murders; those of Charles Humphreys, Troy Burress, and David Spears. She told the court she wanted to "get right with God" by confessing. In a rambling statement, Aileen reiterated that Mallory had raped her, but she admitted "these others did not. They only began to start to," implying the other men might have become violent or she *thought* they were going to. For these three additional murders, she received three more death sentences in May 1992.

Aileen didn't stop there. In June 1992, she pleaded guilty to the murder of Charles Carskaddon and got a fifth death sentence in November 1992. In February 1993, she pleaded guilty to killing Walter Antonio, resulting in a sixth death sentence. The only victim for whom she wasn't prosecuted was Peter Siems, since his body was never found. In total, Aileen Wuornos received six death sentences – an almost unprecedented penalty, reflecting each life she had taken (except Siems). At this point, Aileen essentially stopped fighting her case. She often said she wanted to die and even asked for the death penalty, believing it to be her destiny or perhaps an escape.

It's worth noting that Aileen gave many inconsistent accounts of the killings over time. Initially, she insisted to police and reporters that every single one of the seven men had either raped her or tried to, so she shot them in self-defense. Later on, she changed her story and admitted that robbery and eliminating witnesses was the real reason for at least some of the murders. However, in 2002, in an interview with filmmaker Nick Broomfield, Aileen once again claimed that it *was* self-defense but she said she couldn't stand being on death row anymore and wanted to die, which is why she had dropped the self-defense claims and pleaded guilty. This confusion about her true motive has made Aileen Wuornos a controversial figure. It's likely that the truth lies somewhere in between: her first killing may have been born of genuine fear and trauma, while the subsequent ones were fueled by anger, paranoia, and opportunism.

After her sentencing, Aileen Wuornos joined the tiny population of women on Florida's death row. She was initially housed in the Broward Correctional Institution for women, and later moved to Florida State Prison (the same facility that houses male death row inmates) for her final years. Life on death row did not bring Aileen peace. In fact, her mental state appeared to deteriorate as the years passed. She oscillated between acceptance of her fate and bursts of paranoia and rage.

By 1996, Aileen's mandatory appeals had reached the U.S. Supreme Court, which denied her appeal, effectively affirming her convictions and sentences. With her legal avenues shrinking, Aileen took the unusual step of firing her attorneys and actively volunteering for execution. In 2001, she petitioned the Florida Supreme Court to stop all her remaining appeals and hurry up the execution. In a letter to the court, Aileen wrote a now-famous statement: *"I killed those men, robbed them as cold as ice. And I'd do it again, too. ... I have hate crawling through my system... I'm one who seriously hates human life and would kill again."* She also vehemently denied the suggestion that she was "crazy," insisting she knew exactly what she was doing and was sane. This chilling declaration shocked many, and it came from a woman who seemed determined to embrace her own execution.

Concerned about her mental competence (since it's not legal to execute someone who is insane), the court ordered psychiatric evaluations. Aileen's own lawyers argued she was not in her right mind, pointing to her paranoid writings and statements. However, a panel of court-appointed psychiatrists found Aileen competent. She understood the legal process and the consequence of execution, and if she wanted to die, she had the right to waive further appeals. Florida's Governor at the time, Jeb Bush, even put a temporary stay on her execution in 2002 to review a psychological evaluation, but this was lifted once doctors again deemed her mentally fit to face execution.

While on death row, Aileen's behavior grew increasingly erratic. She accused prison staff of abusing her in various bizarre ways. In letters and interviews in 2002, she claimed that prison guards were spitting in her food, serving her meals dirty, and subjecting her to sonic pressure that was "crushing" her head. She ranted about strip searches, low water pressure, and guards "taunting" her constantly. Aileen even said she overheard officials *"wishing to rape me before execution"* in order to push her to suicide. She became so paranoid and fed up that she threatened to stop showering and eating to avoid potential harassment. One of her attorneys commented that Aileen just wanted to be treated humanely until the day of her execution and that, disturbingly, "She believes what she's written" about the conspiracy against her. These statements reveal a mind overtaken by paranoia. It's very likely that severe mental illness (possibly delusional disorder or the effects of long-term trauma) was playing a role in Aileen's final years.

In the weeks leading up to her execution, Aileen granted a final round of interviews, notably with Nick Broomfield, the British documentarian who had been following her case for years. In her final interview, Aileen's demeanor shifted between calm acceptance and furious outbursts. She talked about how she was excited to "meet God and Jesus and the angels" after death, indicating a form of religious or spiritual fixation. But she also unloaded a lot of anger. At one point, thinking about how society had treated her, she lashed out to Broomfield, *"You sabotaged my ass! ... Society and the cops and the system — a raped woman got executed, and was used for books and movies and shit!"* Her very last on-camera words were, *"Thanks a lot, society, for railroading my ass."* It was classic Aileen: equal parts self-pitying, defiant, and vulgar. (Later, her childhood friend Dawn Botkins said Aileen's anger in that moment was aimed at the whole world, not at the interviewer.) Clearly, even at the end, Aileen Wuornos felt she had been profoundly betrayed, in her mind, by everyone.

On October 9, 2002, after 11 years on Florida's death row, Aileen Wuornos was executed by lethal injection. She was 46 years old. Aileen had declined the traditional last meal (Florida offers up to $20 for whatever the condemned prisoner wants); instead, she just asked for a cup of coffee as her final comfort. Strapped to the gurney at Florida State Prison in Starke, wearing a prison gown and with IVs in her arms, Aileen managed to utter some final words that were as cryptic as they were memorably *on-brand* for her. With a calm tone, she said: *"Yes, I would just like to say I'm sailing with the Rock, and I'll be back, like Independence Day with Jesus. June 6, like the movie, big mother ship and all, I'll be back, I'll be back."* Those were her official last words, referencing the 1996 alien-invasion film *Independence Day* and promising in her own way that she'd return to earth with Jesus. Many people scratched their heads at that remark. Was it delusion? A final act of morbid humor? Or Aileen's way of saying she believed in an afterlife? Only Aileen knew for sure. At 9:47 a.m. Eastern Time on October 9, 2002, Aileen Wuornos was pronounced dead.

Her body was cremated, and per her wishes, Aileen's ashes were scattered beneath a tree in her home state of Michigan by her friend Dawn. In a poignant detail, Aileen had requested that "Carnival" by Natalie Merchant be played at her funeral; a song she listened to often in prison. When the singer Natalie Merchant learned about this, she said she was *"disturbed"* by Aileen's story but still gave permission to use the song in the closing of the documentary *Aileen: Life and Death of a Serial Killer*, reasoning that if her music gave Aileen any solace in her final days, then *"I have to be grateful."*

And with that, the life of Aileen Wuornos came to an end. She became only the second woman in Florida (and the tenth in the U.S. since reinstatement of the death penalty in 1976) to be executed for her crimes. But in many ways, Aileen's story was just beginning its journey into legend through movies, documentaries, and media coverage.

Aileen Wuornos's infamy made her a prime subject for Hollywood and the media, but these portrayals often blurred fact and fiction. Perhaps the most well-known adaptation is the 2003 film Monster, starring Charlize Theron as Aileen Wuornos. Theron's performance was chillingly accurate in appearance. She gained weight and wore prosthetic makeup, becoming a dead ringer for Wuornos. She even won an Oscar for the role. However, *Monster* took some liberties in telling Aileen's story, leading to a bit of controversy about its accuracy.

For one, the film created a composite character named Selby Wall (played by Christina Ricci) to represent Tyria Moore. While much of the dynamic between Aileen and Selby in the movie mirrors the real Aileen-Tyria relationship, some details were changed. More significantly, the tone of the film elicits sympathy for Aileen in a way that not everyone agrees with. For example, in *Monster*, we see Aileen trying to go straight. She earnestly attempts to quit prostitution and find a regular job, only to face rejection and humiliation, which drives her back to the streets. This "down on her luck" portrayal has some truth (Aileen likely did wish for a normal life), but it is exaggerated for the narrative. In reality, there's little evidence Aileen ever filled out job applications as the film shows; by the late 1980s she was pretty much surviving through sex work and theft without attempting conventional employment.

The biggest sticking point is how *Monster* depicts the first murder. The film shows Richard Mallory (though he's not named in the movie) picking up Aileen, then brutally beating and raping her in extremely graphic scenes, before she grabs a gun and kills him in clear self-defense. This scene is very hard to watch, and it certainly makes the audience empathize with Aileen. Who wouldn't think she was justified after enduring such horrific abuse? Family members of Aileen's real-life victims criticized the movie for this reason: they felt it painted her too much as a victim and glossed over the fact that she went on to kill six more men who were not all violent rapists. The truth is complex: while Aileen did claim Mallory raped her, and he had a record of sex crimes, the other murders did not have evidence of attempted rape. By showing the first killing in such a sympathetic light, the film *Monster* risks leaving viewers with the impression that *all* her killings might have been self-defense, which is not what the courts concluded.

Additionally, *Monster* did not consult key figures like the lead prosecutor, John Tanner, who knew the case intimately. If they had, they might have portrayed certain events differently. The film also compresses time and omits the more bizarre facets of Aileen's story. For instance, her 1976 marriage to Lewis Fell and the 1991 legal adoption by Arlene Pralle are skipped entirely. These omissions make for a tighter narrative but also simplify Aileen's character. In *Monster*, Theron's Wuornos comes off as a woman who's been dealt a bad hand by life at every turn (which is true) and who yearns for love (also true), eventually exploding in violence almost *accidentally*. The real Wuornos was a bit more volatile and inconsistent than the relatively coherent character in the film. As one commentator put it, the film made Wuornos *"understandable,"* whereas the real Wuornos was often erratic and much more unapologetically homicidal than Theron's portrayal suggests.

That said, *Monster* does get a lot right: the essence of Aileen's and Tyria's love, the desperation of their situation, and many key moments (like the final betrayal via telephone confession) are drawn from real events. It's just important to remember that *Patty Jenkins*, the writer-director, crafted the story to have a certain tragic arc. One that might smooth out some of Wuornos's roughest edges. For a rawer look at Aileen, the documentaries by Nick Broomfield (*Aileen Wuornos: The Selling of a Serial Killer* (1993) and *Aileen: Life and Death of a Serial Killer* (2003)) offer actual footage of Aileen speaking and reveal some of the behind-the-scenes shenanigans, like how individuals sought to profit from her story. In those docs, you see the real Aileen. Sometimes she is cooperative and charming, other times, she is exploding in anger and profanity at unseen tormentors which underscores how unpredictable she was.

Another dramatization, Aileen Wuornos: American Boogeywoman (2021), attempts to depict Aileen's younger years (including her marriage to Lewis Fell). This low-budget film took even greater creative license and was widely criticized as "wildly inaccurate" and sensationalized, essentially an exploitation flick not to be mistaken for fact. It's safe to say that portrayal bears little resemblance to verified history.

Media narratives also sometimes dubbed Aileen a man-hating "feminist serial killer" or spun her story as a symbol of women's anger. However, Aileen's life of abuse and her crimes form a unique, individual tragedy. It's not neatly symbolic of any movement, and she herself didn't claim to be retaliating against men *in general* (she wasn't targeting men out of ideology; it was personal survival and rage). The focus should really stay on *Wuornos's personal story*, which is what we've detailed here.

In comparing the factual events to the media portrayals, the overarching theme is that Aileen Wuornos's life was messy, sad, and violent and while films and shows might capture parts of that, they inevitably simplify some of the contradictions. The truth of Wuornos's life doesn't excuse her murders, but it provides context often lost in the "monster" caricature. As Broomfield noted in his documentary, *"Aileen Wuornos led a tortured, torturing life that is beyond my worst nightmares."* Her anger *did* explode into incredible violence, but in her quieter moments, there was also a wounded, damaged person underneath.

In the end, the story of Aileen Wuornos is a true crime saga with no winners. Seven innocent (if flawed) men lost their lives. Aileen herself, a product of abuse, abandonment, and systemic failures, ended up on the executioner's gurney. Her case challenged perceptions about women's capacity for serial violence and prompted debates about how society and media label female criminals. But stripped of the media hype, Aileen's life story is ultimately a human one: a girl nobody wanted, who grew into a woman full of pain and fury, leaving a trail of death behind her. It's a story as haunting and complex as any in the annals of American crime, far more complicated than the one-note "monster" portrayed on screen.

Throughout it all, one thing is clear: Aileen Wuornos lived and died on her own terms, for better or worse. As she said herself in one of her last interviews, reflecting on her impending death, *"I'm sailing with the Rock... I'll be back."*. Those words capture Aileen's mix of delusion and defiance. Even in death, she wasn't about to apologize or explain herself further. And perhaps that is how this "Damsel of Death" will be remembered - not as a heroine or a folk devil, but as a damaged soul whose choices were horrific and whose life was a hurricane of misfortune and anger.

FINAL THOUGHTS

As different as these women were—mothers, lovers, loners, liars—they all had one thing in common: they crossed a line most of us can't even imagine approaching.

Some were loud, aggressive, and unapologetic, like Aileen Wuornos and Katherine Knight. Others lived quietly in small towns, raised kids, went to church, and smiled for Christmas cards. Cindy taught Sunday school. Sherri jogged through her neighborhood like any other mom trying to hold it all together. On the surface, these women may have had very little in common. But deep underneath, something darker connected them all. **Evil**.

That word feels heavy, maybe even too easy. But what else do you call it when someone is capable of such destruction? The real question though...the one that lingers long after the trials and headlines fade is: *How*? How can someone smile through the day and kill by night? How can someone love their children and still do the unthinkable? How are some people able to suppress that darkness... while others let it consume them?

What causes it to rise to the surface? Is it trauma? Is it choice? Is it a slow unraveling of something they were barely holding together in the first place?

Maybe that's the part we'll never fully understand. Maybe that's the question that keeps us coming back to these stories. Because if people like them can hide in plain sight... what does that say about the rest of us?

Are we all capable of evil? And if so, what is it that finally lets it seep out? What tears the threads that bind it in and lets it take over? Maybe that's the ultimate unanswerable question.

Finally, I want to sincerely thank you for reading this book and being a part of Mama Mystery. I've always dreamed of becoming an author and telling stories to a large audience. You all have made that dream come true for me and I need you to know how truly grateful I am for your support.

Some of you have been here since 2020 when I started the Mama Mystery podcast and some of you may be fairly new here. But I think of every single one of you as a friend of mine and as a huge part of my life. I can't wait to see what the future holds for us.

Stay curious,
Kelly

(Mama...Mystery...OUT!)

RESOURCES

Susan Smith

- Smith, David, and Carol Calef. *Beyond All Reason: My Life with Susan Smith.* Pinnacle, 1995.

- McGinniss, Joe. *Fatal Vision.* Penguin Books, 1989.

- *Susan Smith: Sex Behind Bars.* Investigation Discovery, 2017.

- "Susan Smith Coverage." *CNN*, Cable News Network, www.cnn.com.

- "Susan Smith." *The New York Times*, www.nytimes.com.

- "Susan Smith." *The State*, Columbia, South Carolina, www.thestate.com.

Cindy Reese

- "Episode 94: The Murder of Michael Reese." *Southern Fried True Crime*, created by Erica Kelley, performance by Erica Kelley, 13 Apr. 2020, podcast.

- Robinson, Carol. "Cindy Reese Convicted of Murder in Husband's Death." *AL.com*, 2 Dec. 2016, www.al.com.

- "Cindy Reese Case Coverage." *The Birmingham News*, www.al.com/birminghamnews.

- Alabama Department of Corrections. *Inmate Search - Cindy Reese.* www.doc.state.al.us.

Katherine Knight

- Lalor, Peter. *Blood Stain: The True Story of Katherine Knight, Australia's Hannibal.* Allen & Unwin, 2002.

- "The Katherine Knight Story." *Crime Investigation Australia*, Foxtel Networks, 2009.

- "Katherine Knight Coverage." *The Sydney Morning Herald*, www.smh.com.au.

- "Katherine Knight." *ABC News Australia*, www.abc.net.au.

Diane Downs

- Rule, Ann. *Small Sacrifices*. Signet Books, 1988.

- *Small Sacrifices*. Directed by David Greene, performances by Farrah Fawcett, Ryan O'Neal, ABC, 1989.

- "Diane Downs Coverage." *The Oregonian*, Portland, OR, www.oregonlive.com.

- "Diane Downs Articles." *The Register-Guard*, Eugene, OR, www.registerguard.com.

Liz Golyar

- "MISSING: Cari Farver." *Crime Junkie*, created by Ashley Flowers, Audiochuck, 2019, podcast.

- "Liz Golyar Coverage." *Omaha World-Herald*, Omaha, NE, www.omaha.com.

- "Cari Farver Case." *Dateline NBC*, NBC Universal, 2017.

- Douglas County District Court. *State of Nebraska vs. Shanna Golyar*, case no. CR16-857.

Betty Broderick

- Stumbo, Bella. *Until the Twelfth of Never: The Deadly Divorce of Dan & Betty Broderick*. Pocket Books, 1993.

- *Dirty John: The Betty Broderick Story*. Created by Alexandra Cunningham, performances by Amanda Peet and Christian Slater, USA Network, 2020.

- "Betty Broderick." *Los Angeles Times*, www.latimes.com.

- "Broderick Case Coverage." *San Diego Union-Tribune*, www.sandiegouniontribune.com.

Sherri Papini

- "Sherri Papini Kidnapping Hoax." *True Crime Brewery*, Tiegrabber Podcasts, 2022, podcast.

- "Sherri Papini Case Coverage." *ABC News*, abcnews.go.com.

- "Papini Articles." *The Sacramento Bee*, www.sacbee.com.

- "Sherri Papini Updates." *Redding Record Searchlight*, www.redding.com.

- U.S. District Court for the Eastern District of California. *United States v. Sherri Papini*, case no. 2:22-cr-00070.

Taylor Parker

- "Taylor Parker Murder Trial Coverage." *Texarkana Gazette*, www.texarkanagazette.com.

- "Taylor Parker Case Updates." *KTBS News*, www.ktbs.com.

- Bowie County District Court. *State of Texas vs. Taylor Parker*, case no. 20F0719-102.

- Texas Department of Public Safety. Press Releases, www.dps.texas.gov.

Brittany Norwood

- Morse, Dan. "Lululemon Murder." *The Washington Post*, 6 Nov. 2011, www.washingtonpost.com.

- "Brittany Norwood Trial Coverage." *The Baltimore Sun*, www.baltimoresun.com.

- Montgomery County Circuit Court. *State of Maryland vs. Brittany Norwood*, case no. 118522C.

- "The Lululemon Murder." *Dateline NBC*, NBC Universal, 2011.

Shayna Hubers

- "Shayna Hubers Case Coverage." *The Cincinnati Enquirer*, www.cincinnati.com.

- "Shayna Hubers Murder Case." *WCPO 9 News*, www.wcpo.com.

- Campbell County Circuit Court. *Commonwealth of Kentucky vs. Shayna Hubers*, case no. 12-CR-00554.

- "Obsessed." *20/20*, ABC, 2016.

Aileen Wuornos

- Wuornos, Aileen, Lisa Kester, and Daphne Gottlieb. *Dear Dawn: Aileen Wuornos in Her Own Words*. Soft Skull Press, 2012.

- *Aileen: Life and Death of a Serial Killer*. Directed by Nick Broomfield, performance by Aileen Wuornos, Lafayette Films, 2003.

- "Aileen Wuornos Coverage." *Orlando Sentinel*, www.orlandosentinel.com.

- "Wuornos Case Articles." *The Tampa Bay Times*, www.tampabay.com.

ABOUT THE AUTHOR

Kelly Evans is the creator and host of the hit true crime podcast Mama Mystery, where she tells some of the most shocking true crime stories with curiosity, compassion, and a no-nonsense approach that listeners can't get enough of. Her husband, Austin, often joins her as cohost—bringing humor, perspective, and just enough skepticism to keep things interesting.

Known for her casual, conversational storytelling style, Kelly has built a loyal following by diving deep into the stories that others gloss over, always mindful of the victims and the lasting impact these crimes leave behind.

When she's not podcasting or writing, Kelly is a busy mom to four beautiful children—Jack, Kennedy, August, and Elliotte—who keep her heart and hands full. She lives in Missouri, where she's probably juggling dinner, TikTok drafts, and a true crime timeline... all at once.

Wicked Women is her first book. But it won't be her last.

KEEP IN TOUCH WITH KELLY

facebook.com/mamamysterypodcast
Instagram.com/mama.mysterypodcast
tiktok.com/mama.mysterypodcast

www.mamamystery.com

ACKNOWLEDGMENTS

I want to thank my husband, Austin.

Austin, you have always seen potential in me that I've had a hard time recognizing myself. You push me to achieve great things, to work toward my goals and see them through to the end. You're the best cheerleader and motivator and you always keep me grounded. You make me laugh daily and you make every day more fun. I used to hate watching romantic movies because I thought that kind of love just wasn't meant for me or that it didn't really exist. I didn't think I'd ever find it and it always seemed so unrealistic. But you have made me realize love like that actually does exist and my favorite love story of all is *ours*. I love you.

www.ingramcontent.com/pod-product-compliance
Lightning Source LLC
Chambersburg PA
CBHW031423270326
41930CB00007B/555